# PERSPECTIVES IN CHILD CARE POLICY

*Lorraine Fox Harding*

*Longman*
London and New York

**Longman Group UK Limited,**
Longman House, Burnt Mill, Harlow,
Essex CM20 2JE, England
*and Associated Companies throughout the world.*

*Published in the United States of America
by Longman Inc., New York*

© Longman Group UK Limited 1991

First published 1991

**British Library Cataloguing in Publication Data**
Fox Harding, Lorraine
Perspectives in child care policy
1. Great Britain. Children. Care
I. Title
362.70941

**ISBN 0–582–08345–1**

**Library of Congress Cataloging-in-Publication Data**
Fox Harding, Lorraine
Perspectives in child care policy/by Lorraine Fox Harding.
p.   cm.
Includes bibliographical references.
ISBN 0–582–08345–1
1. Child welfare—Government policy—Great Britain.   I. Title.
HV751.A6F69 1991                                90–5564
362.7′0941—dc20                                      CIP

Set in Linotron 202 10/12 Bembo
Produced by Longman Group (FE) Ltd.
Printed in Hong Kong

# Contents

Contents

# *Acknowledgements*

I would like to acknowledge the help of the following people in writing this book: Kirk Mann and Mike Stein for reading parts of the draft; Kirk Mann for some stimulating 'supervision sessions'; Bob Franklin for a flow of information and ideas; David Mercer for invaluable help in the arduous task of assembling the footnotes; Jude Cohen and Gena Lodge for helping with the typing; Mary Lance for her sisterly encouragement and support; and my husband David Harding for his help, encouragement and support throughout the whole operation.

# Dedication

This book is dedicated to my great grandfather
William Calvert, 1866–1938, who took an interest
in social policy before the word was invented
and who with his wife brought up nine children
in the shadow of the workhouse.

# *Preface*

This book will be very helpful to those who, over the years, have struggled with the underlying ethical issues which constantly arise in the practice of child welfare. Some of us have become bored with the polemical, even messianic, tone of some texts in child care policy. This is a refreshing (and very thorough) attempt to analyse objectively four powerful themes which recur in the analysis of policy – *laissez-faire* and patriarchy; state paternalism and child protection; the birth family and parents' rights, and children's rights. It will be a godsend to students and perhaps teachers too! But it will also be valued by those many practitioners and managers who want to work on their underlying philosophy of child care, to inform their discussion making and counteract the arbitrary shifts of emphasis to which we have been so prone since the war.

The author presumably believes in the power of reason. Indeed, academics have to do or we would be out of business! Yet it is observable that arguments concerning children in families rouse deep emotions. We can all point to examples of literature in which feelings masquerade as reason and in which one senses a powerful need to persuade readers that one side of the story of families is paramount. Adopters, foster parents, birth parents, children – each take their turn in being placed at the top of the moral tree, to be accorded special priority in law, policy and practice. Even when child protection is afforded unequivocal priority, hidden identification with parental rights and needs can affect practice or there can be genuine doubt as to the extent to which specific children's needs are best met within their birth family. The shifts in emphasis in the law, as the pendulum sways, illustrate this vividly; they both mirror and influence public opinion. The latest Children Act will affect significantly the debate.

We have to learn to live with the tension and ambivalence in this sphere of social welfare policy, possibly more affected by underlying emotion than any other. Those who, as part of the management of ambivalence, have a will to understand intellectually will benefit greatly from an appraisal of the different perspectives which this book offers. Objectivity in the social sciences is a phantasy but at least we can examine our underlying biases more rigorously with the help of such a text.

Professor Olive Stevenson
University of Nottingham
April 1990.

# Foreword

The idea for this book originated in an article published by the author under the name of Lorraine Fox in 1982 in the *British Journal of Social Work*[1] (reprinted in the Open University Reader *Child Care: Concerns and Conflicts*[2] (1989)). The article set out two schools of thought or 'value positions', which may be adhered to in relation to child care policy, and it has been quite widely referred to. This book develops the ideas in the article further, in exploring a four-fold division of positions or 'value perspectives' which builds on and elaborates the original two-fold classification.

## A NOTE ON THE NATIONAL FOCUS OF THE BOOK

This book is written mostly with child care law and policy in **England and Wales** in mind as a context (referred to usually as England/English policy for shortness). References to **British** policy are on the whole not made, as it is recognised that **Scotland**, while it shares some of the English child care legislation, also has some Acts of its own, and in particular has a very different system, based on informal children's hearings, for children in need of compulsory care. Scotland, it is felt, is worthy of a study in its own right, as indeed is Northern Ireland. While to illustrate the different perspectives *in practice* reference is made mostly to actual child care policy in the English/Welsh context, short sections are also incorporated referring to policy in the **United States, Australia and Scandinavia.**

# NOTES AND REFERENCES

1. L. M. Fox 1982 'Two Value Positions in Recent Child Care Law and Practice' *British Journal of Social Work* 12(2) April 1982 265–90.
2. S. Morgan and P. Righton (Eds) 1989 *Child Care: Concerns and Conflicts* (Course Reader) Open University/Hodder and Stoughton.

# CHAPTER ONE

# The importance of child care law and policy

In modern societies it may be thought self-evident that the state should use its power to intervene between parents and their children in order to defend the children from various kinds of ill-treatment, inadequate care or poor upbringing. It is widely known and accepted that not all parents care for and socialise their children well. There is much evidence of various kinds of abuse.[1] From time to time extreme cases of child cruelty leading to death hit the headlines and provoke much media condemnation of the agents of the state. The most famous examples in a British context would be Maria Colwell in the 1970s and Jasmine Beckford, Tyra Henry and Kimberley Carlile in the 1980s.[2] In the United States there was the case of Melisha Gibson in the 1970s and in Canada Kim Popen in the 1980s.[3] In the 1980s sexual abuse of children by parents has been discovered to be more common than was thought. Becoming a parent in the biological sense hardly ensures that an adult will consistently maintain the standards of upbringing which are widely regarded in society as necessary or desirable.

It seems legitimate for society – through the force of law if necessary – to act, when such standards are not achieved. As suggested, in particularly severe cases of abuse and death there is often an outcry – to the effect that the state and its legal machinery should have done more. This can be so marked that attention is deflected from the actual killer of the child. There is a strong popular sense of society's duty to protect children, and social workers already involved with families where a child is killed may be bitterly accused of negligence and incompetence for not having anticipated the severe injury and death and for not having safeguarded the child by removing her. That is, they are criticised for not having used more fully and willingly the powers of the state. Sometimes the actual limits of these powers are

1

misunderstood, but it appears – at first glance – that there must be a consensus here that the state *should* indeed have, and use, extensive legal powers to act against and overrule the apparently 'natural' powers of parents where there is a need to protect the child. Surely there can be no dispute about this?

Such a position, however, becomes increasingly problematic the closer we look at it, and some awkward questions arise. For example, just *when* is the state to intervene? Outright cruelty to, and neglect of, children shade into merely careless or casual care; unacceptable violence shades into methods of discipline accepted by some people; one person's notion of a 'good upbringing' is not another's; and one person's 'good' decision about a child's life and future might be a fearful mistake from another perspective. Should the state act to protect only when harm to a child *has* occurred – or when it is *likely* to occur – and how is such harm to be decided and by whom? How can there be clear guidelines – so that everyone knows where they are – indicating when the state should use its coercive powers, when it should merely offer supportive help, and when it should stay out of the family altogether?

Secondly, how is the state to know when poor quality child care is going on and how are the mechanisms for identifying it to be applied throughout the population? Presumably the powers of the state should be applied consistently to all children, all parents, yet it can be argued that the system is haphazard; while some groups are under greater state surveillance and more likely to suffer the loss of their family autonomy and integrity to the state's control, others, protected by relative wealth and high social status, may get away, almost literally, with murder. Yet to identify and respond exhaustively to *all* child maltreatment would be likely to involve state surveillance on a scale which most people would regard as unacceptable in terms of civil liberties, the costs of which (both in financial and other terms) would be incalculable.

Thirdly, some poor child care is certainly due to circumstances over which parents have no control. They may be struggling with low incomes and jobs which militate against proper child care, living in appalling housing and deprived neighbourhoods, or in poor mental or physical health. They may have been victims of poor child care and depriving environments themselves. Are these parents to be 'punished' by having their children taken away, perhaps permanently? What is the justification when parents are victims themselves?

Fourthly, is the action that the state takes in cases of improper care always helpful, and the alternative care that the state itself may provide necessarily superior to the birth parents' care? It may be additionally damaging to a child to split up the family and/or remove her to a 'substitute home', perhaps depriving her of all contact with her original parents. It is salutary to remember that one of the most notorious child abuse cases in Britain this century – and one that had some influence on the reform of law and practice – the case of Dennis O'Neill, who died in 1945, was of a child *already* in the care of the state because of parental mistreatment, placed with foster parents supposedly 'chosen' and 'supervise' by a local authority (although in fact seized on in desperation and supervised barely at all).[4]

These 'awkward questions' and many others give rise to a situation where there can be no certainty as to what the state should do, when it should do it, or how. Consensus is illusory once the complexities are probed, and differing perspectives on the many problematic aspects of the state's child care role can be identified, while the debate between the proponents of the various views is often heated and emotional. It is difficult to be detached: after all, everyone has been a child while most people have parented one. Disagreements are not merely intellectual therefore, but are bound up with personal feelings and experiences. The debates are significant, because of the serious dilemmas that arise in policy, and because different perspectives point to different policy consequences.

## THE STUDY OF CHILD CARE POLICY

The study of child care policy and the debates surrounding it can be useful and important for a number of groups: firstly for social scientists, secondly for various professionals and policy-makers, and thirdly for a wider audience. As far as social science is concerned, one aspect of the study of society is the study of childhood and its construction by society, of the place and condition of children in society, and by extension the study of age itself – questions of development and maturation over time, of how experience at different ages is defined, and of how society responds to differences in age. The meaning of age and the treatment of different ages are found to vary between societies, between social groups, and over time. Such meanings and practices may be argued to have only a limited connection with biological factors and much to do with the nature of society and the role of different age groups within it. The study of child care law and policy may be argued to have much to contribute to the more general study of childhood. While it is true that the formal child care machinery of the state only involves a minority of children (in England and Wales, for example, less than 1 per cent of the under 18 population are actually in the care of the state at any one time,[5] although others would be under supervision and helped in other ways), the role of the state – in providing care for children as an alternative to parental care, in intervening between parent and child in various ways, and in prescribing certain rules surrounding childhood – can tell us much about childhood in society and how children are perceived and treated. For example, in modern western societies children are not seen as being as fully responsible for themselves as adults are. They are seen as vulnerable and in need of some protection. Their rights are recognised to a degree yet are also highly circumscribed. They are seen as needing to be controlled. They cannot be passed from adult to adult in an unrestricted way. Childhood's special status is reflected in the laws and policies which have been formulated over time, the changes which have been made in these, and the debates surrounding such changes and attempted changes. Where disagreements arise, they may reflect conflicting notions of childhood, as discussion of the four perspectives outlined in this book will attempt to show. Nevertheless, despite disputes, there seems to be a broad consensus about the *importance* of children and of the safeguarding of their welfare. This reflects something of the general position of children in society.

A second reason for an interest in child care policy in the social sciences concerns such policy's relation to the family. The family may be seen as a central social institution, carrying *inter alia* the function of reproducing the next generation and hence the society of the future. The family has excited a great deal of recent interest and study. Two features of this interest have been, firstly, a focus on family *change*, in response to the many changes which are perceived to be occurring, and to be of significance, in western societies (such as a markedly increased incidence of divorce and its consequences); and secondly, a focus on *diversity*, not only of actual family forms, but of norms and beliefs concerning the family. The interest for social science is perhaps essentially that there seems to be no universal consensus either on what 'the family' is, or on what it ought to be.

Children are central to most notions of the family unit. Here again there is both change and diversity of family patterns and approaches. For example, the increased fragmentation and realignment of parent couples may affect children's experience and upbringing profoundly; while children's lives are probably also more heterogeneous than they were; and the conflicting beliefs about what is good for the family, and individuals in families, overlap with the question of what is good for children as a special group. The study of child care law and policy, then, can add another dimension to the understanding of shifting family forms and ideas about the family. Law and policy usually attempt, to some degree, to respond to changes in the family and to the rich variety of family forms and circumstances. They will also be informed by different concepts of, and beliefs about, the family; and the different child care perspectives discussed in this book will also reflect such different family concepts and beliefs. For example, different views may be taken as to whether the family is primarily a biological or a psychological unit; of the importance of early bonds and of stability over time; and of the relative importance of family autonomy as opposed to support and intervention from outside.

A third point concerns the role of the state and the inter-relationship between the state and citizens. As indicated, there is a common belief that the modern state should have legal powers to intervene coercively between parents and children where there has been clear maltreatment. In England, for example, there have been such powers on the statute book for about a century. Intervention may take the form of both prosecution of the offender and removal (or supervision) of the child. Yet the popular concern about child welfare is balanced by a perhaps equally strong concern, which manifests itself in some circumstances, about the dangers of the state having excessive powers and making unwarranted intrusions into the privacy of domestic life. The family may be seen as some kind of 'bastion' against the power of the state. This is neatly illustrated in some cases where it appears that the state, acting through courts, social workers, medical staff and so on, has forcibly removed children from parents without sufficient justification. Here the public and media response is the mirror image of that in cases of child deaths – the agents of the state are execrated for doing *too much*. An example would be the Cleveland child sex abuse cases in England in 1987.[6]

The inconsistency over state intervention arises in societies where there has traditionally been a marked distrust of too large-scale or authoritarian a role for state bodies. This distrust may be in tension with the desire to protect the most vulnerable. A further tension arises between this desire to protect the vulnerable and the reluctance to commit sufficient societal resources, via state or other bodies, to make such protection effective. The point to bear in mind here is that consideration of the workings of the child care laws and machinery of the state, and the ideas underlying them, may contribute to an understanding of the role of the state in general.

The importance of child care law and policy for those who are involved in the child care field as professionals, practitioners, decision-makers, policy-makers and law-makers – those who create, analyse, discuss, influence and implement law and policy at every level – should be self-evidently clear. Within the category of professionals and practitioners might be included, most obviously, the social workers employed by public authorities and their managers, but also social workers with voluntary bodies, doctors and other health professionals working with children, education professionals, other professionals working with children, and magistrates and judges called on to make decisions in a variety of child care cases. In so far as elected representatives in public authorities take decisions in child care practice, they may also be included in this category. Those who train professionals and practitioners are another important group. That there is an overlap with the 'policy-maker' category should be clear. 'Policy' here is taken to mean the ongoing actions of the state of a significant kind and the thinking underlying them. The middle and higher levels of the state organisations responsible for child protection work may be involved in policy-making. Child care legislation in many respects leaves a wide area of discretion to the implementing authorities. For example, decisions and judgements have to be made as to when to bring into operation particular sections of the law, or as to how particular principles enshrined in the law (such as the 'welfare of the child') should be interpreted. Policy is created within agencies as well as at a more centralised level of the state. Similarly, courts which regularly deal with child care cases may evolve particular 'policies' or approaches. Elected representatives at a local and central level are policy-makers in a broader sense, particularly those at the level where laws are passed, along with the state employees who advise them. Various pressure groups and professional bodies may also have a role in policy-making. Members of investigating committees and enquiries, and other experts, specialists, advisers and commentators, also have a policy-making role.

Three specific aspects of a study of child care law and policy suggest themselves as helpful to these groups. Firstly, there is the acquisition of factual knowledge based on, for example, research into child care, historical accounts of law and policy, and accounts of individual cases. Secondly, there is the analysis of the principles, values, beliefs, assumptions and preferences underlying policy and law, which might lead to greater clarity and more meaningful choices. It is in this second field that the analysis of the four competing value perspectives in this book will, it is hoped, make the greatest contribution. Thirdly, there is the more detailed analysis of particular pieces of legislation and decisions in individual cases which can help also to clarify values, assumptions and policy effects, while indicating both current trends and problems and possible likely developments in the future. And where wide publicity is given to individual 'scandal' cases, it is important for professionals and policy-makers to be able to disentangle in an informed and thoughtful way the arguments, ideas and criticisms embodied in the response. There is the same need where official enquiries investigate and report and when specific legislative changes are proposed. In particular, emotive and ill-informed social responses to single issues and cases require careful and knowledgeable dissection and evaluation.

However, it can be argued that an interest in child care law and policy cannot realistically be seen as solely the province of specialists. The actions of child care professionals, courts, legislators and so on, are clearly of interest to a broad section of the general public – or individual cases of children *either* killed/abused *or* taken away from home 'unnecessarily' would not attract the degree of media attention that they do. As indicated, the perception of child care issues is sharpened emotionally by the fact that everyone has been a child and most people have had one (or would like to have one). In the contemplation of particular problems and disputes, it appears that onlookers may emotionally identify with the interests of just one party in the dispute. This may, for example, be the child. It is suggested that the majority of media reports of severe child abuse cases in Britain both reflect and encourage an identification with the child, who is portrayed entirely as victim, while little or no identification is made with the abusing parent. Alternatively in some – though probably fewer – cases, the story is implicitly or explicitly presented entirely from the (supposedly innocent) parents' point of view, encouraging identification with them. An example of an emotional identification by a stranger with the parents, to the exclusion of the child, was the Rayner case in Tameside in England in 1987. A local authority planned to take away a baby at birth from a family where there had been three unexplained child deaths already. A businessman who did not know the family was moved to offer financial aid to help meet their legal bills.[7] More rarely, perhaps, an onlooker in a child care case might identify emotionally with a foster or adoptive parent, with a non-custodial or step-parent, or with the social worker responsible for the case. It might be hypothesised that factors in individuals' own psychological history would have a bearing on which party they feel closest to. Child care is an area of state policy where it is extremely difficult to remain neutral and detached, because of the emotional processes which appear to be involved.

This state of affairs appears to have two consequences. Firstly, there *is* a high level of general interest in child care matters, as indicated, and from the amount of media focus this would appear to have increased in extent in the 1970s and 1980s. Secondly, while there is a high level of interest, much of the debate and discussion is pitched at a *low* level in terms of knowledge, understanding, fairness to all parties involved, balance in considering arguments, awareness of how much is *not* known, and an ability to consider a number of different interpretations of the given facts. Emotion lowers the quality of debate, possibly to the detriment of the quality of decision-making and policy-making. And the area is seemingly not widely recognised as one in which specialist knowledge and experience is needed in order to reach a conclusion. It is suggested that there is a public education need here, then, so that public and media responses to well-publicised cases at least become more sophisticated and balanced.

The importance to society of developing appropriate laws and policies in the child care field should be readily apparent. Children constitute future generations of adults, and the continuities between childhood experience and adult behaviour are widely recognised. For example, those who abuse children are thought to be disproportionately those who *were* abused or neglected as children themselves.[8] There is a strong social investment in ensuring the adequate care and socialisation of the young in order to safeguard the future social order, and the high level of interest and concern about child care matters surely reflects this wider awareness of the needs of society. Unfortunately, however, there can be no clearcut consensus as to what kind of adult – or what kind of social order – it is desirable to produce, or precisely what sort of child upbringing will bring the desired ends about. In considering the importance of child care law and policy we are inevitably drawn back to the question of values – what kind of people and what kind of society? Child care may be important, but recognising this does not tell us what kind of child care we should provide. For example, it might be thought obvious that abuse is a 'bad thing' and that if abused children tend to become abusing adults, abuse is doubly a 'bad thing'. Yet this position presupposes a value judgement about physical violence and social control. In some times, places and cultures, severe physical chastisement might be seen as a legitimate tool of socialisation. If the chastised then go on to chastise others, this would not be construed negatively. The point is that fundamental norms

8

are bound up with notions of effectiveness in child upbringing.

Child care and the role of society acting through the state are rightly seen as of crucial importance to society, but the issues are complex and tied to deep-seated values and feelings. An attempt at systematic analysis of different perspectives in this area may be helpful.

## INTRODUCTION TO THE FOUR VALUE PERSPECTIVES IN CHAPTERS 2 – 5

To recapitulate, there is no certainty and no consensus as to the state's role in child care, and different perspectives can be identified. In an attempt to make sense of the differences, a four-fold classification is put forward in this book. This framework is based on an article published by the author under the name of Fox in 1982, 'Two value positions in recent child care law and practice'[9]. The article outlined only two schools of thought in the child care field: the first, referred to as the 'kinship defenders', stressed the value of biological families for children and the need for state intervention to support and preserve the family unit, rather than putting children into state or substitute care; while the second, called the 'society-as-parent protagonists', stressed a protective role for the state where parental care of children is poor, favouring good, secure foster and adoptive homes, with the exclusion of the birth parents if the child is not to return to them, and a general diminution of parental rights. However this two-fold framework was subsequently found to be an unsatisfactory oversimplification: it did not adequately incorporate the range of diverse views found in child care law and policy, and in particular did not fully accommodate those authors, commentators and pressure groups inclined to a *laissez-faire* or to a 'children's rights' perspective. A *four*-fold classification was therefore developed. The four-fold typology is no doubt not the only possible classification; there may be some blurring of the boundaries between categories; and other categories of view might also be argued to exist. But the four polarities seem currently to be the most significant in understanding child care law and policy. The four positions have been influential to different degrees, and particular positions have been in the ascendant at different historical periods and in different countries.

Because concepts of the state's role in relation to children hinge partly on underlying values – values to do with children, with adults as parents, with the family as a unit, with welfare and suffering, and with

9

the state itself – the four positions are referred to as value positions or perspectives. The term perspective is favoured because each category incorporates a range of views in itself, and 'position' perhaps implies something more definite, fixed and monolithic than is actually found from an examination of the literature and policy. The perspectives are labelled here as follows:

### (i) *Laissez-faire and patriarchy*

This perspective is broadly identified with the nineteenth century but has enjoyed some renaissance in the late twentieth century. It is essentially the position that power in the family should not be disturbed except in very extreme circumstances, and the role of the state should be a minimal one.

### (ii) *State paternalism and child protection*

This perspective may be associated with the growth of state intervention in welfare in the late nineteenth and twentieth centuries. Here extensive state intervention to protect and care for children is legitimated, but state intervention itself may be authoritarian and biological family bonds undervalued. Good quality substitute care is favoured when the care of the biological parents is found to be inadequate.

### (iii) *The modern defence of the birth family and parents' rights*

This perspective may be associated more with the expansion of Welfare States in the post-Second World War period. It is to be distinguished from *laissez-faire* in that state intervention is legitimated, but this intervention is seen as ideally of a supportive kind, helping to defend and preserve birth families. Poorer and socially deprived parents are seen as often victims of heavy-handed state action, rather than – as they should be – objects of help and support.

### (iv) *Children's rights and child liberation*

This perspective, certainly in its extreme form, is more marginal to law and policy, but has been influential in some times and places. The position advocates the child as a subject, as an independent person with rights which, in the extreme form of the position, are similar to the rights of the adult. Children are to be freed from adult oppression by being granted a more adult status.

Each perspective will be related to examples of law, policy and practice in particular times and places.

# NOTES AND REFERENCES

1.  For example, in 1989 NSPCC statistics showed that in 1988, the incidence of registered sexual abuse cases was 6.5 per 10,000 children (or 0.065 per cent). The total number registered as sexually abused was an estimated 6,700 in England and Wales, with 9,700 registered as physically abused, and nearly 27,400 in total estimated as at risk, neglected, or sexually, emotionally, or physically abused. *See* 1989 S. J. Creighton, *Child Abuse Trends in England and Wales 1983–87* London, NSPCC. (Reported in *The Guardian* 5 July 1989.)

    A Department of Health survey of children on Child Protection Registers showed that they numbered nearly 40,000 in England or 0.3 per cent of the under 18 population at 31 March 1988. A quarter were registered as physically abused, and a seventh as sexually abused, with a third giving cause for 'grave concern'. *See* DH 1988 *First National Survey of Child Protection Registers*. (Reported in Social Policy Digest, *Journal of Social Policy*, 18(3), July 1989.)

    A survey by the Association of Directors of Social Services found 41,600 children registered at risk in England and Wales at the end of March 1989. ('41,600 children "at risk of abuse"' *The Guardian* 2 August 1989. *See also*: National Children's Home 1989 *Children in Danger – Factfile 1989*.

2.  Secretary of State for Social Services 1974 *Report of the Committee of Inquiry into the Care and Supervision provided in Relation to Maria Colwell* London, HMSO; London Borough of Brent 1985 *A Child in Trust: The Report of the Panel of Inquiry into the Circumstances surrounding the Death of Jasmine Beckford*; London Borough of Greenwich 1987 *A Child in Mind: Protection of Children in a Responsible Society. Report of the Commission of Inquiry into the circumstances surrounding the death of Kimberley Carlile*; London Borough of Lambeth 1987 *Whose Child? The report of the Public Inquiry into the Death of Tyra Henry*; See also: Department of Health and Social Security (DHSS) 1982 *Child Abuse: A Study of Inquiry Reports 1973–1981* London, HMSO.

3.  For the case of Melisha Gibson, see: J. Goldstein, A. Freud and A. Solnit 1980 *Before the Best Interests of the Child* London, Burnett Books/André Deutsch 141; For Kim Popen, see: His Hon. Judge H. Ward Allen 1982 *Judicial Inquiry into the Care of Kim Anne Popen by the Children's Aid Society of the City of Sarnia and the County of Lambton* Toronto, Queen's Printer. Referred to in K. L. Levitt and B. Wharf (Eds) 1985 *The Challenge of Child Welfare* Vancouver, University of British Columbia Press.

4.  Sir Walter Monckton 1945 *Report on the circumstances which led to the boarding out of Dennis and Terence O'Neill at Bank Farm, Minsterley, and the steps taken to supervise their welfare* Cmd. 6636. London, HMSO.

5.  For example, on 31 March 1986 0.6 per cent of the under 18 population were in local authority care, in England. Source: DHSS *Children in Care of Local Authorities at 31st March 1986, England* London, HMSO.

6.  Secretary of State for Social Services 1988 *Report of the Inquiry into Child Abuse in Cleveland 1987* Cm. 412 London, HMSO. Further comment is made on these cases in Chapter 4 (see footnotes 57 and 58).

7. See press reports, for example: 'Tragedy in Tameside' *The Guardian* 18 November 1987.
8. According to Parton 1985 *The Politics of Child Abuse* (see Chapter 2, footnote 53) the intergenerational link in abuse is perhaps most explicitly stated in: S. Wasserman 1967 'The Abused Parent of the Abused Child' *Children* No. 14 175–9.
9. L. M. Fox 1982 'Two Value Positions'. See Foreword, footnote 1.

# CHAPTER TWO
# *Laissez-faire and patriarchy*

## INTRODUCTION

The terms '*laissez-faire*' and 'minimalism' are used here to describe the view that the role of the state in child care should be a minimal one, while the privacy and sanctity of the parent-child relationship should be respected. Some who take this view would also argue that in extreme cases of poor parental care, state intervention is not only acceptable but preferably of a strong and authoritative kind, transferring the child to a secure placement with a new set of parent figures.

'Patriarchy' here refers to the power of adult males over women and children, particularly in the family.

### (i)  *The main elements of the perspective*

Underlying this first value perspective lies a mistrust of the state and an acute awareness of the dangerousness of its powers. It reflects a liberal democratic culture such as is broadly found in western industrial societies, where there is a strong undercurrent of feeling that the state should in general keep out of certain 'private' areas of citizens' lives, with restricted exceptions. In this perspective citizens have – or should have – strong rights held against the state. In particular, domestic and family life, the home and hearth, are seen as a relatively private arena which should not be invaded by the agents of the state except with due cause, such cause usually being associated with criminality. There is a pervading sense that personal relationships are in general no business of the state's. There is an ideology implied here of a dichotomy between a *private* domain, encompassing the family and seen perhaps as some

13

kind of retreat, a domain particularly associated with a special role for women, and a contrasting *public* arena, in which individuals interact with the wider society and the state, an arena seen as the particular province of men. These two spheres of the private and the public may be seen as somewhat in tension and in opposition to each other. Mount (1982)[1] is one writer on the family (not one focusing on the child care field specifically) who sees the family over the centuries as a desired private unit which individuals have valued and fiercely protected against the incursions of larger institutions, both the state and the church. He comments: 'Only the family has continued throughout history and still continues to undermine the state. The family is the enduring permanent enemy of all hierarchies, churches and ideologies.'

A general emphasis on the desirable separateness of the family from the power of the state appears to mean, in effect, that power *within* the family should lie where it is allowed to fall. In the societies considered here, adults are powerful in relation to children and men in relation to women. This power is partly based on generally superior physical size and strength, but is also, clearly, socially and legally structured and determined. One aspect of such male and adult power would be the relative economic dependence of women and children; another would be legal provisions which allot children, in particular, a less independent status; and other aspects would include institutions such as labour markets, housing markets, education and social security systems, as well as social norms and attitudes and informal sanctions. The relative power positions of men and women in the family have been extensively analysed by feminist writers.[2] The weaker power position of children has been taken up most obviously, perhaps, by those authors who will be categorised in this book as belonging to the 'children's rights' perspective (the fourth to be discussed, in Chapter 5), and, perhaps to a lesser degree, those belonging to the 'state paternalism and child protection' school (the second to be discussed, in Chapter 3). The point to be made here, however, is that a strong emphasis on the value of *not* intervening directly in the family via the state will mean in practice that family power will lie where it falls according to various other institutions and practices, and where it falls, on the whole, is on adults, and, particularly, on men in their role as husbands and fathers or stepfathers.

It may be argued that in modern western cultures such beliefs about the protection of the autonomy of the family from the encroachments of the state remain deeply embedded, notwithstanding the proliferation of modern statutes which *do* give the state a certain amount of power over the workings of the family. For example, in the English context, Dingwall, Eekelaar and Murray (1983)[3] in their study of social work practice in child care cases, found that the social workers (who, it must be noted, were agents of the state who had *as one of their special tasks* the intervention, on a compulsory basis if need be, between parent and child) were in practice reluctant to use their coercive powers. They readily and optimistically accepted parental explanations and excuses regarding the children, and interpreted events in the way most favourable to the parents. Dingwall *et al.* outline the dilemma facing the 'liberal society' which places a high value on family autonomy and privacy (as a check on state power), yet must be concerned with the socialisation of future generations of citizens. In such a society there are considerable structural and cultural limitations to the degree of state surveillance possible.

The main elements of the position of those who, having looked at child care questions, explicitly support a *laissez-faire* role for the state in child care, appear to be:

(a) **a belief in the benefits for society of a minimum state**, a state which engages in only minimal intervention in families. A weaker state entails stronger families, freer individuals, and is generally advantageous, in this view.

(b) **a complementary belief in the value to all, including children, of undisturbed family life** where adults can get on with bringing up their children in their chosen way. It is argued that adults have a right to do this, and in any case it is better for the children too. The bearing and rearing of a child produces a special bond between parents and child, and it is damaging to disrupt it, though it is accepted that it may be necessary to do so *in extreme cases* to avert a greater evil. Where extreme cases do occur, for some of these authors the function of the state, ideally, is to find a new, permanent, secure home for the child, with severance of contact with the family of origin. The state, having intervened authoritatively in this way, then withdraws, according the new home the same autonomy as the original one.

The *laissez-faire* approach to child care does not necessarily entail patriarchy, that is institutionalised power of males over females and children, and in modern child care literature the argument about undisturbed family functioning tends to be put more about *parents* generically than fathers in particular. In this value position in its modern form, it is relatively unfettered *parental* control which is seen as desirable; the state cannot do the *parents'* job for them in any effective way. Parents' and children's interests are, largely, identified, and by implication the interests of the two separate parents are also identified; the family as a whole has a life as a unit whose boundaries the rest of the community should respect. Yet, as indicated, *laissez-faire* tends to be linked with patriarchy in societies where men already have greater power than women. This was very obviously the case, for example, in mid-nineteenth century Britain when the family – though with some class variations – was more overtly patriarchal than it is now. The vastly superior power of men in society was both reinforced by, and explicitly reflected in, the family, and the husband's/father's rights and powers were almost absolute under the common law. There was also a belief that such male authority was *divinely* ordered and 'natural'. In this situation, a weak child care role for the state in effect reinforced patriarchy by very limited intervention in the patriarchal family, while *vice-versa*, belief in the value of patriarchy could be used to reinforce the notion of a weak, non-interventionist state in child care matters. So justificatory arguments about the divinely inspired nature of patriarchy could be deployed when the state was asked to exercise power in relation to children. Paternal power should not be interfered with because of its 'natural' and god-given quality. In modern society patriarchy is less overt and support for it less blatant. Yet it may be argued that the difference is only one of degree, and that patriarchy and notions of minimalism or *laissez-faire* continue to support and reinforce one another. Also patriarchal authority today is not without its defenders, as will be shown later. There are elements of support on the political right for a return to a 'traditional' patriarchal family which is freer from state intervention, while academic authors not necessarily on the right have also appeared to regret the passing of the more obviously patriarchal family and the extension of intervention in the family by the state.

(ii) *Some authors associated with the perspective*

The most notable child care authors associated with the minimalist and *laissez-faire* position on child care are Goldstein, Freud and

Solnit, who set out their views in two works, *Beyond the Best Interests of the Child* (1973, 1979)[4] and *Before the Best Interests of the Child* (1980).[5] In their earlier work Goldstein *et al.* note first that the law distinguishes between adults and children, with the law for adults being by and large designed to safeguard their right to order their personal affairs free of government intrusion, while for children, who are presumed to be not fully competent to safeguard their interests but dependent on adults, the state 'seeks to assure each child membership in a family with at least one such adult whom the law designates "parent"'. The degree of state intervention in parent-child relationships varies, but the traditional goals of such intervention have been to serve 'the best interests of the child'. However, Goldstein *et al.* feel that, while decision-makers have recognised the need to protect the child's *physical* well-being, they have not understood, or have undervalued, the need to safeguard *psychological* well-being. The authors use psychoanalytic theory to develop child placement guidelines which would safeguard the child's *psychological* needs. Such theory, they believe, shows the child's need for *continuity* of relationships. Of importance here are two 'value preferences' which the authors state. The first is that the law must make the child's needs paramount (this being in society's best interests), and the second is a value preference for privacy and minimum state intervention. This stems from the need to safeguard the child's need for continuity, and therefore to safeguard the right of parents to raise their children as they see fit, free of government intrusion except in cases of neglect and abandonment. The value preference is reinforced by the view that the law is a crude instrument, incapable of effectively managing complex parent-child relationships.

Goldstein *et al.* go on to consider child-parent relationships and the psychology of children, emphasising the importance of *psychological* rather than biological ties, and then to elaborate some guidelines for the laws of child placement. They delineate five guidelines for decision-makers concerned with placements, based on the beliefs that children whose placement becomes the subject of controversy should be placed with adults who are, or are likely to become, their psychological parents, and that the least detrimental available alternative should be found for the child. The guidelines they put forward are as follows:

(1) **Placement decisions should safeguard the child's need for continuity** (continuity of environment and relationship being

17

more important than in adulthood). The authors comment: 'The advantages of continuing, ongoing "imperfect" relationships must be weighed even in neglect proceedings against those of the alternative placements that can be made available.'

(2) **Placement decisions should reflect the child's, not the adult's, sense of time**, the child's sense of time being different at different stages of development. The younger the child, the shorter the interval before absence is experienced as a permanent loss. Speedy decision-taking is thus more important the younger the child.

(3) **Placement decisions must take into account the law's incapacity to supervise interpersonal relationships and the limits of knowledge in making long-term predictions**. The law is a relatively crude instrument in the field of individual relationships, and the capacity to predict in this field is limited.

These are three component guidelines for a fourth, more general one:

(4) **Placements should provide the least detrimental alternative for safeguarding the child's growth and development**, this being the placement which maximises the child's opportunity for being wanted and maintaining a continuous relationship with a psychological parent. The traditional standard, 'in the best interests of the child', the authors feel, is unrealistic and fails to convey that in these cases the child is *already* a victim of adverse circumstances. It is damage limitation which is required, it seems. Also, the traditional guideline had come to mean something less than the child's best interests, with these interests sometimes being made subordinate to adult interests.

(5) **The child in any contested placement should have full party status and the right to be represented by counsel**. This guideline has much in common with the children's rights perspective which will be discussed in Chapter 5. Goldstein *et al.* note that the law presumed that parents were generally best suited to represent and safeguard the child's interests, but that such a presumption should not prevail in disputes over placement. Nor should it be presumed that the *state* or child care agency represents the child's interests necessarily. The

child's interests should therefore be represented *independently*. However, in their later book they appear to retreat somewhat from this position.

Goldstein *et al.* then devote a chapter to rewriting a judge's decision in an actual case in accordance with their fourth guideline, the overall guideline of the least detrimental alternative. A final chapter asks 'Why Should the Child's Interests be Paramount?'. The answer put forward is firstly that these interests should be paramount once the child's placement becomes the subject of official controversy, but *not before*. Before this, the law must safeguard the rights of parents to raise their children as they see fit, free of state intervention and of harassment by other adults, in order to accord with the continuity guideline. When the child *is* the subject of conflict however, there is a danger that his needs will not be regarded as primary. Judges, for example, may see the parents as innocent victims, whose needs override the child's needs. But the paramountcy of the *child's* interests, the authors believe, serves the well-being of the greatest number (the child and psychological parents) as well as protecting future adults and therefore future generations of children.

In their later work, *Before the Best Interests of the Child*, Goldstein *et al.* develop further their theme of parental control undisturbed by state intervention except in extreme cases. They reiterate their view that before state intervention occurs, when the best interests of the child is not the criterion, family autonomy and minimum state intervention should be supported, commenting: 'So long as a child is a member of a functioning family, his paramount interest lies in the preservation of his family'. The question posed in their book is essentially when the state is justified in overriding the autonomy of families, but firstly the authors defend further the principle of minimum intervention. They argue that parents are legally presumed to do what is 'good' for their children; and that the dependence of childhood requires day-to-day care which provides the basis of attachment. This attachment is an essential element in socialisation. The 'complex and vital developments' of childhood and adolescence 'require the privacy of family life under guardianship by parents who are autonomous'. Thus:

> When family integrity is broken or weakened by state intrusion, his [the child's] needs are thwarted and his belief that his parents are omniscient and all-powerful is shaken prematurely. The effect on the child's developmental progress is invariably detrimental. The child's need for

safety within the confines of the family must be met by law through
its recognition of family privacy as the barrier to state intrusion upon
parental autonomy in child rearing.

Two underlying purposes here are to provide parents with an uninter-
rupted opportunity to meet their child's needs, and to safeguard the
continuing maintenance of family ties. Psychological bonds which are
not based on biological ties also merit protection, for the same reasons.
So, 'rights which are normally secured over time by biological or
adoptive parents may be lost by their failure to provide continuous care
for their child and earned by those who do'. Thus long-term substitute
caretakers should be granted the same respect for their autonomy as
biological parents. Goldstein *et al.* also reiterate their argument that
the law does not have the capacity to supervise complex parent-child
relationships.

The authors' position is thus that, 'A policy of minimum coercive
intervention by the state thus accords not only with our firm belief as
citizens in individual freedom and human dignity, but also with our
professional understanding of the intricate developmental processes of
childhood'. The authors recognise however that parents may fail, and
that, 'Family privacy may become a cover for exploiting the inherent
inequality between adult and child'. Where family privacy becomes a
threat to the child's well-being, state intervention *is* justified. Yet even
then state intrusion may make things worse – what is offered by the
state or other agencies as alternative care is not necessarily better, or
able to compensate children for what they lose in their own homes. In
every case the law should ask 'whether removal from an unsatisfactory
home is the beneficial measure it purports to be'. Identifying children
in serious jeopardy requires revision of the relevant statutes so as to
protect families. In their quest for minimum intervention, the authors
ask and seek to answer the question: what ought to be established
before the 'best interests of the child test' is invoked over rights to
parental autonomy and family privacy?

In subsequent chapters Goldstein *et al.* set out a framework for the
law's response to the question of justifying coercive state intervention,
including here **fair warning** to parents, **restriction of the power of
state officials**, and **greater precision**; they then outline appropriate
**grounds** for such intervention. There are seven very restricted
grounds where compulsory intervention between parent and child
would in their view be acceptable.

(1)  The **first** of these grounds is where a parent has *asked* the state to
     terminate their rights (without further justification required) or

to determine custody. But custody agreements between parents would be respected.

(2) **Secondly**, intervention would be justified where psychological bonds existed between a long-term parental caretaker and a child, and the caretaker sought to retain the child or to become the legal parent. Goldstein *et al.* specify time periods for children of different ages after which legal recognition could be granted to the new parent–child relationship, and the old one terminated with the original parents losing their rights. In this event, adoption is seen as the most favourable outcome, or failing that, 'care with tenure' which appears to be close to the notion present in English law from 1975 to 1991 of custodianship, a form of legal custody less comprehensive and irreversible than adoption. Placements without tenure are seen as producing insecurity in the child, although some placements are recognised as genuinely temporary.

(3) The **third ground** accepted for intervention is the death, disappearance, hospitalisation or imprisonment of parents, together with their failure to make provision for the child's care; these circumstances are seen as examples of gross failures of parental care which deprive the child emotionally.

(4) The **fourth ground** is the parent's conviction of a sexual offence against the child, also seen as a gross failure of care producing emotional harm. It should be noted that conviction or acquittal because of 'insanity' is required.

(5) The **fifth ground**, also a gross failure, is serious bodily injury, interpreted narrowly. Where such harm has been inflicted by the parent, parental rights should always be terminated, and the child should be permanently placed elsewhere. Corporal punishment is condemned by the authors, but is not included in the ground; emotional damage alone is also not included.

(6) A **sixth ground** for intervention relates to the failure to authorise medical care, *but only* where denial of such care would result in death *and* where supplying such care would give the child a chance of a normal life or a life worth living. The narrowness of the ground is said to acknowledge the law's limited capacity for making more than gross distinctions in this field, and to respect diverse parental beliefs and values.

(7) The **seventh ground** put forward is where the child needs legal assistance, and the parents request it or there is an establishment on any of the other grounds for modifying or terminating parental relationships.

The seven grounds are on the whole narrow and relatively clearcut. And in cases stopping short of the grounds, usually no intervention is seen as justified. Where they *do* apply, the original parent-child relationship would often be severed and a new one created.

Running throughout *Before the Best Interests* is the theme of the **adverse effects of state action** on the parent-child relation, and the **need to keep such action to a minimum**. At the beginning of Chapter 2, 'The Framework', for example, the authors call for the identification of circumstances which justify 'invading the right of parents and their children to feel at home with one another and to be secure in their persons and dwellings' – a fairly value-laden description of child protection work. Later in the chapter they comment: 'any interference with family privacy alters the relationships between family members and undermines the effectiveness of parental authority', while children react to the infringement of parental autonomy 'with anxiety, diminishing trust, loosening of emotional ties, or an increasing tendency to be out of control'. The final chapter is entitled 'Too Early, Too Late, Too Much or Too Little'. Noting that there is no consensus about what is best for children, the authors state the tension between fear of encouraging the state to violate family integrity *before* intervention is justified, and fear of inhibiting the state until it is *too late* to protect the child. Under the existing grounds for intervention at the time (the authors were writing in an American context) agencies could be held to do *too little*, too late, for example in returning battered infants to parents, or to do *too much* or to do it too early on insufficient evidence, for example in the duty to report cases of suspected child battering. Goldstein *et al.*'s own emphasis is clear. They seek 'to hold in check our rescue fantasies and to ensure that the state be authorised to intervene if and only if it provides the child in jeopardy with a less detrimental alternative'. The limits of knowledge and the limitations of those who seek to help are stressed. Coercive intervention – intervention by force of law – should be restricted to 'objectively' definable grounds. This means leaving out some children we would wish to protect; but overinclusion on the other hand means that state agents have too much discretion. Harm is inherent in every violation of family integrity; so the preferred error is on the side of non-intrusiveness.

Goldstein *et al.* will be discussed further below. Brief mention can be made here of two groups of British child care authors who may also arguably be put in the *laissez-faire* camp, although they also have points in common with other value perspectives.

Firstly, Morris, Giller, Szwed and Geach (1980)[6] in *Justice for Children* evince concern for parents' civil liberties and call for less compulsory state intervention. These authors are associated with a pressure group of the same title as their book, which will be referred to in discussing the children's rights perspective. Their argument is put on the grounds that the state does not necessarily act in the best interests of children; state-employed professionals are seen as having excessive discretionary power. Not only does state intervention and 'treatment' not work, but the costs to the child may outweigh those of leaving well alone. Morris *et al.* say: 'Parental autonomy in child-rearing must be respected . . . there is no "proper" way to raise children.' Of most interest here are the policy recommendations which the authors outline in their last chapter, 'New Directions: a Family Court'. Supporting the introduction of a comprehensive family court (something which has been argued for for some time in Britain[7]) which would emphasise 'rights' rather than 'treatment', they propose six interrelated principles as a basis for intervention with non-offending children, to replace the subjective 'best interests' test. These are:

(i) **the principle of respect for family autonomy**. Here diversity in child-rearing, and the importance of respecting it, is stressed. The presumption in favour of parental autonomy should only be rebutted where there is specific harm or the disruption/absence of parental ties; even then, there should be a presumption against removing the child.

(ii) **principle of voluntary services**. That is, help should be given on a non-compulsory basis to assist parents to keep their children.

(iii) **the principle of limited intervention** in the lives of children and families. Criticising certain grounds for compulsory intervention in the English system, the authors advocate more restricted intervention on narrower, strictly defined criteria – where there has been physical harm or neglect or sexual abuse or abandonment. There may also be a need for some intervention with the siblings of abused children. The alleged criteria would have to be proved in court.

(iv) **the principle of least restrictive alternative**. Where there *is* a case for compulsory intervention, such intervention should minimise disruption and promote the child-family relationship. Various forms of substitute care are seen as damaging to the child. Thus the proving of a criterion for intervention would

23

not automatically lead to intervention, let alone removal from home. Other types of measure should be possible.

(v) **the principle of the parties' right to legal representation**. The child should be a full independent party to the proceedings, as should the parents.

(vi) **the principle of visibility and accountability of decision-making**. Discretion should be limited and there should be firm guidelines for decisions and scope for appeal.

These six principles are broadly in line with the minimum intervention position of Goldstein *et al.* However, there is also in Morris *et al.*'s approach an element of the fourth value perspective to be described in Chapter 5, the children's rights perspective. This is seen in their emphasis on the child as subject rather than object, for example in their fifth principle that the child should have separate legal representation, also discussed in Chapter 7 of their book. Morris *et al.* also say: 'Our proposals are not a legitimation of a *laissez-faire* approach *towards social inequalities* [my italics] . . . limiting compulsory intervention means the corresponding expansion of voluntary services.'

Their second principle of intervention stresses the importance of assistance to parents on a non-compulsory basis to keep families together. There are echoes here of the third value perspective to be discussed in Chapter 4, the modern defence of the birth parents, which advocates supportive intervention to help parents fulfil their role. Morris *et al.*, like proponents of the pro-parent perspective, believe that many parents *can* be helped to care better by the provision of various social services.

Secondly, Taylor, Lacey and Bracken (1980)[8] in *In Whose Best Interests?* argue in a broadly similar vein to Morris *et al.*, although concerned mainly with young offenders. They defend 'natural justice' and parents' and children's rights and liberties held against the state, and propose restricted grounds for compulsory state intervention based on a limited list of specific harms to the child. Again, the 'best interests' principle is criticised. Taylor *et al.* state the principle: 'No child should be received into care or committed to the care of a local authority unless it has been previously determined that such a course of action constitutes the least restrictive, or least detrimental available alternative.' They put forward proposals, based on a formulation by Wald,[9] for grounds for intervention with non-offending children. First the statement is made that 'Coercive societal intervention should be premised upon specific harms to a child, not on the basis of parental conduct'. Intervention would only be permitted where it would not cause a greater harm; and would be permitted for the following specific harms:

(a) **injury** causing disfigurement, impairment of bodily functioning or severe bodily harm; or the substantial likelihood of this;
(b) serious **emotional damage** where the parents are unwilling or unable to provide or permit the necessary treatment;
(c) **sexual abuse** by a member of the household;
(d) need for **medical treatment** to prevent serious physical harm where the parents are unwilling or unable to provide or permit this.

The slightly broader grounds for intervention accepted by these authors may be noted. Emotional damage is acknowledged as a justification for compulsory intervention, as is refusal of medical treatment in other than life-or-death situations. The (substantial) *likelihood* of injury is also accepted as a ground. On the other hand the parents' disappearance from the child's life and/or the formation of strong bonds with a substitute caretaker are not referred to. There is an attempt to narrow the grounds for coercive state intervention, which is in keeping with a general *laissez-faire* approach.

The child's right to separate legal representation is supported and Taylor *et al.* include in their book charters of rights for children in care and in institutions. There is an affinity with the children's rights school again. Taylor *et al.*, like Morris *et al.*, favour state intervention stopping short of compulsory measures; families should be helped before the point of legal action. For example, voluntary programmes are suggested for non-criminal misbehaviour. This emphasis is in keeping with the *third*, pro-parent value perspective. Nevertheless, the views of Taylor *et al.*, like those of Morris *et al.*, seem to have more in common with *laissez-faire* than with the other schools of thought.

## (iii) *Rationale and underlying values*

A number of elements of Goldstein *et al.*'s rationale may be outlined. An article by Freeman (1983)[10] is helpful here and will be drawn on in identifying the different elements. The first element is the *psychological* aspect of the rationale. This concerns the notion of *psychological parenthood*, which has been touched on. Goldstein *et al.* argue for the sanctity, not of the biological parent-child link *per se*, but of the *psychological* bond between the child and whoever parents her, based on day-to-day caring, interaction and attachment. The psychological parent role may indeed be carried by the biological parent, and in practice often is, but it can equally well be played by unrelated adults who want the child and are its principal carers. It is thus the psychological aspects of the relationship, rather than its biological or legal basis, which are important. In *Beyond the Best Interests* Goldstein *et al.* argue that children have no psychological conception of relationships by blood tie till quite late in their development; it is day-to-day interchanges with people who care for them which are more important. They comment that while having produced a child normally has far-reaching psychological meaning for the *parents*, for the child the physical realities of his conception and birth are not the direct cause of his emotional attachment. Attachment results from day-to-day attention to his physical and emotional needs. Only a parent who provides for these needs will build a *psychological* relationship to the child, will become the *psychological* parent. The absent biological parent is a stranger. In discussing the 'wanted child' the authors say that only a child with a person he can love and who feels love can develop healthy self-esteem. If such a positive emotional environment is missing from the start, the individual's love and regard for himself – and therefore his capacity to love and care for others – are damaged.

In *Before the Best Interests* the concept of psychological parenthood is emphasised again. The authors comment that 'constantly ongoing interactions between parents and children become for each child the starting point for an all-important line of development that leads towards adult functioning. What begins as the experience of physical contentment or pleasure that accompanies bodily care develops into a primary attachment to the person who provides it.' The assignment of parental rights does not guarantee that either biological or adoptive parents will establish significant psychological ties to their child. And in cases of separation of parent and child, legal entitlement cannot prevent the establishment of psychological bonds between children and others – their longtime substitute caretakers.

In a sense this view departs from the traditional or conventional one of the family, in that the importance of the family is construed in social and psychological rather than genetic terms. As Hodges (1981)[11] comments in a review of Goldstein *et al.*'s works: 'importantly, they reorganise the notion of the family around psychological ties rather than birth or the "blood tie".' This means that Goldstein *et al.*'s approach differs significantly from earlier forms of *laissez-faire*, which saw the sanctity of the *blood tie* itself as requiring protection. Such thinking about the importance of the blood tie as a separate factor does still emerge in some modern judicial decisions however, and it is also present in some modern policy trends.[12] It can also be noted that Goldstein *et al.* do clearly recognise that in practice in most cases the psychological/biological distinction does not need to be made: the biological parent *is* also the psychological parent. In these cases the biological parent, except in extreme situations, should be left undisturbed.

But it is the notion of psychological parenthood which is deployed by Goldstein *et al.* to defend the policy of minimum state intervention. True psychological parenthood – necessary to the child – cannot be achieved unless the family's sanctity is respected. Psychological parents must be autonomous, within certain broad limits. *Beyond the Best Interests* makes the point that interference with the tie to the psychological parent is extremely emotionally painful for the child, and this may be so even where the tie is to a psychological parent who seems 'unfit'. The authors comment: 'Whatever beneficial qualities a psychological parent may be lacking, he offers the child the chance to become a wanted and needed member within a family structure.' This, according to the authors, is usually *not* provided in an institution, where there are *no* psychological parents. The fostering situation also has little chance of 'promoting the psychological parent-wanted child relationship'. Foster parents are deprived of the usual base of parental devotion, that is being the 'undisputed sole possessor' of the child, while the child feels the insecurity of the arrangement, which clashes with his need for emotional constancy. It is also difficult for the child to react to two sets of parents for more than a short time. The second ground for compulsory intervention, that there are bonds between the child and a longtime caretaker, as set out in *Before the Best Interests*, also derives its justification from the concept of psychological parenthood. Children should not be kept 'in limbo' or separated from psychologically real parents who wish to continue to care for them. These bonds also deserve protection from state interference.

The notion of psychological parenthood is the main plank in Goldstein *et al.*'s justification for their policy position; others will be briefly discussed. There is a *philosophical* rationale to their viewpoint; minimum state intervention, as mentioned, accords with a belief 'in individual freedom and human dignity'. Freeman sets the emergence of Goldstein *et al.*'s ideas in the context of the early 1980s' popularity of libertarianism and the minimal state. While Goldstein *et al.* do not make an explicit connection between their arguments on child care and those political authors who advocate a more limited role for the state in general, there is, argues Freeman, a strong compatibility between their views and a 'philosophy of extreme liberalism, of an individualism which treats all rights as though they were private property'. The state is seen here as having (ideally) very limited functions, for example, enforcing contracts and protecting individuals against crime. This is congruent with Goldstein *et al.*'s argument for 'strict limitations upon state intervention in matters which intimately concern parent-child relations', such interventions being characteristic of the growth of the Welfare State. The family is seen by them as 'a private area outside the law'. There may be an unstated economic rationale here also – highly limited state intervention is consonant with lower levels of public expenditure.

Then there are the more pragmatic arguments. The law is too blunt and too slow an instrument to supervise complex parent-child relationships; and the legal system itself cannot act like a decision-making parent. Furthermore, state intervention is often not effective in averting the ill-treatment of children. A further line of argument stresses the injustice of using vague standards in assessing the adequacy of parental care. Parents who are judged by courts and social workers may not know what is expected of them, the point at which their standard of care becomes unacceptable, and this uncertainty can be seen as unfair. Also, the child-rearing standards of one class or ethnic group may be unfairly imposed on another. When the various legal powers are used against parents, the assessments made of the parents may have much to do with subjective perceptions, personalities, and the relationship between the parents and those doing the assessing. The civil liberties of parents are thus under threat from the discretion of those who define the situation – the agents of the state – and from the absence of consistent, objective yardsticks for the care of children. And once particular parents have been labelled as inadequate, or their children as at risk of abuse and neglect, subsequent events may be interpreted to fit the label. So there is a labelling *process* in which individuals can be unfairly stereotyped. A related problem to the vague standards used is the difficulty of predicting the long-term damage to the child of leaving her in an inadequate home or removing her to an alternative. This is particularly so when *emotional* as opposed to physical abuse or deprivation is the issue.

It would be tempting to identify the underlying political values of the *laissez-faire* or minimalist position in child care with the values of the radical right concerning the state, individuals and the family more generally. In both cases the freedom of individuals *from* state control is stressed; the state is seen as threatening, as a force to be kept within bounds; and counterweights to state power are highly valued. The family may be seen as a locus of alternative power. It is also seen as a locus of serious responsibility. However, not all of those who support a more restricted state role in intervening compulsorily between parent and child belong, politically, on the right. Morris *et al.* and Taylor *et al.* put their critique of state intrusion more from a left radical point of view. For example, Morris *et al.* seem to see the development of compulsory intervention in children's lives as part of a more general class-linked structure of social control, stating: 'The recognition of childhood was one device by which control of the property-less class was achieved.' They are also conscious of class dominance in models of what 'good' child-rearing practices are. Taylor *et al.* emphasise that they do not 'subscribe to some crude "self-help" theory of society', but that any concern with natural justice and rights in child care involves confronting *present* social work ideology and practice (the implication being that such state intervention could be improved). It is perfectly possible from a left-wing perspective to see the exercise of state power in a capitalist society as potentially oppressive to most people, as consideration of the third position to be discussed in Chapter 4 will hopefully make clear. Thus it is not necessarily a conservative world view which underlies the minimalist approach and its distrust of the state.

A final point about underlying values is that at least in the Goldstein *et al.* version of *laissez-faire* – particularly their latter work – the child as a discrete individual with a viewpoint of her own does not make much of an appearance. Decisions and judgements are made *on behalf of* children by parents and other adults. The child's different sense of time is emphasised, as are other aspects of the child's perceptions, but generally children's interests are imputed to them by others, and conflict is seen as lying between *parents* and the state. True, in *Beyond the Best Interests* the authors put forward the guideline that the child in a contested placement should have party status and the right to be represented. It is said here that the presumption that parents or the state represent the child's interests should not prevail in disputes; the child needs his own counsel whose goal is to determine the least detrimental alternative for his client. The child's interests may conflict with those of the adults or the agency, and therefore require *independent* interpretation. However, in *Before the Best Interests* a somewhat different position is put. Legal assistance is only seen as appropriate for the child whose parents believe he needs a lawyer and cannot get one for him, or whose parents have been disqualified as the exclusive representatives of his interests. It is argued that the appointment of a lawyer for the child *without* regard to the wishes of the parents should not take place until the presumption of parental autonomy is overcome with the establishment of one of the grounds for intervention. Short of this situation (for example where there is only a *charge* of one of the grounds) the same lawyer can usually represent both parents and child. Thus parents' and children's interests are to a great extent identified. This is very different from the approach of the children's rights perspective. This identification of parent and child is less marked with Morris *et al.* and, especially, Taylor *et al.* – both of whom support separate representation for the child, for example.

## (iv) *Criticisms of laissez-faire*

### (a) *Empirical support*

*Beyond the Best Interests of the Child* has been criticised by Katkin, Bullington and Levine (1974)[13] for lack of empirical support for its propositions. They point out that the book 'does not contain a single reference to any empirical study in the extensive literature on adoption and foster placement. In fact, its references to material from the social sciences include only a single citation to non-psychiatric or non-psychoanalytic literature'. Goldstein *et al.* do, however, quote some child studies, such as those by Bowlby and others on the effects of maternal deprivation, and some on child abuse; but in the view of Katkin *et al.* they are not sufficiently aware of the criticisms of these studies. They also, it is argued, overlook the *limitations* on what can be inferred from the evidence they introduce; for example, they base assertions on a single case study and confuse causality and correlation. The issue here, Katkin *et al.* say, is whether Goldstein *et al.* 'fulfilled the responsibility, implicit in all scholarly efforts to influence social policy, to demonstrate not only the justifications for action, but also the bases for uncertainty'. Katkin *et al.* also find that some of the Goldstein unsubstantiated claims contradict everyday experience, for example the assertion that separation from the parent for more than just a few days may result in permanent emotional scarring in a pre-oedipal child, regardless of the adequacy of the interim care. Nor do Goldstein *et al.* always acknowledge where among the views they take there is controversy about what actually is the case. For example, they fail to do this with the question of the harmful effects of separation from the parent *per se*, regardless of subsequent deprivation. In fact, Katkin *et al.* say, many of the studies cited in support of this position deal with *deprivation*, not separation. An additional criticism is that the authors do not deal with the totality of psychoanalytic theory and literature relevant to their study. Nor do they examine competing explanations and positions but merely advocate their own. Perceptively, Katkin *et al.* comment that in law advocates are expected to amass only the evidence that supports their own position, but in *Beyond the Best Interests* 'neither Professor Goldstein nor the others is practising law; and in any event the usual condition of advocacy – that another side be present – has not been fulfilled'. In their conclusion, Katkin *et al.* ask: 'Why was such a limited range of literature consulted, and why did the authors ignore evidence of the weakness of basic studies used to support their propositions?' Relating the problem to the sociology of knowledge, they see the answer as lying partly in the fact that the three authors are particularly prestigious psychoanalysts who may have become insulated and protected from outside criticism.

So Goldstein *et al.* in their earlier book are open to some degree of criticism for their disregard of evidence and its limitations; indeed, the charge is a serious one given the importance and the firmness of their recommendations. *Before the Best Interests of the Child* refers to more studies of children and their development – for example the notes list studies on maternal deprivation and early childhood development, on later childhood, on adoption, institutional care, sexual abuse, and other forms of abuse, as well as legal material, psychoanalytic writings, and their own earlier works. Nevertheless, it seems that the evidence of some child studies is dismissed in this book,[14] and that Goldstein *et al.*'s position derives largely from psychoanalytic theory, from findings in individual cases in clinical practice, and from analyses of court cases and other individual cases.

To consider the other authors briefly, Morris *et al.* make use of government figures relating to children and the interventions of the legal system, and of research studies, including their own. Examples would be the finding by Cawson[15] that over 30 per cent of young offenders subject to care orders in 1975 had no previous court appearances; Milham's study of secure units;[16] and Holman's evidence of the under-use of the powers to do preventive work.[17] The authors also quote individual cases. They aim to show, broadly, that the state system for dealing with both offending and non-offending children and young persons is unsatisfactory and more coercive than it needs to be. A problem arises with the *interpretation* of the data, however. If, for example, Cawson's figure of 31 per cent is higher than might be expected or hoped, what is the yardstick that is being used to reach this conclusion?

Taylor *et al.*'s initial concern arose from experience of about a hundred child care cases handled by the British mental health pressure group MIND, which provided a social work advocacy service for parents and children involved in care and other proceedings in the juvenile court. The authors also quote extensively from research and government statistics to support various aspects of their case. Examples would be the finding by Thorpe *et al.* (1979)[18] that a third of young offenders apparently not requiring residential care received a care order on their first court appearance; Cawson's finding again; figures showing the increased number of young offenders sent to penal institutions over the 1970s; and evidence of life inside institutions. The type of data used, and the intention in using it, are similar to Morris *et al.*'s approach. It is aimed to show that state intervention is too coercive and could and should be less so. Similar problems arise as with Morris *et al.*'s work: what do the statistics actually tell us? Differences of view arise about the appropriate disposition for children appearing before the courts (whether for offences or because of their own need for protection). Differences of view mean that from one angle a given set of statistics makes the system look too coercive, and from another angle not coercive enough. A similar reservation must be entered about the use of individual cases. Judicial decisions, for example, *may* reflect a current trend or presage a new one, but do not necessarily do so; and different judges arrive at different judgements when faced with similar cases in the same historical period (indeed, the existence of an appeals system reflects and assumes such differences). Consideration of one case may suggest that the system is too coercive, and consideration of another that it is not coercive enough. Overall conclusions are difficult to arrive at from isolated instances, although such instances may be useful to illustrate particular ways of thinking and are usually of intrinsic interest in themselves.

(b) *Problems with the implications for policy*
The implications for policy arising from Goldstein *et al.*'s work have been outlined – their **five guidelines** for disputed child placement, encompassing: one overall guideline, the 'least detrimental alternative'; three component guidelines (concerning continuity, sense of time, and the law's incapacity); and a guideline on legal representation; and their **seven grounds** where compulsory intervention between parent and child would be justified (parental requests, bonds with a psychological but non-biological parent, disappearance etc. of the parents, conviction of a sexual offence, serious injury, failure to authorise life-saving medical care and need for legal assistance).

Some difficulties may be found with the overall placement guideline, that is, the 'least detrimental alternative'. It may be thought just as potentially subjective as the 'best interests' test and just as problematic in terms of interpretation. The first three component guidelines are meant to feed into and give substance to the general guideline. The first guideline, the emphasis on the child's sense of time, would seem to be helpful and well-founded. The second, 'continuity' guideline seems, however, virtually to elevate continuity above all other values. As Freeman comments: 'At the very least the breaking of ties cannot be "invariably detrimental" [ie as Goldstein *et al.* claim]. If that were the case no state intervention into the family could ever be justified.' The third guideline, the law's incapacity in the field of parent-child relationships, may be recognised as valid; it is only one possible response to that problem, however, to recommend that as far as possible the law should withdraw. Another possible response is to advocate an improvement in the functioning of the law and state machinery, for example through more sophisticated systems for assessment and substitute care.

Greater difficulties arise with the recommendations in the second work. The main problem with the seven grounds for compulsory intervention is their narrowness and inflexibility. With the **first ground**, where the parent asks the state to intervene, no such intervention is seen as justified where parents come to an agreement about the child's care; thus divorce or separation are not sufficient grounds for intervention in themselves; yet it may be argued that the machinery of the state should (as it does under some jurisdictions) satisfy itself as to the nature of arrangements for children in these cases even where parents *are* in agreement. The time limits laid down in the **second, psychological bonding ground**, after which a substitute caretaker who wished to have parental rights over the child could be granted them, are inevitably arbitrary – a point which Goldstein *et al.* concede themselves. The time periods are twelve months with the caretaker for a child up to three at the time of the placement, and twenty-four months for a child older than this at the time of the placement. Beyond this time, legal recognition could be granted to the 'new' relationship and the previous one terminated (although the authors allow for a special hearing in certain cases to determine psychological parenthood). Specific time periods are seen as the least intrusive mode of intervention, giving advance warning to the parents. Objections to this approach, however, arise because of the rigidities of such a clear cut-off point in time, and because of fears that parents who are aware of the time limit may remove their child – when it is perhaps not appropriate to do so – just before it expires. Furthermore, such fixed time limits take no account of *why* the child has been in another's care for so long.

With the **third ground**, the death, disappearance etc. of the parent, it should be noted that if the parent has provided for the child's care by delegating it to another, for example through a will, Goldstein *et al.* take the view that the parent's wishes should be respected. This allows parents a high degree of autonomy to make private arrangements for their children, which conflicts with the notion, present in English law for example, that the state should have a degree of responsibility for the surveillance and regulation of such arrangements. With the **fourth ground**, the sexual offence against the child, the insistence upon conviction (or acquittal by reason of insanity) may be objected to. The high standard of proof required in obtaining a conviction means that no compulsory intervention would be possible in many cases of alleged or suspected abuse, and that therefore the child could remain in the alleged offender's care, a situation where there are at least grounds for regarding the child's welfare as being at risk. Goldstein *et al.* take the view, however, that the justification for removing the child *is* best left to the *criminal* law with its high standards of proof; thus: 'the authority to assume the risks of intervention, including the termination of parental rights, arises only after the parent–child relationship has been severed by the *criminal process*' [my italics]. Many would regard this position as not going far enough in cases where there is suspicion, or indeed clear evidence, of sexual abuse. Also, as Freeman points out, the trend in the treatment of sexual abuse within the family has been to move away from a penal response – the criminal law can also be a clumsy instrument. It also tends to involve delays. And not all abused children wish for their parent to be criminalised (they wish for the abuse to stop – which is different). A further point is that Goldstein *et al.* focus only on the *emotional* harm arising from sexual abuse. Any physical harm, they argue, is covered by the fifth ground (serious injury). Yet it may be thought that the consequences of sexual abuse cannot be categorised in this simple way.

The **fifth ground** is *serious* bodily injury inflicted by the parent, or repeated failure to prevent the child suffering such injury. Goldstein *et al.* are clear that seriously injured children should be removed; yet no such provision is made for less serious injury or emotional injury. Parents, as they see it, should be protected from unwarranted intrusions arising from undefined terms such as 'denial of proper care', 'emotional damage' or the 'unfit home'. There is no consensus about these concepts, they say, which are too imprecise to ensure fair warning to parents. Again, it may be argued that the proposed ground does not extend far enough to provide adequate protection for the child. Severe corporal punishment would occasion no state action, nor behaviour which might reasonably be regarded as physical and/or mental cruelty but which inflicts no actual injury. There is also an apparent inconsistency in the authors' argument. Serious bodily injury, they argue, has the effect of *psychological* harm – the destruction of the child's trust in the parents and his feeling of safety with them. Yet surely less serious injury and neglect may be argued to produce the same psychological results – yet they are not covered by this ground. Again, in the delicate balancing act involved in protecting children from their parents, and parents from intrusive state agencies, Goldstein *et al.* clearly identify with the *parents*.

The **sixth ground** relates to the failure to authorise life-saving medical care but only where such care would give the child a chance of normal development or a life worth living. Goldstein *et al.* argue that when death is not a likely consequence of exercising a medical choice, there would be no justification for government intrusion; courts and doctors must not impose their preferences in medical care. In cases in which there can be disagreement about whether life after treatment will be 'normal' or 'worth living', the parents should be left free to decide; parents 'must have the right to act on their belief within the privacy of their family'. The authors acknowledge that the ground would allow parents to decide 'whether their congenitally malformed newborn with an ascertainable neurological deficiency and highly predictable mental retardation should be provided with treatment which might avoid death, yet which offered no chance of cure'. 'Families' (ie parents) know their own values here and have to live with the consequences; they may feel the death option is their forced choice. If their autonomy here is not respected, then the state must take on itself the burden of providing the resources that the child needs.

Goldstein *et al.*'s comments make it plain that treatment could be withheld from a handicapped child on the ground that it could never have a normal life or a life worth living, and Freeman's discussion of the case of the Down's Syndrome child Philip Becker, in the light of Goldstein *et al.*'s guideline, underlines this point, highlighting dramatically what the Goldstein model of parental autonomy *might* imply if the sixth guideline were rigidly applied. Philip Becker was an eleven-year-old American child with Down's Syndrome who also had a heart defect which could be corrected by surgery, although with the risk of post-operative complications. Without surgery he would positively deteriorate and probably die; with it, if successful, he would develop into a healthy, although never 'normal' adult. Although his parents were not caring for him and were in only intermittent contact, they refused to consent to surgery, and the courts upheld their decision. The parents' refusal of consent was based partly on the grounds that the child's life was not worth living and should not therefore be prolonged by surgery.[19] While Goldstein *et al.* have not commented specifically on this case, it does highlight the narrowness of permissible state intervention under their sixth ground.

Another point may be made in response to their argument that if parental choice in such cases is not respected, then the state must take on the 'burden' of providing the needed resources for the child. Many would argue that the state should indeed do precisely this for handicapped children, both wanted and unwanted; that this is the *child's* right; and that there are other potential caretakers in society who are willing to take on a handicapped child rejected by his own parents.

The **seventh ground** for compulsory intervention is the child's need for legal assistance. This has already been discussed in the context of Goldstein *et al.*'s tendency not to differentiate the child as a separate person and to identify child and parental interests to a high degree. Again the narrowness of this ground, and the emphasis given to *parental* choice, may be noted. Only where one of the other grounds has been established may the child have separate legal representation regardless of parental wishes. It may be objected here that it is not at this late stage that the child *needs* a lawyer. The authors again illustrate their value preference in their conclusion on this point: 'Protection of the family, protection of the child from the state – not from his parents – is central . . . to what we propose as criteria in this ground for the appointment and function of counsel for children.'

Besides the narrow and clearcut nature of the grounds for state intervention in Goldstein's work, there is the further characteristic of somewhat draconian intervention when the grounds *are* proved. While in cases of problematic child care which stop short of the grounds, *no* intervention (certainly no compulsory intervention – and only minor reference is made to voluntary intervention) is seen as justified, however where the grounds *do* apply, state intervention would usually be sweeping, with the original parent-child bonds being severed and new ones created. The approach is essentially black and white. State action is seen as primarily coercive, rather than supportive to parents who may not care for children well, but could be helped to care better. The scope for prevention of family break-up is overlooked, and in this the Goldstein position differs sharply from the third value perspective to be discussed in Chapter 4, the pro-parent perspective. As Katkin *et al.* comment, Goldstein *et al.*, 'while obviously concerned about the effects of separation on children, seem uninterested in how separation occurs initially'. Freeman makes a similar point with respect to the second, 'psychological bonding' ground for intervention, that it is strange 'that the reason why a child is in care should count for absolutely nothing'.

It is clear that the authors do not adopt a *totally laissez-faire* approach, as drastic intervention by force of law is permitted in certain extreme cases. They also do not apparently object to compulsory education or legal restrictions on child labour. These powers exercised by the state also limit parental freedom but are seen as unproblematic. Like other thinkers on child care policy, Goldstein *et al.* do see the need to draw a line *somewhere*, bounding parental autonomy. But it may be argued, with Freeman, that they 'have drawn the line in the wrong place' – 'too close to the parents' interests and too far from the children's'.

Some similar problems arise with Morris *et al.*'s and Taylor *et al.*'s recommendations for child care policy. Morris *et al.*'s grounds for compulsory intervention are self-confessedly narrow. These grounds make a distinction 'between situations in which harm or neglect has actually occurred and situations of possible future risk, and also between physical and emotional harm'. *Possible* abuse is excluded because of the difficulty of predicting accurately, and emotional harm because of the subjectivity and unreliability of such judgements. The authors favour 'concern with conduct based on identifiable and objective criteria'. So, for example, child abuse registers should only include those children about whom a court has made a specific finding, not those merely 'at risk'. The authors concede: 'We accept that such a narrowing of criteria may entail risks.' Such risks may be found unacceptable. While Taylor *et al.*'s grounds for intervention are broader in some ways, in that emotional injury and the *likelihood* of injury are included, abandonment, for example, is overlooked. Both groups of authors, however, do not anticipate the rather draconian severance from the family of origin – together with integration into a new family – envisaged by Goldstein *et al.* as a necessary consequence of intervention; on the contrary, Morris *et al.* argue for the disposition which does *least* to sever the child's bonds with

37

his family, while Taylor *et al.* clearly wish to reduce the number of children in care.

### (c) *Problems of rationale and underlying values*

Further objections may be put to some of the ideas underpinning the Goldstein minimalist approach. Firstly, the notion of 'psychological parenthood' may be seen to have much validity; but the degree of emphasis put upon it by Goldstein *et al.* may understate the importance of biological and genetic ties, or even deny their existence. The present author in a paper on surrogate motherhood[20] suggests that biological ties *per se* may still be of importance to people. For example, the fact that some adopted individuals have attempted to trace their original family suggests that pure biology without a psychological link can be important.[21] Two other points made are that:

> while childhood carers are of crucial importance, the people with whom one shares part of one's *genetic* make-up – not only parents but also siblings, grandparents, aunts, uncles, cousins – do tend to resemble oneself in certain respects. This resemblance can form a basis for affinity, fascination, curiosity, insight into self, and relationship – even when one has not known these people early in life. The second point is that, Goldstein, Freud and Solnit notwithstanding, society still tends to define families largely in biological terms – so unseen relatives may still be socially construed as relatives regardless of the lack of a close interactional link – and their absence may be acutely felt.

The paper also makes the point that the Goldstein argument seems to ring most true when applied to very young children who do not understand the psychological-biological distinction themselves. A further point is made by Katkin *et al.*:[22] 'psychology does not offer the same guarantee of clear-cut issues as biology', and it therefore leaves more scope for judicial discretion.

Secondly, criticisms may be put of the argument that true psychological parenthood can only be achieved when there is minimum intervention from outside in the parent-child bond. Goldstein *et al.*'s position – that there should be only two psychological parents, or, if the two are separated, only one, functioning in an autonomous way – overlooks the possibility that children can relate happily to *a number* of parent figures who are not co-resident, and can benefit psychologically from doing so. This point will be referred to further in discussing the third, pro-birth parent perspective, which takes a far less exclusive view of parental roles towards children. It may be noted here that there is evidence that, for example, children may benefit from contact with their birth parents, notwithstanding that they are cared for on a long-term basis by foster parents, or benefit from contact with a non-custodial parent after separation/divorce. Holman (1975),[23] for example, argues that the 'inclusive' type of foster care, where contact with the natural parent is favoured, is positively related to fostering success (absence of fostering breakdown and of child problems), while Benians (1982)[24] has identified five ways in which a non-custodial parent's access can contribute to the child's well-being. Children may perhaps also benefit from their relationships with part-time caretakers, teachers, social workers and other adults. Goldstein *et al.*'s insistence that, in effect, the basis of emotional health is exclusive parental *possession* of the child is, to say the least, questionable.

To deal with Goldstein *et al.*'s political philosophical rationale briefly: this rationale is not set out in the same detail as the psychological rationale, but appears to bias their work in a particular direction and to lead them to make certain assumptions. One, the implicit assumption that major state responsibility for the care of handicapped children is undesirable, has already been mentioned. Another is a rather poor opinion of the abilities of legislators, judges and professionals, in their work in the field of child care; and another the apparent dismissal of any benefits in institutional care. The authors emphasise at many points in their writings the *dangers* arising from an over-intrusive state. Their preoccupation is with the *rights* of parents as well as the *needs* of children. Their ideal state thus acts in a narrow, legalistic way.

Various arguments may be put against the extremely restricted view of the role of the state taken by Goldstein *et al.* With reference to children, the most obvious are that the vulnerability of children requires strong state protection (associated most clearly with the second value perspective to be described in Chapter 3, the paternalist perspective) and that there is a social responsibility to care for *all* children and therefore to help parents in their role (more likely to be put by proponents of the third, pro-parent value perspective). Wider arguments concerning the welfare role of the state relate to notions of collective responsibility, social rights, the meeting of needs and the creation of greater equality, arguments which will not be explored here. Perhaps the main point to note is that these *laissez-faire* proponents do not, on the whole, see state intervention as benign. Yet it may be argued powerfully that the state in its welfare role, for all its obvious faults, has achieved much, particularly for dependent groups. Furthermore, it may do much to protect such groups from the exercise of the 'individual freedom' which Goldstein *et al.* appear to find so appealing. As Freeman[25] puts it: 'in a world of basic structural inequalities individual freedom can be so exercised as to undermine not only the freedom of others but also their human dignity. The parent–child relationship is a microcosm of this imbalance.' Finally, the suspicion of a hidden economic rationale here has been mentioned. The general advocacy of a reduced welfare role for government has much to do with support for a reduced level of public expenditure (and lower taxes).

The various other arguments put by Goldstein *et al.* may be conceded in principle. Yes, the law is a blunt instrument; standards can be vague and may involve personal and class prejudices; professional discretion is a potential threat to liberty; prediction is difficult; and the momentum generated by a labelling process may result in unfairness to individuals; while it is conceded that the state child care machinery is often ineffective (as cases of children abused and killed while under state supervision make tragically clear). As has already been said, an alternative response to Goldstein's to this state of affairs is to seek to *improve* the response of the law and the child care agencies rather than to curtail it. Further, as Freeman also concedes, what is engaged in here *is* a line-drawing exercise; some boundaries *should* be drawn around state power – *but* Goldstein *et al.* have drawn their line in the wrong place.

The underlying values and rationale of the two other groups of authors identified as belonging in the modern *laissez-faire* camp are not so well-developed, although some of the same themes are identifiable. These include the limits of knowledge and prediction, the unsatisfactory nature of much substitute care, and the problems of excessive discretion. However, while anxious to see a shrinking of the state's role in compulsory intervention, Morris *et al.* envisage both a *concentration* (rather than a reduction) of resources, and the provision of extensive services on a voluntary basis. Taylor *et al.* stress both natural justice and children's rights, here having much in common with the third (pro-parent) and fourth (children's rights) value perspectives, but do not want their book to be regarded as a plea for legalism. They are acutely aware of the *lack* of state resources which causes the need for substitute care to arise.

A final critical point to be made here relates to the overlooking of the child as a separate entity with rights of her own. A few issues may be mentioned. The first is the absence of emphasis on the child's *own wishes*, which may be seen as a serious shortcoming in the Goldstein minimalist school. Perhaps it is assumed that children do not have wishes or that if they do, these do not accord with their 'best interests' and can therefore be disregarded. It may be objected that in the real world children may have strong views and feelings about, for example, with whom they should live; that children vary; and that while their wishes may not always be consonant with what psychoanalytic theory would prescribe for them, perhaps this should call into question psychoanalytic theory as much as it does the validity of the child's viewpoint. A second issue is that of independent legal representation for the child, which has already been discussed. A third is the notion of the child's right to proper care, somewhat overlooked in the Goldstein approach which assumes a higher value for continuity, 'psychological parenthood', and being a 'wanted child'. It is interesting in the light of these concerns to note the contrast with some versions of the children's rights school, which would see child placement decisions as resting *with the child* – thus, presumably, largely obviating the need for guidelines and formal grounds for intervention to guide adults in their decisions.

## (v) *The perspective in practice*

The main elements in this value perspective, the work of some authors associated with it, the underlying rationale, and some problems found, have been discussed. Brief accounts will now be given of some developments at two different historical periods which illustrate the workings of the perspective in practice. The accounts given are illustrative only – this is not a comprehensive review of the periods when *laissez-faire* has been influential. The accounts are intended to give some idea of what the value perspective may mean when translated into law, policy and practice. The topics covered are nineteenth century English child care law, and American child welfare law and practice in the 1970s and 1980s. In a slightly different vein, a note will be added on the slow apparent decline of patriarchy and recent attempts at its revival.

## *LAISSEZ-FAIRE* IN NINETEENTH CENTURY ENGLISH CHILD CARE LAW

A striking illustration of an early and extreme form of *laissez-faire* is afforded by the situation of children and child care in England in the nineteenth century, particularly the earlier part of the century. Only gradually was the common law presumption that the rights of fathers were virtually absolute eroded by various statutes which first gave some rights to mothers and, later, some protection to children. (It is worth remembering that animals gained statutory protection from cruelty well before children did.) Even early in the century, however, some interventions in paternal rights *were* allowed for, in what were then regarded as extreme cases – for example in 1817 the poet Shelley's atheism and intention to bring up his children without religion were regarded as sufficiently serious to constitute grounds for depriving him of custody.[26] On the other hand, even much later in the century, a strongly *laissez-faire* viewpoint could still be demonstrated in judgements in court cases where the custody or upbringing of children was at issue.

A well-known example was the case of the Agar-Ellis family, regarding whom there were a number of court hearings under the wardship jurisdiction[27] in the 1870s and 1880s.[28] This was an English upper class family where there was a dispute between the estranged parents about the religious upbringing of the three daughters, aged 12, 11 and 9 at the time of the first proceedings in 1878. The Protestant father, having initially promised his wife that their children would be brought up as Roman Catholics, changed his mind and, in the face of resistance by the children to being brought up as Anglicans, started an action to have them made wards of court, with a summons in the action concerning their religious education. The mother then petitioned with a view to the children being brought up as Roman Catholics. Her petition was initially dismissed by the first court to hear the case, and on appeal by her, the father's rights to decide were again upheld, although the judgement hinted that it might be for the children's welfare to remain Catholics. Of interest here are the fact that the court refused to examine the children, who were well past infancy, and some of the comments made by the judges concerning paternal rights. The Vice-Chancellor in the first judgement,[29] for example, criticised the mother for having forgotten 'that by the laws of *England* by the laws of Christianity, and by the constitution of society, when there is a difference of opinion between husband and wife, it is the duty of the wife to submit to the husband', later going on to say that the court never interfered between a father and his children, except when the father brought them up irreligiously (quoting the Shelley case[30]), or where there was immoral conduct (quoting Wellesley v. Wellesley[31]), or where the father had been guilty of the abandonment of parental duty. In the appeal case, while the mother's lawyers argued that the interests of the children should be considered when the children were wards of court,[32] the judges made comments like the following:

> The right of the father to the custody and control of his child
> is one of the most sacred of rights. No doubt the law may take
> away from him this right or may interfere with his exercise of
> it, just as it may take away his life or his property or interfere
> with his liberty, but it must be for some sufficient cause known
> to the law.

The perception of paternal rights as comparable to other basic civil liberties is symptomatic of a marked *laissez-faire* position.

In 1883 the Agar-Ellis family returned to court with their dispute; this time the problem concerned restrictions put by the father on the mother's access to the second daughter, now aged 16.[33] A petition had been presented by mother and daughter asking that the daughter be allowed to spend her vacation with her mother and that the mother be allowed free access and communication in the future. Although the children were still wards of court, the courts refused to interfere with the exercise of the father's rights and dismissed the petition. Again, the mother's lawyers argued for the child's benefit to be considered; again, the courts came down on the side of paternal authority. It is of interest that economic arguments came into this case. The father's lawyers stated that the father, if he were not allowed to bring up his children in his own way, would consider himself discharged from all legal and moral obligation to maintain them (and that no offer to maintain had been made by the mother's side, while only a small fund was available to the court). The court refused to see the daughter, and the judges made similar comments to those made in the 1878 case, such as: 'The rights of a father are sacred rights because his duties are sacred duties,' and: 'It is not in our power to go into the question as to what we think is for the benefit of this ward.' It was said that the court could not bring up a child as successfully as a father 'even if the father was exercising his discretion as regards the child in a way which critics might condemn'. There are strong similarities with the Goldstein *et al.* emphasis on parental autonomy here.

Another way in which nineteenth century *laissez-faire* can be illustrated is by looking at those changes in the law which *moved away* from *laissez-faire* and the debates which these changes stimulated. The fact that specific measures were introduced to protect the rights of women and children – and that the measures were opposed – is an indicator of what *laissez-faire* had meant, and its strength. Two strands may be identified in the legislative changes. At various points during the century, legislation eroded the near-absolute common law paternal rights by granting some restricted rights to married women in relation to their children. For example, in 1839 an Infants' Custody

Act introduced into the Commons by Talfourd gave married mothers restricted custody and access rights in cases of marital separation. Interestingly, the Bill was argued against in terms of its propensity to undermine marriage by reducing the woman's incentive to remain in her marriage. Nevertheless, it passed, and later legislation extended maternal custody, access and guardianship rights further. By 1886, the mother had the right to apply for custody of, or access to, a minor child up to the age of 21, and had rights to appoint a testamentary guardian and act jointly with one appointed by the father. Even so, maternal rights were not yet equal to paternal ones.

The second strand in legislative change concerned greater protection for children. As is widely known, child labour in much of the nineteenth century was still extensively exploited under harsh conditions and education was for most children rudimentary (as was the case in previous centuries); there was also no specific statutory protection against cruelty by adults (until 1889) and child criminals over the age of seven still tended to be treated in a similar way to adult offenders. Pinchbeck and Hewitt (1969)[34] point out that the statutory protection of children only became a subject of serious concern in the nineteenth century, and even then there was a long struggle to bring it into being, requiring 'a revolution in contemporary attitudes to social responsibility', attitudes in which ignorance and religious views were both a factor. Also, to undermine parental responsibility was, it was feared, to undermine family stability and therefore the stability of society itself. Interestingly, both laws restricting child labour and those introducing compulsory education were opposed on the grounds that they constituted an unacceptable intrusion by the state into *family* responsibility and parental rights. So control of the working hours of children (and women) could be argued against on the grounds that their care and protection was a family responsibility which state intervention would tend to break down. A related argument was that the parent had the right to do what he liked with the labour of the child as long as he provided adequate support. Similar arguments were advanced against the growth of state education; education could be seen as a family responsibility, which would be damaged should the state intervene. Compulsory education could be seen as an abrogation of the parental right to the child's services. The factory reformer Shaftesbury saw it as an infringement of the parent's right to bring up the child as he saw fit, and as encouraging undesirable dependence on the state.[35]

It was not until the 1880s that effective campaigns were mounted against child cruelty within the family. The concept of the father's absolute right to custody had to be attacked – these campaigns, it may be noted, were being conducted around the same time as the Agar-Ellis judgements discussed earlier. A Prevention of Cruelty to, and Protection of, Children Act was passed in 1889; prior to this cruelty to children was not a specific criminal offence, and the only recourse at law was for the minor or his 'next friend' to sue the parent or for the Poor Law authorities to prosecute, where they were responsible for the child. Behlmer (1982)[36] attributes the slowness of change in this field largely to the persistence of the idea that parent–child relations were immune to government regulation. In fact, the 1889 Act made only restricted interventions possible.

In conclusion, it should be remembered that the *laissez-faire* of nineteenth century England was different in significant ways from the modern form of *laissez-faire* which has been the main focus of this chapter. In particular, it concentrated on the *blood tie* to the *father* (rather than, as Goldstein *et al.* do, on an *emotional* tie to a *psychological parent*); did not – even nominally – give first priority to the child's interests; and allowed for a narrower scope for state intervention in more extreme cases. Nevertheless, it had certain points in common with modern *laissez-faire* and illustrate where the logic of *laissez-faire* might lead. Both positions see state intervention as inherently undesirable and only reluctantly accepted when extreme circumstances justify it. Both positions see the child's interests – in the vast majority of cases – as lying *really* in remaining with the parent and under parental control. Compare, for example, the following two statements, one made by a judge in one of the Agar-Ellis cases in 1883, and the other by Goldstein, Freud and Solnit in 1980:

> when, by birth, a child is subject to a father, it is for the general interest of families, and for the general interest of children, and really for the interest of the particular infant, that the Court should not, except in very extreme cases, interfere with the discretion of the father, but leave to him the responsibility of exercising that power which nature has given him by the birth of the child.

> We believe that a child's need for continuity of care by autonomous parents requires acknowledging that parents should generally be entitled to raise their children as they think best, free of state interference. This conviction finds expression in our preference for minimum state intervention and prompts restraint in defining justifications for coercively intruding on family relationships.

The rationales and the language might be different, but the central themes regarding state policy are much the same.

## *LAISSEZ-FAIRE* IN THE 1970S AND 1980S IN UNITED STATES CHILD WELFARE LAW, POLICY AND PRACTICE

The modern form of *laissez-faire* appears to have attracted a stronger following in the United States, particularly among the legal profession, and Goldstein, Freud and Solnit have been more influential there, than in Britain. It is American policy and legislation which will be drawn on here to illustrate the workings of *laissez-faire* in recent times. It must be stressed firstly that the child welfare system in the United States is extremely heterogeneous (owing to different laws in different states), and that it encompasses preventative and rehabilitative work with families as well as child protection tasks of a more interventionist kind.[37] But the underlying notions and approach of *laissez-faire* are present in certain strands of child welfare policy and thinking in a way in which it seems they are not (or not yet) in the United Kingdom. For example, McGowan (1983)[38] reviewing developments in the United States in child welfare from the early 1970s to the early 1980s, comments that child welfare agencies were now being attacked for 'their failure to keep children out of placement, minimize costs while maintaining appropriate resources for children who must be placed in temporary substitute care, and move children back into their own families or permanent adoptive homes as quickly as possible'. Such critiques of the agencies are contrasted with earlier ones which sought broader services for a wider population of children and families. Now the expectation was rather 'that the child welfare field should serve only those children for whom state intervention is essential to ensure a minimal level of care and protection and that these children should be cared for in as rational, time-limited, and cost–efficient a manner as possible'. This emphasis is highly compatible with the *laissez-faire* approach. McGowan further suggests that the status and significance of child welfare services were diminishing, while their accountability was being tightened up. Interestingly, McGowan comments: 'We now seem to be in a period in which the most universal desire is to turn back the clock to return to the fantasized comfort and certitude of earlier periods in American history, and to rediscover ways of hiding or rationalizing the social problems and forces that threaten to disturb the general peace.'

A further insight into recent American child welfare policy is provided by Costin and Rapp (1984)[39] who list among major service trends from the early 1970s to the early 1980s: methods for facilitating placement in *permanent* homes; widening of the definition of an 'adoptable' child and increased adoption of some children previously excluded from it; and cuts in welfare programmes, along with proposals to relax certain child labour laws and reduced support for research on children and families. Alongside these trends they also note broadening public mandates for child welfare agencies – more responsibilities, more services – and laws requiring the reporting of suspected abuse and neglect, trends which apparently point in the opposite direction to *laissez-faire*. However, they also note 'Increasing reluctance on the part of social workers to assume responsibility for removing children from their homes, even when their situations are recognised as hazardous to their well-being'.

It has been mentioned that the *laissez-faire* approach has attracted particular support in American legal circles. A notable legal proponent of *laissez-faire* is Wald (1975 and 1976),[40] who is also often quoted by other authors. As Costin and Rapp say, Wald 'endorses a narrowing of the scope of coercive state intervention in matters of neglect'. In his 1975 publication, Wald advanced the thesis 'that a reappraisal of the neglect jurisdiction of juvenile courts is . . . necessary. . . . I submit that a narrowing of neglect jurisdiction is needed'. Wald saw a temptation to intervene too often, with insufficient restraint on the exercise of coercive state power in relation to children. His article developed statutory standards for neglect proceedings based on specific harms and the principle of parental autonomy. Wald's arguments are very close to those of Goldstein *et al*. In considering termination of parental rights, among other things, in his 1976 publication, Wald was critical of existing laws for being vague about termination and focusing on parental fault. He favoured termination based on the length of time the child had been in care and the likelihood of its harming or helping the child. Termination 'would be the norm after a child has been in care a given period of time unless there are specific reasons why termination would be harmful to the child', for example, when the parent-child relationship was close. The relevant time periods would vary with the child's age.

Another legal supporter of *laissez-faire* is Mnookin (1973 and 1975).[41] For example, in his 1973 publication, Mnookin proposed new child care standards to limit removal to cases of immediate and substantial danger to (physical) health where there was no reasonable means of protecting the child at home, and to ensure that children who *were* removed were provided with a stable environment. He opposed excessive judicial discretion in imposing personal values when deciding on the best interests of the child. Again, continuity and stability were emphasised, as was the difficulty of predicting the outcome of different placement decisions for the child. Termination of parental rights, adoption and guardianship, should be provided for at the end of a fixed time limit in foster care (ie 'in care' in the British sense).

A further example from the legal profession is Duquette (1981),[42] who, while acknowledging that child abuse laws in all states aimed to facilitate benevolent intervention to strengthen family life, goes on:

> The idealistic goals of child protection laws must not obscure the
> fact that government intervention in family life infringes fundamental
> personal liberties of both parents and children, and may not fulfil its
> idealistic and benevolent promise. The personal freedoms of parents to
> have children in their care and custody and to raise them as they see fit
> and the correlative rights of children to live with their parents unfettered
> by government interference must be protected and must be set aside
> only under carefully defined circumstances.

Nevertheless, if the deficiencies which led to intervention were not corrected, then 'the interests of the child in having a permanent and stable home are served by termination of the natural parents' rights and placing the child for adoption or in some other permanent placement'. These illustrations give the flavour of some of the thinking. Two themes are marked – the restriction of intervention, and the provision of a single, stable home if intervention is unavoidable.

An example of one aspect of *laissez-faire* in action would be a requirement to bring a child in foster care before a court if she has not been returned to her parents within a specified time period. Duquette suggests that after six months of care the social worker should attempt to decide whether to seek termination of parental rights or another out-of-home plan for the child, or return of the child to the parents. Cole (1979)[43] in an article refers to legal changes in Minnesota whereby, if a voluntarily placed child had not been returned home 18 months from the day of placement, a petition had to be filed with the court for dependency, neglect or termination of parental rights. Parents unable to resolve difficulties standing in the way of the child's return home could have their rights terminated under new grounds: 'neglected and in foster care'. The emphasis here is on one definite home for the child, and on clearcut grounds for deciding whether this should be with the original parents or not. Further examples may be gleaned from Katz *et al.* (1975),[44] who reviewed child neglect laws in the various American states. In California a child could be declared free from parental custody if, *inter alia*, he was in foster care for two consecutive years and return to the parent would be detrimental, along with certain parental failures.

In Maine parental rights could be terminated altogether after *one* year from the child's committal to care after a neglect hearing. In New York parental rights could be terminated one year after the child's placement or committal, if the parent failed (under certain conditions) to maintain contact or plan for the future. Another example of the approach would be the use of statutory review procedures. Freeman (1983)[45] points out that (at the time he wrote) some twenty-three states in America had review procedures for children in care, involving a party other than the agency, which was usually a court but could be a panel of citizens. For example in New York, since 1971, the agencies were required to petition the Family Court to review the foster care status of all children in voluntary placement for two years. It was found that children moved more quickly through the system where there was such a review structure. Again, the emphasis is on a definite plan for the child, giving long-term security.

Finally, something must be said specifically about a dominant theme in recent United States child welfare policy already referred to indirectly, and that is 'permanency planning'. This has also been influential in Britain. 'Permanency planning' means basically a policy of finding a permanent home as soon as possible for a child who comes into foster care, *either* by returning her to her original family, *or* by finding her an adoptive or permanent foster family. Time spent 'in limbo', in 'temporary' (but possibly long-term) foster care should be reduced to a minimum. Such an approach is heavily influenced by the Goldstein model of a single, secure, continuous parental home for the child which has virtually total control. Proper planning for children in care or at risk of care would be important to achieve this goal. Talking of the 'permanent planning revolution', Costin and Rapp characterise permanence as implying intent, commitment, continuity, a sense of common future, and belonging. Legal and social status are an important element in this. Case reviews are an essential part of permanency planning, facilitating movement out of foster care; contracts with parents also help the movement to permanency. The examples of provisions for termination of parental rights mentioned above also illustrate the permanency approach – if the child cannot be returned to the parents within a fixed time period, parental rights can be lost. However, the author is reluctant to identify the permanency movement only with the *laissez-faire* perspective. It is also highly consonant with the child protectionist position, or, if the greater emphasis is placed on return to the birth family, with the third, parents' rights perspective. It seems that there are different forms of permanency planning, which may give different degrees of weighting to the birth family, the long-term foster home, or the adoptive home. Permanency will be discussed further in considering the child protection point of view.

## Note on the decline and defence of patriarchy

The value perspective outlined in this chapter has been dubbed '*laissez-faire* and patriarchy'. So far, most direct attention has been paid to the principle of *laissez-faire* , but is it worth saying something more about patriarchy in its own right. As has been said, *laissez-faire* tends to support patriarchy where men already have greater power than women in the family. Since the nineteenth century, however, specific inroads have been made into the formal patriarchal power of men within families by means of statutes affording some rights to women and some protection to children. Some of the English legislation of the nineteenth century giving mothers certain custody, access and guardianship rights over their children has been referred to. In addition there were Acts granting married women greater rights in divorce and to control their own property.[46] The situation was still far from legal equality, however. In the twentieth century, English legislation has moved towards establishing at least a formal equality for women both in the family and outside it; the 1925 Guardianship of Minors Act, for example, began: 'Whereas Parliament by the Sex Disqualification (Removal) Act, 1919, and various other enactments, had sought to establish equality in law between the sexes, and it is expedient that this principle should obtain with respect to the guardianship of infants and the rights and responsibilities conferred thereby:' then stating in Section 1 that in custody and related proceedings the court was to regard the child's welfare as the first and paramount consideration, and was not to consider 'whether from any other point of view the claim of the father, or any right at common law possessed by the father . . . is superior to that of the mother, or the claim of the mother is superior to that of the father'. Later legislation, in the 1970s,[47] equalised maternal and paternal rights in general, that is before custody or other disputes arose, and thus carried the 1925 principle further.

In a situation of formal equality for women, is it fair to associate the modern form of *laissez-faire* with patriarchy? It might be thought, as Goldstein *et al.*'s wording suggests, that the discussion is only about *parents* and in no sense favours the power of fathers over that of mothers. Indeed, in a context where women as primary caretakers are more likely to be construed as the main 'psychological parent', and certainly in practice are more likely to gain custody or actual care of the child on divorce, it might be thought that *laissez-faire* entails *matriarchy* rather than patriarchy. Single parents are now a sizeable minority among families (about a million families in Britain in 1986 or about 14 per cent of families, this representing about 1.5 million children or 14 per cent of children; over 14 million children in the United States or about 24 per cent of children[48]) and most single parents are mothers (over 90 per cent in Britain, and a similar proportion in the United States[49]). As well as divorced motherhood, it may be noted, unmarried motherhood is becoming more common. (In Britain in 1988, over 25 per cent of births were outside marriage,[50] although many of these births were registered by both parents.[51]) In an increasing number of cases, then, the parent who has sole day-to-day care of the child is the mother. Parental autonomy would then mean *maternal* autonomy – the right of mothers to conduct their family life in their own way, without interference from either child care agencies or other adults – including, among these other adults, non-custodial fathers, if the Goldstein model is followed.

The point may be conceded to a degree with regard to single parents; although single parent mothers remain vulnerable to the forces of patriarchy in the wider society. Where there are two co-resident parents, however, it may be argued that males still have greater *de facto* power, for example economic power, with male violence within the family being an extreme manifestation of power. Parental autonomy could then mean greater autonomy for fathers than mothers. Offsetting this, mothers may have much scope for day-to-day control and minor decisions. Relative maternal and paternal power in the family perhaps deserves further investigation, although it is beyond the scope of this book.

However, before leaving the first value perspective, a modern connection between *laissez-faire* and patriarchy should be commented on. There is a school of thought which would like to see *both* a reduction in the welfare and therapeutic interventions of the state, *and* a reassertion of male authority within the family (and this school also tends to be deeply antagonistic to single parent families). Berger and Berger (1983)[52] have characterised this school of thought as a 'neotraditionalist' perspective on the family, and as essentially a backlash phenomenon. It contains strands of anti-permissiveness, anti-feminism, and a moral anxiety about the breakdown of the family and the wider moral order.[53] It favours traditional role divisions within the family and permanent marriage. In the British context, a pressure group called the Conservative Family Campaign, formed in 1986, numbered among its aims: 'to put father back at the head of the family table',[54] although it was vague about how this might actually be achieved. Other bodies with this type of objective have also appeared. And the right-wing Institute of Economic Affairs issued a publication on the family, also in 1986,[55] which spoke of: 'the normal family . . . the husband being the principal if not the only breadwinner', lamenting a perceived transfer of power and responsibility from family to state.

As mentioned earlier, support for patriarchy is not confined to the political right. Two academic examples may be cited. Lasch (1977)[56] deplores the decline of the patriarchal family over the last century, seeing state control over the family and child-rearing as having been extended in an undesirable way, while paternal authority has been weakened by capitalism, consumerism and market forces. Donzelot (1979)[57] sees family authority as no longer endorsed and supported by the state but 'colonised' in a patriarchy *of* the state, through the interventions of various 'experts'. These therapeutic interventions, working through mothers specifically, are distrusted as apparatuses of control. It appears that the reduction of paternal power is regretted. The support for patriarchy is more subtle in these authors' work, but is nevertheless arguably present.[58] Certainly patriarchy is seen as being weakened as the welfare role of the state has expanded – and both trends are apparently lamented. Reversing the trend would appear to mean reinstating a strong form of patriarchy.

# SOME REFERENCES RELEVANT TO THIS PERSPECTIVE

E.S. Cole 1979 'Conflicting rights' *Adoption and Fostering* 95 35–40

L.B. Costin and C.A. Rapp 1984 *Child Welfare Policies and Practice* 3rd edition New York, McGraw-Hill

D.N. Duquette 1981 'The Legal Aspects of Child Abuse and Neglect' in Ed K.C. Faller *Social Work with Abused and Neglected Children* New York, Free Press

M.D.A. Freeman 1983 'Freedom and the Welfare State: Child-rearing, Parental Autonomy and State Intervention' *Journal of Social Welfare Law* March 1983 70–91

J. Goldstein, A. Freud and A. Solnit 1973, 1979 *Beyond the Best Interests of the Child* New York, Free Press

J. Goldstein, A. Freud and A. Solnit 1980 *Before the Best Interests of the Child* London, Burnett Books/André Deutsch

P. Hodges 1981 'Children and Parents: Who Chooses?' (a review of J. Goldstein *et al.* 1973 *Beyond the Best Interests of the Child* and 1980 *Before the Best Interests of the Child Politics and Power* 3

D. Katkin, B. Bullington and M. Levine 1974 'Above and Beyond the Best Interests of the Child: An Inquiry into the Relationship between Social Science and Social Action' *Law and Society Review* 8(4) 669–687

S. Katz, R.-A.W. Howe and M. McGrath 1975 'Child Neglect Laws in America' *Family Law Quarterly* IX I

B.G. McGowan and W. Meezan (Eds) 1983 *Child Welfare Current Dilemmas, Future Directions* Illinois, Peacock Publishers Inc.

R.H. Mnookin 1973 'Foster Care: in Whose Best Interest' *Harvard Educational Review* 43(4) 599

R.H. Mnookin 1975 'Child Custody Adjudication: Judicial Functions in the Face of Indeterminacy' *Law and Contemporary Problems* 39

A. Morris, H. Giller, E. Szwed and H. Geach 1980 *Justice for Children* London and Basingstoke, Macmillan

L. Taylor, R. Lacey and D. Bracken 1980 *In Whose Best Interests? The unjust treatment of children in courts and institutions* London, Cobden Trust and MIND

M. Wald 1975 'State intervention on behalf of neglected children: A search for realistic standards' *Stanford Law Review* 27 985–1040

M. Wald 1976 'Neglected Children: Standards for Removal of Children from their homes, monitoring the status of children in foster care, and termination of parental rights' *Stanford Law Review* 28 622–70

## NOTES AND REFERENCES

1.  F. Mount 1982 *The Subversive Family* London, Cape.
2.  There is a wide range of feminist writings encompassing the family; for example: M. Barrett and M. McIntosh 1982 *The Antisocial Family* London, Verso; J. Brannen and G. Wilson 1987 *Give and Take in Families. Studies in resource distribution* London, Allen and Unwin; A. Oakley 1976 *Housewife* Harmondsworth, Penguin; A. Oakley 1982 *Subject Women* Glasgow, Fontana; B. Thorne and M. Yalom (Eds) 1982 *Rethinking the Family. Some feminist questions* New York/London, Longman; D. Gittins 1985 *The Family in Question. Changing Households and Familiar Ideologies* Basingstoke, Macmillan Education.
3.  R. Dingwall, J. Eekelaar and T. Murray 1983 *The Protection of Children: State Intervention and Family Life* Oxford, Blackwell.
4.  J. Goldstein, A. Freud and A. Solnit 1973, 1979 *Beyond the Best Interests of the Child* New York, Free Press.

5. J. Goldstein, A. Freud and A. Solnit 1980 *Before the Best Interests of the Child* Chapter 1, footnote 3.
6. A. Morris, H. Giller, E. Szwed and H. Geach 1980 *Justice for Children* London and Basingstoke, Macmillan.
7. A Family Court was recommended in the Finer Report on One Parent Families 1974 *Report of the Committee on One Parent Families* Cmnd. 5629 London, HMSO. There was sporadic interest and campaigning around this issue after the Finer Report, increasing in intensity with the government review of child care law (see Chapter 4, footnote 23) in the mid-1980s. The Children Act 1989 went some way to achieving the features associated with the 'family court' model, though it did not institute a family court as such.
8. L. Taylor, R. Lacey and D. Bracken 1980 *In Whose Best Interests? The unjust treatment of children in courts and institutions* London, Cobden Trust and MIND.
9. M. Wald in M. K. Rosenbaum (Ed) 1976 *Pursuing Justice for the Child* University of Chicago Press; as referred to in L. Taylor *et al.* 1980 *In Whose Best Interests?* footnote 8.
10. M.D.A. Freeman 1983 'Freedom and the Welfare State: Child-Rearing, Parental Autonomy and State Intervention' *Journal of Social Welfare Law* March 1983 70–91.
11. P. Hodges 1981 'Children and Parents: Who Chooses?' (a review of J. Goldstein *et al.* 1973 *Beyond the Best Interests of the Child* This chapter, footnote 4, and 1980 *Before the Best Interests of the Child* Chapter 1, footnote 3) *Politics and Power* 3 1981.
12. For example, the 1975 Children Act (Section 26) allowed adults adopted as children access to their original birth certificate, hence possibly the opportunity to trace their original, biological parent(s). Changes in the law have also given more rights to unmarried fathers and to 'illegitimate' children. Under the Legitimacy Act 1959 and the Guardianship of Minors Act 1971, an unmarried father could apply for custody or access. The Houghton Report 1972 (see Chapter 3, footnote 64) sought to strengthen the unmarried father's position, as did the ensuing Children Act 1975. A number of subsequent reports from the Law Commission recommended effectively strengthening the unmarried father's legal position: 1979 *Illegitimacy. Working Paper No. 74*; 1982 *Illegitimacy. Report 118;* 1986 *Illegitimacy (Second Report). Report 157* Cmnd. 9913 London, HMSO. The proposals of the last of these were embodied in the Family Law Reform Act 1987, implemented in 1989, which abolished illegitimacy as a legal category, and allowed fathers to apply to a court to share parental rights with mothers. Under the Children Act 1989 an unmarried father can obtain 'parental responsibility' either through a court application or a formal agreement with the mother. All these moves, which have in general weakened the legal distinctions between father-child relations in and out of wedlock, suggest, *inter alia*, a stress on the importance of biological bonds.

    'Blood tie' cases include Re: E 1981, where a county court gave custody to a putative father who was a stranger to the child. However, this decision was reversed on appeal. (Re: E (an infant) Court of Appeal 25 June 1981; reported in *Adoption and Fostering* 106(4) December 1981.)

13. D. Katkin, B. Bullington and M. Levine 1974 'Above and Beyond the Best Interests of the Child: An Inquiry into the Relationship between Social Science and Social Action' *Law and Society Review* Vol. 8(4) 669–87.

14. See Freeman 1983 'Freedom and the Welfare State' 71–2. This chapter, footnote 10.

15. P. Cawson *et al.* 1978 *Young Offenders in Care* Preliminary Report (unpublished); later, DHSS Social Research Branch; as quoted by Morris *et al.* 1980 *Justice for Children* This chapter, footnote 6.

16. S. Millham 1978 *Locking up Children* Farnborough, Saxon House; as quoted by Morris *et al.* 1980 *Justice for Children* This chapter, footnote 6.

17. R. Holman 1976 *Inequality in Child Care* London, Child Poverty Action Group, Poverty Pamphlet 26; as quoted by Morris *et al.* 1980 *Justice for Children* This chapter, footnote 6.

18. D. Thorpe, J. Paley and G. Green 1979 'The making of a delinquent' *Community Care* 26 April 1979; as quoted by Taylor *et al.* 1980 *In Whose Best Interests?* This chapter, footnote 8.

19. 156 Cal. Rptr. 48 1979, *cert. denied* 1980 100 S.Ct. 1597; as quoted in Freeman 1983 'Freedom and the Welfare State' This chapter, footnote 10. See Freeman for a fuller discussion of this case.

20. L. M. Harding 1987 'The Debate on Surrogate Motherhood: The Current Situation, Some Arguments and Issues; Questions Facing Law and Policy' *Journal of Social Welfare Law* Jan. 1987 37–63.

21. Further evidence of the importance of biological links may be found in the (often considerable) efforts of some individuals (including some conceived by artificial insemination) to trace their unknown biological fathers; and the efforts of those who as children were emigrated by child care agencies to (then) colonies such as Canada and Australia, to search much later in life for their original, biological families.

    On the search for the missing biological father, see, for example: J. Cunningham 1983 'When a father is a missing link' *The Guardian* 2 November 1983; P. Toynbee 1985 *Lost Children*; On the emigrated children: P. Bean and J. Melville 1989 *Lost Children of the Empire* Unwin Hyman.

    However, it should also be noted that of adopted adults eligible for access to their original birth certificate only a small minority seem to have exercised this right, and of those who do apply for such access, again only a small minority actually want to make contact with their birth parents as opposed to just obtaining information. See: J. Triseliotis 1970 *In Search of Origins: the experience of adopted children* London, Routledge Kegan Paul (on Scotland, where the right of access to the birth certificate has existed for longer); *The Guardian* 21 October 1977, 14 September 1983; J. Melville 1983 'Looking for a Mother' *New Society* 8 December 1983; DHSS 1984 *Second Report on the Children Act 1975*.

22. D. Katkin *et al.* 1974 'Above and Beyond the Best Interests of the Child'. This chapter, footnote 13.

23. R. Holman 1975 'The Place of Fostering in Social Work' *British Journal of Social Work* 5(1) 3–29. See also: R. Holman 1982 'Exclusive and inclusive fostering' in Family Rights Group *Fostering Parental Contact*.

24. R. Benians 1982 'Preserving parental contact: a factor in promoting healthy growth and development in children in Family Rights Group *Fostering Parental Contact*' footnote 23.

25. M.D.A. Freeman 1983 'Freedom and the Welfare State'. This chapter, footnote 10.

26. Shelley v. Westbrooke 1817, Jac. 266n.

27. For many centuries, the wardship jurisdiction of England and Wales has enabled the state through the courts effectively to act *in loco parentis* towards certain children. Under this jurisdiction, application can be made to the court for a child to be placed under its control. The court can then appoint a guardian for the child or make it a ward of court, in which case all significant decisions are taken by the court itself. The power derived from the notion of the sovereign as *parens patriae* (parent of the country) and thus protector of the weakest. However, in mediaeval times wardship was primarily a means of ensuring that guardians of minors administered their affairs fairly and handed over property intact at the ward's majority. The jurisdiction later came to be used to settle disputes about children's upbringing, and in the 1970s and 1980s was used by local authorities to protect children where other child care legislation seemed inadequate. However, the Children Act 1989 restricted such usage by local authorities. See: N. V. Lowe and R.A.H. White 1979 *Wards of Court* London, Butterworths. 2nd ed.: 1986 London, Barry Rose; N. Finnis 1980 'Wardship: a fairer way of caring?' *Community Care* 3 July 1980.

28. In re Agar-Ellis 1878 10 Ch.D. p.49; In re Agar-Ellis 1883 24 Ch.D. p. 317.

29. In re Agar-Ellis 1878, footnote 28. This case reference is to the appeal case.

30. Shelley v. Westbrooke This chapter, footnote 26.

31. Wellesley v. Wellesley 2 Bli. (N. S.) 124 (as quoted in Agar-Ellis 1878 case report).

32. In re-Agar Ellis 1878 Op. cit. This chapter, footnote 28.

33. In re-Agar Ellis 1883 Op. cit. This chapter, footnote 28.

34. I. Pinchbeck and M. Hewitt 1969 *Children in English Society* Vol. II. London, Routledge Kegan Paul.

35. Ibid.

36. G. K. Behlmer 1982 *Child abuse and moral reform in England 1870–1908* Stanford, California, Stanford University Press.

37. See, for example: J. Pierson 1983 'The American Way' *Community Care* 13 October 1983; P.A. Sinanoglu 1984 'From drift to permanency: the US 1980 legislation' *Adoption and Fostering* 8(4) 10–14.

38. B. G. McGowan 1983 'Historical Evolution of Child Welfare Services: an Examination of the Sources of Current Problems and Dilemmas' in B. G. McGowan and W. Meezan (Eds) *Child Welfare Current Dilemmas. Future Directions* Illinois, Peacock Publishers Inc.

39. L. B. Costin and C. A. Rapp 1984 *Child Welfare Policies and Practice* 3rd edition. New York, McGraw-Hill.

40. M. Wald 1975 'State intervention on behalf of neglected children: A search for realistic standards' *Stanford Law Review* 27 985–1040. M. Wald 1976 'Neglected Children: Standards for Removal of Children from their

homes, monitoring the status of children in foster care, and termination of parental rights' *Stanford Law Review* 28 622–70.

41.  R. H. Mnookin 1973 'Foster Care: in Whose Best Interest' *Harvard Educational Review* 43(4) 599. R. H. Mnookin 1975 'Child Custody Adjudication: Judicial Functions in the Face of Indeterminacy' *Law and Contemporary Problems* 39.

42.  D. N. Duquette 1981 'The Legal Aspects of Child Abuse and Neglect' in K. C. Faller *Social Work with Abused and Neglected Children* New York, Free Press.

43.  E. S. Cole 1979 'Conflicting rights' *Adoption and Fostering* No. 95. 35–40.

44.  S. Katz, R.-A. W. Howe and M. McGrath 1975 'Child Neglect Laws in America' *Family Law Quarterly* IX(I) Spring 1975.

45.  M.D.A. Freeman 1983 *The Rights and Wrongs of Children* London, Frances Pinter.

46.  In divorce, the relevant Act in the nineteenth century was the Matrimonial Causes Act 1857. In the field of married women's property, nineteenth century Acts included the Married Women's Property Acts of 1870, 1882, and 1884.

47.  Guardianship of Minors Act 1971. Guardianship Act 1973. See: S. Maidment 1976 'A Look at Equal Parental Rights' *New Law Journal* 126.5572 14 October 1976.

48.  Facts on U.K. one parent families from: National Council for One Parent Families (NCOPF) 1988 *Helping One-Parent Families to Work A Programme for Action* London, NCOPF; and other NCOPF sources. Central Statistical Office *Social Trends 1988* London, HMSO; Office of Population Censuses and Surveys (OPCS) 1989 *Population Trends* 55 London, HMSO.

Facts on U.S. one parent families from: M. Meade King 1988 'Unpaid dues' *The Guardian* 1 March 1988.

49.  Ibid.

50.  While in 1980 13 per cent of live births in England and Wales were outside marriage, by 1983 the proportion had risen to 19 per cent, and by 1986 to over 21 per cent. The latest figure at the time of writing was for 1988 when the proportion was over 25 per cent. Sources: OPCS *Birth Statistics* as quoted in NCOPF 1988 *Helping One-Parent Families to Work* Footnote 48; *The Guardian* 3 September 1984 and 30 June 1989; Family Policy Studies Centre *Family Policy Bulletin* No. 7, Spring/Summer 1989.

51.  In 1987 (when births outside marriage had reached 23 per cent) 68 per cent of these births were registered by both parents, of whom 70 per cent gave the same address. Source: Family Policy Studies Centre *Family Policy Bulletin* Footnote 50; Official estimates are that at least half of all babies born to unmarried parents are being cared for by both of them living together. Source: *The Guardian* 30 June 1989.

Also see: P. Moss and G. Lau 1985 'Mothers without marriages' *New Society* 9 August 1985. A. Spackman 1988 'Why the family is crumbling' *Independent* 13 June 1988.

52.  B. Berger and P. L. Berger 1983 *The War over the Family. Capturing the Middle Ground* London, Hutchinson.

53.  For a development of this analysis relevant to child care, see: N. Parton

1981 'Child Abuse, Social Anxiety and Welfare' *British Journal of Social Work* 11(4) 394–414; N. Parton 1985 *The Politics of Child Abuse* London, Macmillan; N. Parton 1985 'Politics and practice' *Community Care* 26 September 1985 22–4.

54. Conservative Family Campaign press release: 'Putting Children First' 14 March 1986.

55. D. Anderson and G. Dawson 1986 *Family Portraits* Social Affairs Unit/Esmonde Publishing Ltd.

56. C. Lasch 1977 *Haven in a Heartless World. The Family Beseiged* New York, Basic Books.

57. J. Donzelot 1980 *The Policing of Families: Welfare versus the State* London, Hutchinson.

58. See the discussion of these authors' work in M. Barrett and M. McIntosh 1982 *The Antisocial Family* This chapter, footnote 2.

# CHAPTER THREE
# *State paternalism and child protection*

## INTRODUCTION

The term 'state paternalism and child protection' is taken to indicate the school of thought which favours extensive state intervention to protect children from poor parental care. Where parental care is inadequate, finding the child a new permanent home where good quality care will be provided is favoured. The rights and liberties of parents are given a low priority; the child is paramount.

### (i) *The main elements of the perspective*

In striking contrast to the *laissez-faire* school of thought, the second perspective envisages a very considerable role for the state in intervening (coercively if need be) in families, in order to protect children from cruelty or inadequate care. The approach may be seen as rooted in a stronger awareness that (birth) parental care is not always good, indeed may be intensely damaging; higher standards would be set for appropriate care than in the *laissez-faire* perspective, norms of child-rearing would be more likely to be defined and imposed, and there is a tendency to be more punitive towards parents who fall short of particular norms and standards. The paternalist/protectionist orientation to parental care is complemented by the view that children should have a high priority in society, that they have rights to a good standard of care, and should at all costs be protected, using the force of the law where necessary, from ill-treatment. Thus parental rights are not valued highly in this approach; it is the parental *duty* to care properly for the child which is prominent, and where this duty is not met, the state may well be justified in removing the child permanently to other caretakers. The child's well-being is paramount, and adult needs, interests and rights must if necessary be sacrificed to this end. There is thus a strong sense of identification with the suffering child. While in a sense the state paternalist perspective emphasises children's *rights*, it focuses on the child's right to adequate nurturance and care rather than to self-determination, in contrast to the fourth, 'children's rights' perspective. That is, the child is seen as essentially dependent, vulnerable, and with needs which are different from those of the adult; the child's rights are, in effect, to the presence of caring adults who will then meet his needs – and are thus different from adult rights. As children are not perceived as responsible for themselves in the way adults are, the child's welfare is largely imputed to him by adults, in this case usually the agents of the state, and possibly the substitute parental caretakers. There is not the same assumption as in the minimalist school that the birth parents generally know and do what is best for the child – but it seems that *other* adults *are* expected to do so.

Somewhat overlooked in the second value perspective is the possible strength of the child's bonds with the original parent even when this parent is deemed to be unsatisfactory. Proponents of this school share with Goldstein, Freud and Solnit an emphasis on *psychological* rather than *biological* bonds; but their attitude to continuity with the original biological and psychological parent seems to differ. Goldstein *et al.* would see value in a child remaining with an unsatisfactory parent who has nevertheless psychologically parented the child; the threshold of mistreatment at which, in their view, removal would be justified is relatively high. With the state paternalist perspective, removal, or at least some form of intervention, could take place at a much lower threshold of problematic care, with the child's welfare more readily seen as lying with other, better caretakers, with whom psychological bonds could be formed in the future. Continuity *per se* is not so highly valued, nor is the original family's integrity and autonomy.

The concept of the state in this approach also stands in marked contrast to the first value position. Much greater faith is placed in the value of beneficent state action to protect children's welfare. The state not only has the *duty* to intervene where there is inadequate care or suspicion of it, but also the *capacity* to provide something better for the child. The state decision-makers – courts and social workers – are seen as able to make sound and valid assessments of what would be best for the child. Substitute care through adoption and (secure) fostering is also positively valued, and in particular adoption tends to be seen as an extremely favourable solution for the care of the child whose original parents are found to be wanting. There is a lack of emphasis on the possible negative aspects of state intervention, and a highly favourable image of the 'rescue' of suffering children to other, better homes. There is neglect of the insidious class element in state care where, broadly speaking, middle-class decision-makers pass judgement on working-class parents and, again broadly, children from deprived homes are placed in somewhat better-off ones. Also overlooked are the difficulties of arriving at a judgement of what *is* best for the child's future welfare; and the problems and stresses attendant upon the substitute care provided by the state. The concept of adoption and foster care is perhaps over-idealised, with the problems of relationships within adoptive and foster families, of lost biological and early psychological ties, of the child's being removed from her cultural origins, being played down.

Furthermore, the emphasis is on good quality child care as judged by professionals and experts. Such a judgement may in reality be experienced as oppressive and intrusive, and both the parent's and the child's viewpoint as to the most preferable option may be undervalued here (although one variant of the view would give *some* emphasis to the child's own wishes). The state in the paternalist perspective is construed as neutral and wise, taking the best course of action for children. Yet the controlling aspect of the state's role is perhaps not fully acknowledged. The implied role of the state is one of extensive surveillance of, and intervention in, child-rearing; but the civil liberties implications of such a role may be disregarded, as may the possibility of misjudgements of abuse and the unnecessary – and traumatic – separation of parent and child. Parents would be highly accountable to the state – a notion in conflict with the traditional one of (relatively) autonomous and private family units. The child protection machinery of the state takes on a potentially authoritarian character in this perspective. What perhaps is underestimated is the degree of resistance by individuals to what is perceived by them as excessively heavy-handed state action. Nor is the essentially political nature of the state sufficiently recognised, it seems. The state is not seen as a political creation defending particular interests and systems, as an institution which may have undeclared political reasons for taking the actions it does; the state is perceived more as a 'good parent', acting wisely to protect the weak, and blind to divisions of class, ethnicity and gender. Another way in which the viewpoint may be described as apolitical lies in the way that apparently 'bad' parenting is construed. This is largely seen as stemming from personal pathology rather than from oppression and deprivation, as some would argue.

In summary, in the paternalist and child protection value perspective, those birth parents who do not bring up their children 'well' cannot expect to keep them. When they fail, state power should be readily and extensively used to provide something better for the children. This would usually be an adoptive or secure, long-term foster home. (It might also be a residential home, although residential care is not on the whole favoured in this perspective.) The original unsatisfactory parents would then tend to be excluded from the child's life and would lose their rights. The state in this perspective has a much broader role than in the *laissez-faire* view and would act authoritatively at a much lower threshold of parental mistreatment. The focus is very much on the child as a separate individual rather than the parents or the (birth) family as a unit. Other possible terms for this position are the 'child salvationist' or 'child rescue' approach.

## (ii)  *Some authors associated with the perspective*

A considerable number of authors have, broadly speaking, supported strong state intervention in child care matters, and favoured adoption and fostering as alternative methods of child care to the birth family. The first example to be discussed is Kellmer Pringle, who in *The Needs of Children* (1974)[1] was extremely critical of a societal emphasis on biological parenthood which she saw as detrimental to the child. In her view society over valued children's ties with their birth parents and was too slow to cut them permanently. Society suffered from a misplaced faith in the blood tie and an over-romanticised picture of parenthood. Kellmer Pringle identified an idea that children belong to their parents like their other possessions, over which they may experience exclusive rights; she sees this as a view which has no factual foundation and should be rejected. Children should be seen rather as only on temporary loan to their parents. Kellmer Pringle argues for a concept of responsible and informed parenthood and a recognition that the ability and willingness to undertake the responsibilities of parenthood are not dependent on, nor necessarily a consequence of, biological parenthood.

The stress on psychological parenthood is in line with Goldstein, Freud and Solnit's. Where Kellmer Pringle parts company with them sharply, however, is on the preferred role of society, acting presumably largely through the state, in intervening between parent and child. She suggests that we go too far in asserting that the way parents bring up their children is solely their own concern. In law and policy, she says, we often act as though the overvalued blood tie ensured satisfactory parenting, with the result that the child's well-being is sacrificed; for example, abused children may be returned to parents when there is a high risk of their being abused again, while thousands of children are condemned to remain in care without permanent substitute parents, in the hope that biological parental interest might be re-awakened. Kellmer Pringle would see support to parents to enable them to care for their children adequately as lying on a continuum with other, more coercive forms of state intervention. One quotation is revealing; she says: 'Bringing up children is too important a task to be left entirely to those parents who are patently in need of support, guidance and, where necessary, sanctions on the part of the community.' Paternalistic control, it seems, extends to the parents as well as the children. Kellmer Pringle might also be deemed to be punitive towards parents and too prepared to prejudge them in a rather rigid way. For example, she comments: 'Those who have been deprived of adequate parental care . . . have little chance of becoming in turn responsible parents themselves', and argues that it is a myth that the maternal role will be fulfilling to a single girl who has herself been rejected in childhood; in the argument that the girl should keep the child and will be helped by this to maturity, the child's welfare is sacrificed to the adult's.

Kellmer Pringle's comments on (then) existing law and policy must be seen in the context in which she wrote, the early 1970s in Britain. In a later publication in 1980[2] she put greater emphasis on prevention of poor child care through wide-ranging support services to families, thus falling into line more with the third value perspective to be discussed, the pro-birth parent view; although the child's rights to loving care, and the parental duty to provide it, were still stressed. The theme of support services occurs elsewhere in Kellmer Pringle's writing,[3] but the 1974 publication remains an interesting example of the protectionist approach.

Like other authors associated with this perspective, Kellmer Pringle is keenly aware of the problems of inadequate child care and failure to meet children's needs. Some authors whose particular pre-occupation is child abuse see a need to make child welfare an overriding social priority and therefore to have strong state intervention in child care. Dingwall, Eekelaar and Murray[4] (1983) quote one example, A. W. Franklin[5] (1982), who says:

> What is needed is for all countries, including our own, to accept the overwhelming importance of the growth and development of children to their full potential and of the need to make this a conscious goal.

> Each country should then accept certain responsibilities – to examine the ways in which this goal can be achieved, to examine those attitudes and practices which hinder the achievement of this goal and to renew, in the context of their own society and culture, the priority to be given to the achievement of this goal.

Dingwall *et al.* comment: 'The heavy-handed paternalism and religiosity of these sentiments are characteristic of many of the best-known writers on child mistreatment. It is argued that child welfare should and must be an absolute social priority. Anyone failing to accept this whole-heartedly may then be justly criticised.' The analysis favoured by Dingwall *et al.*, however, 'depicts agencies as balancing several partially conflicting objectives and points to the real disadvantages of an unreflective pursuit of child protection as an overriding goal'. The failures of child care agencies then are 'not necessarily ignoble'. This point will be taken up later.

Another example of a child abuse author is afforded by Howells[6] (1974) who in an anecdotal book *Remember Maria* – a reference to the Colwell case of 1973 – argues against giving excessive weight to biological parent-child bonds, stating that 'We are forced to conclude that the parent-child bond is not mystical, nor is it ever-present' and that 'The capacity to relate does not depend upon gender role, legal status, mental status etc., but upon the relating experience of that person in his own preceding family'. Separation from the birth family may be beneficial to the child, leading to loving care elsewhere. The implication of this is presumably that such separation must sometimes be enforced or forcibly maintained. However, Howells favours non-coercive therapeutic work with families as well as greater surveillance and coercive action in some circumstances.

The type of approach advocated by some child abuse authors is characterised by Dingwall *et al.* as a 'strict liability' approach. Such an approach regards all injuries or disorders in children as unequivocal evidence of neglect or abuse, and of deficiency in the parents. That is, the emphasis is on *clinical* rather than *social* evidence, and the approach is particularly associated with the medical profession. It may also be linked with a strict moral code and absolute standards; departures from the ideal in this approach would indicate psychopathology. Dingwall *et al.* in fact, in their research, found the approach to be a minority one; most of their informants took the view that clinical evidence must be supplemented by considerations of the child's general state and social environment in identifying abuse.

An overweening concern with abuse may also give rise to definitions which broaden the concept of abuse, and therefore the grounds on which society may be deemed justified in intervening. For example, Gil[7] (1975) puts forward a 'value-based definition' of child abuse as follows: 'any act of commission or omission by individuals, institutions, or society as a whole, and any conditions resulting from such acts or inaction, which deprive children of equal rights and liberties, and/or interfere with their optimal development, constitute, by definition, abusive or neglectful acts or conditions'. Such a broad definition of abuse contrasts sharply with the *laissez-faire* attempt to *restrict* the definition. Gil sees the fundamental cause of child abuse as lying in the society's basic social philosophy and value premises; in this case, criticism is put of non–egalitarian and competitive philosophies. While interpretations of society's deficiencies may vary, others who are particularly concerned about abuse also sometimes link this with a wider, if rather unfocused, social or moral concern. And Parton[8] (1981) sees the identification of child abuse as a social problem as being part of a more generalised moral anxiety in Britain in the 1970s about the failings of the family as an agent of socialisation, and about the social order.

Perhaps a logical conclusion of extremely pronounced concern about child abuse is the concept of licensing for parenthood. As early as 1974 Lord and Weisfeld[9] suggested that this had already been advocated or predicted, with a similar rationale as for licensing people to drive. They commented: 'Perhaps in the 21st or 22nd centuries such legislation and licensing programs may end – or diminish – child abuse, battering, and neglect. In the meantime . . .?' The absolute goal of elimination of child cruelty is here linked with stringent limitations on the liberties of adults.

Strict liability, a broader concept of abuse, and licensing for parent-hood – all indicate where concern about child abuse may lead, taken to its logical conclusion. A less extreme position can also be taken, however, which might also be argued to lie broadly within the state paternalist camp. Although Dingwall *et al.*, as shown, are somewhat critical of the position of some of the child abuse authors, they occupy at least a moderate state paternalist/protectionist position themselves, stating in an article[10] that in their view 'children are not the property of their parents. Parents are trustees for their children's interests: as with any trust, if they fail in the duties involved, they should be discharged. The only body with the legitimacy to monitor and enforce such duties is the state.' To reiterate an earlier point, Dingwall *et al.*'s research showed that in practice social workers preferred the least stigmatising interpretation of what had happened to a child and the least coercive form of intervention. They erred, in other words, on the side of using power too little. Dingwall *et al.* do not seek a sweeping extension of state power, although they recommend, among other changes, a power to make *parental* supervision orders which would give local authorities more power in child protection cases where children were not actually taken into care. The authors argue in their article that 'the central issue in child care law is the adequacy of parental conduct' – the system should place parental conduct at its centre. The proper alternative to removing a child, they contend, is a power to supervise *parents* – the existing supervision orders only confer power to direct the *child's* conduct, an absurdity in protection cases. A parental supervision order should give authorities the power to direct parents in the discharge of their duties, which might include presenting the child for medical inspection or bringing her regularly to a nursery, for example. Staff would also have a right of entry to the home and an emergency power to remove the child for a short time. However, because of the sweeping nature of the parental supervision powers, the order should be limited to one year (and not be renewable) with parents able to apply for revocation after three months. Dingwall *et al.* also advocate some legal provision to cover children at risk of abuse without having to wait until the damage has actually been inflicted.

Dingwall *et al.* are aware that child protection walks a 'delicate tightrope' between libertarian critics on the one hand and authoritarian critics on the other; in fact, they see the present balance in English child care as about right, albeit 'maybe even excessively respectful of the non-interventionist case', and support only 'a measure of consolidation and evolutionary change'. The paternalist or protectionist emphasis is present but in an attenuated form. In their main publication the authors say that while their 'personal conclusion might be that agency staff are over-respectful of parental liberties and that "justice for children" may require more rather than less state intervention', they see the deficiencies arising, not so much from the failings of the agencies, as from the limitations of 'the licenses and charters which we, as citizens, have granted to them'. They explain the dilemma facing the liberal society and state within which child care agencies operate, a state which is different in concept from the 'absolutist "paternal" state' advocated by the more extreme of the child abuse authors. In the liberal state the family is seen as an important check on state power, yet childhood is a critical point in moral socialisation. The problem for the liberal is how to regulate the moral socialisation of children and make child-rearing into a matter of public rather than purely private concern, without destroying the ideal of the autonomous family as a counterweight to state power. While the liberal model of society outlined here would seem to be compatible with Goldstein's *laissez-faire* approach, Dingwall *et al.* in fact identify a 'liberal compromise' which has occurred in the society they are studying ie Britain. The result of this compromise 'is a system which is fully effective neither in preventing mistreatment nor in respecting family privacy but which lurches unevenly between these two poles'. The problem is that agencies 'cannot be given the legal power to underwrite an investigative form of surveillance without destroying the liberal family. At the same time, the state cannot opt out.' There is a need for state surveillance of the well-being of future citizens, but the state 'will always remain vulnerable to criticism from Utopian libertarians whose ideals break on the brute physical reality of children's dependence on adults'. Dingwall *et al.* discuss the liberal state and society sympathetically, but perhaps the wording of this comment, as well as the actual policy recommendations that they make, illustrates the distance they stand both from *laissez-faire* and, as will be shown, the children's rights school.

Other authors whose research work may be associated with the state paternalist/protectionist school of thought will be considered briefly. Tizard[11] (1977) puts a case for greater readiness to terminate parental rights and place children for adoption, based on her study which compared children in institutional care in early life who were subsequently adopted, with similar children who were restored to their natural parent. The findings led Tizard to conclude that the adopted children were the more fortunate group – they had fewer problems than the restored children (although this was related to social class). With reference to the natural mothers whose children had been restored to them, she commented 'The blood tie by no means implied a love tie', and that the adoptive mothers were warmer and more affectionate on the whole than the natural mothers. In Tizard's view, fostering did not offer the security of adoption; the uncertainty disturbed the children and contacts with the natural parents aroused anxiety in them. Her study suggested that social work decisions (at that time – the research was done in the late 1960s and early 1970s) were influenced by a number of assumptions including the primacy of the blood tie and the primacy of natural parental possession; it was accepted that children should be put in care while parents made up their minds whether to relinquish them finally or not. Parental contact, though irregular, prevented the child from forming an alternative parent-child relationship. Tizard argued that her study, together with others, suggested that attempts to restore a child to his natural family may not be in his best interests. In this view, children need someone who is unconditionally and permanently committed to them; it is difficult to see why a parent who takes no responsibility for a child's care has a right to prevent someone else from doing so. There is some resemblance here to Goldstein *et al.* However, Tizard does acknowledge that the issue is complicated by social inequality; in some cases, parents would have been able to keep the child if minimal material assistance had been available.

Other research also appears to show favourable outcomes for the adoption of children, particularly when adoption is compared to leaving a child in what might be thought to be a deprived natural home. For example, Lambert and Streather[12] (1980) using data gathered for the National Child Development Study, studied illegitimate children who were adopted, those who were not adopted, and legitimate children not adopted, at the age of eleven. The illegitimate who had *not* been adopted were on the whole disadvantaged in unfavourable circumstances compared with both those who had been adopted and the legitimate, although the authors emphasise the effects of favourable environments here rather than adoption *per se*. There is also evidence that adoption is preferable to *fostering* because of its greater security; Tizard, as indicated, argues this, and Wolkind[13] (1984), for example, states that there is overwhelming evidence that adoption is more successful than foster care.

Another study which has been used to defend a state paternalist/protectionist position was an investigation which was influential in child care policy in Britain in the 1970s – that by Rowe and Lambert[14] (1973) on children in long-term care, *Children Who Wait*. This broadly supported the view that permanent substitute parents should be found for these children. It was found that decisions about placements were often long delayed while efforts were made to solve the (birth) family's problems, yet rehabilitation back with the family was only expected for about a quarter of the children studied, and there was little actual contact with the birth parents. Most of the children judged by their social workers to need placement, needed a *permanent* rather than a temporary substitute family. Rowe and Lambert believed that social workers should be more committed to placements in permanent homes, and *Children Who Wait* had some influence on policy and practice at the time. Either the child should be speedily returned to his own family or he should be securely established in a substitute one.

Finally, the publications of the organisation British Agencies for Adoption and Fostering (BAAF), should be mentioned. BAAF is an organisation linking adoption and fostering agencies, most notably local authorities functioning in this role, which publishes a journal and pamphlets, sponsors research, conducts conferences, and generally links together and informs various professionals in this field. BAAF may be broadly associated with the child protectionist position. Although it has claimed in the 1980s that it *is* aware of the vital role of birth parents,[15] the tenor of most of its publications over time, and particularly in the late 1970s, has been in favour of permanence in good substitute care.– adoptive and foster homes – as an alternative to poor parental care, with involuntary termination of parental rights accepted more readily than in some other quarters.

The approach is illustrated by two practice guides to the 1975 Children Act produced by the then Association of British Adoption and Fostering Agencies (ABAFA) in 1976 and 1977. These guides dealt with the 1975 Act in general,[16] and with the assumption of parental rights over children in voluntary care,[17] respectively. They aimed to help social workers understand the Act, making use of case histories and similar exercises. The emphasis was on the termination of parental rights in favour of long-term fostering and adoption. One commentator, Tunstill[18] (1977), pointed out that in three out of four case histories in the guide to the assumption of parental rights, the only possibility of a 'happy ending' was by means of such steps. Children were seen as needing long-term substitute families if their own parents could not meet all their needs – if, for example, there was no consistent or affectionate relationship with the parent, or if contact was only sporadic.

A slightly later ABAFA publication, *Terminating Parental Contact*[19] (1979), a collection of papers by various authors, considered whether, and in what circumstances, a parent might be prevented from having contact with a child in care. The need to make plans for children based on a realistic assessment of whether or not rehabilitation with the birth parents was possible, and to consider the *purpose* of parental contact and its effects on the child, was stressed. The starting point in assessing the value of contact should be: is it of benefit to the child? and if so, how? The authors saw this as a somewhat uncommon approach to the problem at the time, when access to children in care was more often discussed in terms of the benefit to the parents. They took the view that if there was some doubt about the child returning home it was necessary to ask if the benefits of contact outweighed the drawbacks. Visits might strengthen bonds with a parent who was unlikely to resume care, and then constitute an obstacle to finding an appropriate placement. There was concern about certainty and security in the placement. Uncertainty and lack of continuity made it hard for the substitute parents to make a strong commitment to the child *and* include the natural parent. The concluding chapter went on to say that since 'there is an assumption in our society that the blood-tie or relationship with the parent is the ideal, then any alternative is seen as a failure rather than as something in the child's best interest'. This attack on society's overvaluation of the blood tie resembles Kellmer Pringle's. The tendency to see alternatives as second best, the ABAFA pamphlet argued, inhibited decisions. If decisions were not made, then:

> foster parents and natural pparents often make them for us by making things happen. This can be very damaging for the child. The consequences of not making a decision must be recognised. Too often we may receive a child into care and then do nothing. Yet it is at this crucial time that the child will be forming attachments to substitute caretakers, and parents will begin to deal with their pain and loss by becoming more detached.

The notion of 'permanency planning' has already been referred to in discussing *laissez-faire* in American child welfare policy. It was noted that there are different forms of permanency planning which give different weight to the original family, the foster home or the adoptive home. A form of permanency which stresses secure fostering or adoption where parental care is deemed inadequate, and a readiness to terminate parental rights as a means of achieving this, is compatible with the child protectionist perspective, and particularly with the approach of ABAFA/BAAF in the latter half of the 1970s. As indicated, ABAFA publications of the time stressed good care for children in secure foster or adoptive homes, and were (relatively) sceptical about attempts to maintain active contact with, or seek return of the child to, parents who were unlikely to be able to care adequately again. Forward planning and positive decision-making were emphasised – preferably at an early stage of entry to substitute care. As a later BAAF publication[20] (1983) noted: 'A child in care cannot have a permanent home'. State intervention is favoured; but as a means to hasten movement through care to permanency.

## (iii) *Rationale and underlying values*

The first point to note about the rationale and underlying values here is that the child is differentiated from the parents and family, and the focus on the child's welfare is paramount. A number of justifications may be found for this. Firstly, there is the moral duty to relieve suffering, especially when inflicted on those who are too weak to defend themselves. Secondly, there is the liberal argument that children are in a different category from adults in that they do not enter into contracts freely. The parent-child relationship is not one which the child chose, and therefore the state has a special duty to protect the child from mistreatment suffered in that relationship. Commenting on this 'classic liberal exemption of children' from full individual responsibility, Dingwall *et al.* say, in their article already cited: 'Although conservative intellectuals have argued for the deregulation of marriage, as a private contract between freely consenting adults, parenthood is different. Children do not enter the relationship freely. As such the state has a duty to protect them until they are capable of making rational judgements about their participation in this contract.' Thirdly, there is the more instrumental argument that children represent the society of the future, and therefore all of society, and in particular its organised expression, the state, has an interest in their socialisation. It is widely accepted that ill-treated children are likely to become delinquent or disturbed adult individuals; that, specifically, there is a link between being ill-treated as a child and ill-treating one's own children. There is a perceived social investment in treating children well, in attempting to ensure that they receive the type of upbringing that will enhance their development and produce well-socialised adults. As suggested earlier, this does raise the more fundamental question of what sort of upbringing will do this, as well as what sort of adult it is thought socially desirable to produce.

Children in this perspective are seen as essentially vulnerable, dependent and in need of protection. Their psychological needs are construed as somewhat *different* from those of adults. Kellmer Pringle, whose most relevant work here is in fact entitled *The Needs of Children*, outlines children's psycho-social needs in a four-fold classification: the need for love and security; for new experiences; for praise and recognition; and for responsibility. If these needs are not met, there is the possibility of long-term damage; indeed Kellmer Pringle comments: 'If one of the basic needs remains unmet – or inadequately met – then development may become stunted or distorted.' For example, if the need for love and security is not met adequately, 'the consequences can be disastrous later on, both for the individual and for society'. Thus it seems children are different from adults in their vulnerability to the frustration of their needs.

A knowledge, or perhaps a particular view, of child psychology, underlies this value perspective as it does the first, but the emphasis is far less strongly on the child's bond with the original parental caretaker(s). Goldstein *et al.*, for example, would recognise the biological parents as also the psychological parents in most cases. The proponents of the second perspective are, by and large, more prepared to discount this when the standard of parenting is poor and the relationship does not seem to the social worker to be good. Cooper[21] (1979) in a chapter in *Terminating Parental Contact*, admits that early attachment may exist in the face of some cruelty and neglect, but 'in this situation it may be relatively easily replaced by a stronger attachment to a warmer and more nurturing maternal figure'.

The emphasis on children as psychologically different from adults means that their rights are also different from adult rights. Freeman,[22] an author who will be considered further in discussing the fourth, children's rights perspective, summarises the perception of these rights in a protectionist perspective well. This category of children's rights, he suggests, is *overtly* concerned with protection, stressing the vulnerability of children. He says that:

> When rights are spoken of in this context, it is to inject more
> responsibility into the parental role. This approach to children's rights
> is the oldest and the most firmly entrenched. It is the concept which is
> to the fore every time a tragedy occurs and a child dies or is seriously
> injured as a result of parental ill-treatment.

Freeman further suggests that when rights are spoken of in the protection framework the attention is on certain *freedoms* that we believe children should have – freedom from abuse and neglect. But this perspective is based on 'the premise that children are unable to care for themselves and so need adult protection, care and guidance'. As Freeman points out, claims to protection are very different from claims to autonomy. The notion of protection rights constitutes 'a highly paternalistic notion. We do not ask children whether they wish to be protected'.

A second element of the underlying rationale concerns how parenthood is seen. There are some important differences in the concept of parenthood from the almost sacrosanct notion largely held by those who subscribe to the *laissez-faire* position. Parenthood is seen more as a conditional trust which, if abused, can and should be removed. The status of socially recognised parenthood is, or should be, dependent upon the provision of good quality child care; being a parent *per se* confers no special rights. Any rights contingent on parenthood are dependent on the appropriate exercise of duties; and thus adult freedoms are rightly limited by the presence of children. Kellmer Pringle carried this further than many were prepared to go by at one stage arguing that motherhood should necessarily be seen as a full-time job.[23] This could be construed as a denial of the rights and freedoms of women. This point will be taken up later. Dingwall *et al.* say in their main publication that it seems meaningful to talk in terms of children's rights 'which justify placing appropriate duties on their caretakers'. While such duties exist within a context which also ascribes certain *rights* to parents (and these rights, Dingwall *et al.* correctly point out, have a *longer* history of recognition than rights ascribed to children), the rights of parents are different from rights over property. Dingwall *et al.*'s characterisation of parents as trustees has already been mentioned. In their book they maintain that parental rights 'must be exercised for the child's benefit. In this respect the rights of parents also have some of the characteristics of duties. As Eekelaar (1973) argued, they are "duty-rights" which parents are not free to abandon, extinguish or waive so long as the child is in their care'. Trustees' rights must be used in the interests of the beneficiaries; in the case of parents, the trustees must promote the child's welfare. Where trustees prove deficient the beneficiaries have a ground for legal action in respect of the negligent discharge of their trustees' duties. But as many mistreated children are unable to initiate their own remedies, others must be licensed to do it for them.

Another way in which the child protectionist school tends to characterise parenthood is its construction of poor parenting as being largely due to individual psychopathology and history, with larger structural determinants of parenting styles tending to be de-emphasised. In this, as will be shown, it parts company with the third pro-parent value position. Kellmer Pringle, as indicated, saw those who had been deprived of adequate parental care themselves as having little chance of becoming responsible parents. Individual characteristics of abusing parents were a focus of interest for early child abuse writers, and it is still widely held, as an article by Cooper (1985) in a BAAF publication *Good Enough Parenting*[24] puts it, that:

> A harsh, neglectful or otherwise unsatisfactory upbringing . . . makes it hard for parents, in many ways, to empathise with their children and to show the necessary awareness, patience and tenderness, and the ability to put the child's needs before their own. Most abusing and neglectful parents . . . lacked adequate affection, interest and concern when young and they are now swamped by their excessive need for these supports in adult life.

A comment in an article by Loney[25] (1987) is of interest here; noting the key role of medical practitioners in concern about child abuse in the 1970s and 80s, he suggests: 'This may help to explain the overwhelming focus on the pathology of the individual abuser or his or her family. . . . there is a danger that the equally important social and cultural factors which contribute to abuse will be omitted'.

A third strand underlying the protectionist position concerns its view of the state. The state is seen as capable of beneficent, competent and unbiased action in removing children from inadequate homes and providing them with alternatives. Such a role for the state is seen as entirely justified. The state is not generally viewed as an unwarranted threat to civil liberties, or as acting differentially towards parents of different social groups. In fact, the class element in child care is not perceived as significant, whereas other positions may see a class pattern both in parenting styles and problems, and in the actions of the state towards parents. In the protectionist perspective, as already shown, it tends to be the state's universally protective role towards those in need of care which is prominent – the state as *parens patriae*, the parent of the country. There is a relatively high degree of faith in the professional servants of the state, although this may be implied rather than explicit. When social workers etc. are criticised, it is characteristically for respecting the birth parent-child bond too much. There is a belief that the state can indeed arrange a better future for the child.

The implied view of the state in this perspective accords neither with a right-wing or classically liberal concept, nor with a more left-wing radical critique. It is a view of a heavily paternal state which presumably devotes considerable resources to the searching out of, and response to, child mistreatment. Substitute care represents a cost to the state, as does investigation and supervision of children in their own homes. On the other hand, foster family care, which is generally preferred to care in residential homes, is also usually cheaper than residential care, while adoption, once it has been accomplished, may represent no definable cost at all. While the notion of large-scale supportive services to families is not completely overlooked by the proponents of this perspective, it is emphasised much less than the interventionist response to particular families where there are clear child care problems. The notion of the state here is perhaps less of a Welfare State than of a family-policing state. The existing economic and political system is often taken as given, and the state's focus in child care matters is seen as a narrow one. This point will be taken up again in considering criticisms of this perspective. It may be noted here that while some subscribers to the paternalist and protectionist viewpoint might present their position as apolitical, rather as though child care matters arose in a political and social vacuum,[26] critics might see their perspective as politically naive. It may be seen as naive, for example, to view state child welfare agencies and courts, and the principles by which they operate, as independent of the forces of class and political power.

## (iv) *Criticisms of state paternalism and child protection*

### (a) *Empirical support*

In general, the second, state paternalist value perspective seems better supported than the first, *laissez-faire* one by empirical studies relating to children and the state's child care system. Two major aspects of the empirical support for this perspective will be critically examined here: studies relating to adoption, and a study relating to children in care. In addition, brief reference will be made to the role of individual cases of extreme child abuse as support for the protectionist position.

Tizard's and Lambert and Streather's studies have been referred to. Tizard found that the adopted children in her study compared favourably with those who were restored to their natural mothers. She gives a positive picture of the effects of adoption on the child's development and the creation of an affectionate family unit, as compared with both restoration and long-term fostering. In her concluding chapter Tizard states:

> The findings of this study suggest that of the children who came into residential nurseries as infants for long-term care, the most fortunate were those who were subsequently adopted. Of course, not all the adoptions had a happy outcome; . . . Yet as a group the children were in a more stable situation, had fewer emotional problems, and were intellectually and academically superior to the fostered, institutional and restored children.

Lambert and Streather's data from the National Child Development Study showed that the illegitimate adopted compared favourably with the illegitimate non-adopted. Earlier data from the NCDS showed a similar trend. For example, it was found that at the age of seven, despite their poor start in life, the adopted children did as well as or better than others in various aspects of ability and attainment, and better than others in general knowledge and oral ability. Conversely, the illegitimate children who remained with their own mothers did relatively badly, and this was so even when they grew up in a middleclass home.[27]

Criticisms of this type of empirical support for the child protection perspective revolve firstly around the degree of significance to be afforded to the dimension of social class. Clearly the observed beneficial effects of adoption stem in part from the tendency of adoption to move children to a somewhat higher social class than that of the family of origin. Holman (1978),[28] in an article analysing the class nature of adoption, notes the gross under-representation found in studies of adoption of Classes IV and V among adoptive parents. The adoption studies themselves acknowledge the class factor. Tizard was aware of the social differences between the two groups of families, although she also cautions: 'much more than social class differentiated the natural and adoptive parents'. Lambert and Streather emphasise the powerful effects of environment, stating: 'Some children were fortunate and lived in an exceptionally favourable environment, and many of the adopted children were among this group.' If class, and the advantages/disadvantages arising from the class position of parents, are the key to adoption success, then adoption *per se* is not necessarily the beneficial strategy for deprived children that the paternalist school of thought claims. Another, quite different strategy, might be proposed: to equalise the class advantages of all parents! This goal might of course be dismissed as 'pie in the sky' and of no immediate help to children in need. Furthermore, there is a strong argument that other, not immediately class-related characteristics make the adoptive home superior.[29] Even so, the class character of adoption arouses some unease about the benefits claimed for it as a method of care.

Another type of reservation concerns the *long-term* effects of adoption, which may damage personality and identity. It may be that most existing studies of adoption are not sufficiently long-term to demonstrate these effects.[30] There is some evidence that adopted children make greater use of the psychiatric services than the general population, though this could also be due to class factors.[31] In general, it is more difficult to trace adoption breakdown than foster home breakdown, as the families concerned will not necessarily return to the agencies involved in the original placement. So again, it can be argued that adoption is in fact a less successful aspect of child care policy than it appears.

Another type of research which may be used to support the child protectionist position consists of studies of children in care, most notably Rowe and Lambert's *Children Who Wait*, which has already been referred to. Investigating children in care whose social workers wanted to find homes with substitute families for them, the study found that 22 per cent of the whole group of 2,812 children studied – who had all been in care for six months or more – were thought to need a substitute family; permanent substitute families were being sought for three quarters of these. Forty per cent of the children needing placement were considered to need permanent foster homes, 6 per cent direct adoption, and 26 per cent a foster home with a view to adoption. However, these judgements were only the *social workers'* assessments – the research team did not themselves make a decision as to which children ought to be placed in what type of placement. Rehabilitation was only expected for about 25 per cent of the children studied; 61 per cent were expected to remain in care until they were 18. Most of the children had been in care for the greater parts of their lives. Contact with the birth parents was limited – only 5 per cent of the children saw their parents as often as once a month; while 18 per cent saw one parent at least once a month, 35 per cent saw one or both parents occasionally, and 41 per cent had no parental contact. The longer the children stayed in care the less parental contact they had. But children in residential establishments were more likely to be in touch with their parents and return to them than children in foster homes.

The Rowe and Lambert study was widely taken to support a policy of permanency in good substitute homes when children have been in care for some time, but other interpretations of their data are possible. Firstly, the social workers' judgements were presumably not the only ones that could have been made of the preferred future for the child. Taking the social workers' views as the object of study inevitably carries this sort of limitation. Secondly, on the issue of parental contact specifically, it may be argued that absence of contact did not necessarily indicate parental indifference, that parents may find many obstacles in the way of remaining in touch with their children in care,[32] and that social workers could and should have done more to facilitate an active parent-child relationship while the child was in care. For example, a study by Thorpe (1974)[33] of long-term foster children also found little parental contact, but a quite different conclusion has been drawn from the findings. The point here is that Rowe and Lambert's data are open to a number of interpretations.

Finally on this question of empirical support, individual cases of extreme child abuse, particularly abuse leading to the child's death, lend considerable emotive power and apparent empirical support to the child protection position. Such is the compelling horror of these cases that it is tempting to conclude that *any* disadvantages arising from the protectionist position would be tolerable if a protectionist policy prevented such cases from occurring again. The obvious reservations are the relative rarity of such extreme cases, the assumption that in principle they could be stopped, and the weighting of the prevention of such child deaths as against other values and objectives.

(b) *Problems with the implications for policy*

The clearest and simplest policy implication of the paternalist position would seem to be that the state, acting chiefly through courts and local authorities, should have more power to intervene between parent and child and should use those legal powers which it does have more readily and extensively. This value perspective, then, could imply the widening of the legal grounds for coercive intervention by the state – this could occur, for example, in the English context, in the grounds for care proceedings in court, for taking parental rights over children already in care on a voluntary basis,[34] and for dispensing with parental consent to adoption. Grounds could be widened to cover situations where the child's welfare might be at risk but could not be adequately protected under existing provisions. Greater powers could also be given to block parental access to children in care where it was thought that parents would never care satisfactorily for their children again. Foster and prospective adoptive parents could be given more rights to achieve legal security and control of the child.

Many of the policy preferences of the modern paternalist school of thought found expression in the English legislative and policy changes of the 1970s. The way in which this occurred will be shown in discussing the value perspective in practice. It should, however, be noted that detailed blueprints for change do not emerge from the authors in this school in the same clearcut way as they do from the writings of Goldstein, Freud and Solnit, although *some* detailed recommendations are made. The discussion here will focus on three general aspects of the policy implications which seem most problematic: the resources aspect; the civil liberties aspect; and the potential clash with women's aspirations and feminism.

To deal briefly with the resources aspect first: it is clear that the paternalist position, if effectively implemented, has considerable implications for societal resources. Such resources could be drawn from voluntary child care agencies but would probably mostly come from the state (which may also partly fund voluntary bodies). The extensive surveillance of children and families thought to be at risk of various types of maltreatment, for example; the initiation and following through of court proceedings; the finding and supervision of substitute placements; the investigation of prospective adoptive homes, all carry a manpower – and a training – cost. The provision of residential homes is notoriously expensive, and although this form of care is not favoured by the child protection school, it is likely to be needed in the short-term for some cases. Foster homes are much cheaper, but in the case of some children who are recognised as difficult to care for, a larger than usual allowance can be paid to the foster parent(s), approximating more closely to a salary. It is now also possible in Britain for local authorities to pay an allowance to adopters in some cases.[35]

Paternalism without adequate resources is likely to result in poor planning and decision-taking and inadequate substitute care. The case of Dennis O'Neill, removed from his parental home for neglect in England in the mid-1940s, but killed in his supposedly supervised foster home, is a tragic reminder of an earlier form of state paternalism which was unsophisticated and under-resourced.[36] There have, however, been other child deaths in foster homes since that time.[37] A sufficiently resourced child care service is needed to prevent the interventions of the state making an unsatisfactory situation worse. Paternalism is more expensive than *laissez-faire*; at the same time, however, it may reasonably be argued to be cheaper than the policy implications of the third value perspective which is to be discussed. Rapid movement of children, even large numbers of them, through care to adoption or secure fostering, is likely to be cheaper than proposals to build better support services for all families, or even the most vulnerable, and to work actively for the rehabilitation of those children who do enter care.

Arguments about resources are particularly pressing at a time when government policies aim to reduce overall expenditure on welfare. Where fixed limits are set on expenditure, devoting more resources to child care carries the opportunity cost of reducing resources for other groups in need such as elderly and disabled people. Some authors who support the state paternalist perspective are well aware of this problem; both Dingwall *et al.* and Howells, for example, mention it.

The second problematic aspect of the implications for policy concerns the threat to civil liberties. Intensive surveillance of children and families to safeguard against ill-treatment or unsatisfactory care carries consequences for such liberties – this may be so, for example, where professionals visit the home, where records are kept on families, and where there is a stigmatising labelling process at work. Concern has been expressed specifically at the keeping of registers of children living with their own families thought to be at risk of abuse. There is fear that there is no adequate mechanism for *removing* children and families from these lists. The exclusion of parents from reports, case conferences and meetings where serious charges may be laid against them, which they have no opportunity to answer, also gives rise to this type of civil liberties concern. The power to remove parental rights over children already in care merely by a *resolution* of a public body, a power which was in existence in Britain for a century, long aroused opposition because of its similar 'behind closed doors' nature. Although resolutions could only be passed on specific grounds, and were basically to protect children whose parents seemed unlikely ever to care for them again, the fact that the decision was taken not in court but in a committee (to which – until 1984 – the parent was unable to make representations, where the local authority acted as judge in its own case) was seen to be a denial of natural justice.[38] It was no surprise that the 1989 Children Act abolished these resolutions, requiring care proceedings instead.

Even the relatively modest proposal of Dingwall *et al.* for parental supervision orders may be objected to in civil liberties terms. The local authority could acquire express power to direct parents in the discharge of their duties; so parents might be required, for example, to bring the child for regular medical inspection, to comply with prescribed treatment, or to participate in a particular remedial programme. There would be a right of entry to the home and an emergency power to remove the child for a short period (eight days), with this period being extended if the case were being prepared for a full care order.[39] Such powers would occupy an intermediate area between full-scale removal of the child, and leaving parents to bring up the child as they see fit or only offering supportive, non-coercive help. A dangerous erosion of civil liberties may be thought to be implied in this rather 'grey' approach, which contrasts with the more clearcut specifications of the *laissez-faire* school. The child is neither wholly removed nor left under parental control, but kept under some kind of shadowy state control in her own family home. Civil liberties protagonists might see another area of dangerous 'greyness' in provisions that would enable legal action in cases of *likely* harm (as is now the case under the 1989 Act).[40] The ill-defined nature of such a specification, it might be thought, leaves scope for oppression of and injustice to parents. The threat of such action is also a form of control, with the authoritarian possibilities which accompany such power.

There is, in other words, a head-on clash here, between parental civil liberties in relation to the state and the wish to protect children via the mechanisms of the state. It is the awareness of this conflict which leads the *laissez-faire* school to attempt to restrict the state's room for manoeuvre.

There is another more general sense in which adult liberties are restricted by the policy implications of the child protectionist school. The ideal of parenthood which it promotes gives a low priority to adult freedoms. Kellmer Pringle proposes as one of the basic features of parental love 'that the constraints imposed upon parental freedom of movement, upon time and upon finance are accepted without resentment or reproach'. That is, the ideal is of unrealistically high standards which could be experienced as oppressive. The ideal of parenthood is an unreasonably self-sacrificing one. To the extent that such an ideal is imposed via child care policy, parental liberties will be firmly limited and parental anxiety and insecurity raised.

This brings us to the question of women's liberties in particular and the extent to which the policy implications of the protectionist school may be construed as anti-feminist. Kellmer Pringle, notably, appears to be explicitly so in some respects. For example she has argued that:

> women should no longer be subjected to the twin social pressures to marry and have children, yet to feel they are 'wasting their education' or are otherwise 'unfulfilled' if they devote themselves full-time to child-care. While it was the destiny of yesterday's woman to raise a family, today it can be her choice. Henceforth only those willing to devote some years to this task should contemplate it; and they should then receive recognition for undertaking one of the most crucial tasks for society's future.

At a later point Kellmer Pringle suggests that the rights of children, particularly the very young, are 'subtly but insistently and dangerously, being undermined by the women's movement, aided and abetted by the media', adding: 'While a woman certainly should have the right not to become a mother, the current dogma that "a baby should not be allowed to make any difference to a woman's life" is not only double-think but also ignores the basic needs of young children.' Kellmer Pringle further suggests the possibility of sufficiently generous allowances to enable a parent to look after young children full-time, and investigation of 'how many mothers (or fathers) would wish during these earliest years to exercise this option in preference to an outside paid job?' This proposal does at least seek to diminish the economic dependence on men which feminists might find an objectionable concomitant of full-time motherhood; and in fairness to Kellmer Pringle she also emphasises the role of fathers and the sharing of parenting between the genders. But through much of her work there appears to run the assumption that it is usually mothers who are the primary parenting figures in the early years. Furthermore, the implications of Kellmer Pringle's 'ten commandments' for child care might alarm feminists concerned about *women's* well-being and interests and women as ends in themselves rather than means to serve the ends of others; for example:

1. Give continuous, consistent, loving care . . .

2. Give generously of your time and understanding . . .
3. Provide new experiences and bathe your child in language . . .

and:

10. Don't expect gratitude; your child did not ask to be born –
    the choice was yours.

The impression is conveyed that the parent – chiefly the mother – is the means to the end of the child's well-being; there seems little room for female self-determination here.

### (c) *Problems of rationale and underlying values*

A first objection to the rationale and underlying values of this perspective is shared with the criticisms of the *laissez-faire* school, and concerns psychological parenthood. This is emphasised over and above biological parenthood, and a (perceived) overvaluation of biological ties is criticised by proponents of this perspective. The converse problems of over emphasising *psychological* bonds in parent-child relationships, to the near-exclusion of birth and genetic links, have been discussed in the previous chapter and will not be re-iterated here. It should be remembered that supporters of the protectionist school are more prepared on the whole than the *laissez-faire* protagonists would be to break existing biological *and* psychological links in order to establish psychological ties in a more caring substitute home.

A second problem is also common to both the first and second perspectives, and concerns the devaluation of children's rights in the sense of rights to self-determination, and the overlooking, to a degree, of the child's own wishes and viewpoint. The psychological differentiation of children in this perspective, as shown, leads to the conclusion that their rights are different from those of adults. Their rights are essentially to better standards of care, not to freedom, in the sense of the freedom to choose, to be independent, or to care for oneself. It is consistent with this emphasis that Dingwall *et al.* are sceptical about separate representation for the child in court. They see protective care proceedings as essentially an adversarial dispute between *parents* and state agencies over the appropriate care of a child. *Parents* therefore should be full parties to the proceedings with access to legal aid; but as far as separate representation for the child is concerned 'the arguments in favour are so weak that such provision ought to be regarded as an extravagance in the present economic climate'. Dingwall *et al.* see an element of unreality in the concept of independent representation of the child's interests, as if these 'were an objectively discoverable entity which only awaited a mouthpiece'. Dingwall *et al.* elaborate their argument fully and convincingly; but the basic problem remains: the child as a separate individual, with a view of her own, is generally excluded.

Another problem with the child protectionist school is partly political and partly psychological; this is its implicit (or explicit!) authoritarianism. The potential threat to civil liberties from the type of policy preferences which tend to emerge from this perspective has already been examined in the previous section. The power of professionals and courts militates against parental autonomy, and overidealised notions of standards of parental care may be experienced as oppressive, particularly to women. The general authoritarianism of the protectionist position is found in its characterisation of the state as benign and class-neutral. Criticisms of this view are essentially that the power of the state can worsen situations as well as improve them, even in terms of the child's welfare; that the state acts differentially towards different groups, for example it may discriminate against the lower socio-economic classes, ethnic minorities, and 'deviant' family forms; that the state may impose judgements of child-rearing practices which are not universally shared – and this again would tend particularly to penalise minorities; that state intervention may be resented however well-intentioned. Furthermore, the coercive actions of the state in protecting children may be seen as missing the point. It may be argued that unsatisfactory child care arises largely from conditions of deprivation, conditions in the labour market, the inadequate provision of daytime care, the low social status accorded to parenting etc., and that the child protectionist standpoint is merely concerned with reacting to the *symptoms* of wider social divisions which cause child-rearing problems to arise. It is an authoritarian response because it gives a high profile to individual culpability, overlooking those social factors over which families have no control, and because it seeks to replace supposedly unsatisfactory parents, rather than assisting them. Thus the most powerless groups in society are punished for their powerlessness by the break-up of their family life. This type of criticism of child protection policies is characteristic of the third, pro-kinship perspective.

The psychological dimension of the authoritarianism of the paternalist/protectionist viewpoint is revealed in its somewhat exacting approach to standards of parenting. It is perhaps illuminating that Kellmer Pringle chooses a 'Ten Commandments' format for her advice on child care. The ten commandments of the Old Testament were absolutes and were delivered by God.[41] There is a greater tendency in this second value perspective than in the others to lay down what parenting ought to be like. Parents who themselves received 'bad' parenting tend to come badly out of this. They tend to be represented as so damaged that they are unlikely to reach satisfactory standards of care with their own children. Kellmer Pringle is particularly cautious about very young parents also, and recommends a social climate 'in which it is considered irresponsible to have children before, say, the age of twenty-two or twenty-three'.

The logical conclusions of such an approach are not necessarily followed through, but could surely include notions of licensing for parenthood and compulsory removal of the children of severely damaged or highly unsuitable people at birth. Kellmer Pringle lays stress on conscious preparation for parenthood, which again may be construed as a somewhat authoritarian approach. Furthermore, the interpretation of who is likely to make a good parent may be seen as over deterministic. The uncertainties about intergenerational continuities in behaviour are overlooked.[42] It may be argued that predictions in individual cases cannot be made with any certainty even from general trends. But it sometimes seems that for the child protectionists, certain potential parents are written off in advance.

A final general aspect of the rationale for this second value perspective which may be criticised is the single-mindedness of its preoccupation with child welfare. This can lead to a crusading, almost messianic tone in some of the writing. Dingwall *et al.* (here defined as only *moderate* paternalists) bring this out well with their quotation from Franklin already referred to, pointing out the religiosity of the sentiments and the emphasis on child welfare as an absolute priority. While not all the authors completely overlook the needs of other groups, there is a general tendency in this perspective to value childhood far above other states and stages of life. It is rather as though children were a separate race with highly privileged claims, rather than ordinary individuals in the process of becoming adults. The obvious criticism is one of lack of balance. Child care policy is only one area of social policy, and needs represented by other policy areas also clamour for attention. Children's welfare is also significantly affected by other, more general social policies. To, in effect, split children off from the rest of society may be seen as ill-founded. Furthermore, the approach, by focusing on the child in isolation, disregards the importance of the (original) family as a unit. The family, rather than the individual child, may be seen as the proper object of policy. Finally, an implied perception of parents only as means to the satisfaction of their children's needs not only diminshes the parents as people, but may be counterproductive. As some authors who deal with the treatment of child abuse in fact recognise, parents may need to have *their* needs met before they can satisfactorily respond to the needs of their child.

## (v) *The perspective in practice*

As in the previous chapter, the discussion has covered the main elements of the value perspective, some authors associated with it, the underlying rationale, and some problems and criticisms. Again, the value perspective will be illustrated by reference to actual policy developments in two different periods. These are both in the English context and cover firstly, the early part of the twentieth century up to the Second World War, and secondly, the 1970s. These were periods in which paternalism – in rather different guises – was particularly prominent in child care policy.

## PATERNALISM AND PROTECTION IN ENGLISH CHILD CARE LAW AND POLICY IN THE EARLY TWENTIETH CENTURY

As shown in the last chapter, the nineteenth century was largely dominated by *laissez-faire* as far as law and policy on children were concerned; nevertheless, some statutes were passed to protect their interests in various ways, and in particular the last decade or so of the century may be seen as marking a distinct shift towards greater concern for child welfare and greater acceptance of state intervention in this field. It was a time when there was great anxiety about the survival and well-being of young children, particularly those of the urban working class, as the birth rate dropped while the infant mortality rate remained high. The first Act to prevent child cruelty was passed in 1889, and other statutes gave greater powers over children to the Poor Law authorities and attempted to regulate parents' private arrangements for foster care.

The early years of the twentieth century saw a continuation of the trends of the 1890s. Behlmer (1982)[43] comments that: 'By the early twentieth century, acute public concern about the health and safety of children was forcing the state to assume greater responsibility for the welfare of its citizens.' Reforms brought in by the Liberal government of 1906–08, such as those relating to the feeding and medical inspection of school children, early notification of births, the probation of young offenders, and the establishment of juvenile courts 'signaled [*sic*] a clear perception of children as England's most precious resource'. An important influence at this time was the poor state of recruits for the Boer War of 1899–1902, a considerable proportion of whom had had to be rejected on physical grounds.[44] Anxiety about physical standards produced concern about the health of the working class population in general, and that of their children in particular. Although infant mortality decreased after the beginning of the century, reports of the falling birth rate were nevertheless still causing alarm, and helped to produce greater attention to infant welfare and mortality. The instrumental aspect of this concern for the young should be stressed. One MP in a debate in 1905 claimed that care for children was 'good economy and good Imperialism'.[45] Nevertheless, it had important practical effects, and by the end of the 1900s there was an impressive array of statutes.

The general picture in the very early years of the century, then, was of a further softening of attitudes to children; there was also a more scientific interest in their development, and an acceptance of wider state involvement in their welfare and therefore in the family.[46] A more modern concept of childhood had begun to emerge, possibly in response to the need to socialise and control the large numbers of young.[47] Specific issues of concern included private fostering, neglect, Poor Law children, young offenders, and child health.

With regard to private fostering, protection of these infants was extended under the Children Act of 1908. Private foster homes were now inspected and regulated by the authorities where there were children up to the age of seven. Concepts of neglect widened, as did the power of the state to intervene between parent and child in order to protect children's health and safety. There was better treatment of those children who were the responsibility of the Poor Law, with fewer of them placed in workhouses and more in specialised children's homes or boarded out with supervised foster parents, and more emphasis on the education and development of the Poor Law child and a reduction of stigma. The 1909 Report on the Poor Laws[48] rejected the principle of 'less eligibility' for children, that is, took the view that Poor Law children should not necessarily receive worse treatment than other children; but separation of the pauper children from their family of origin was seen – as it had been in the nineteenth century – as more or less permanent. The approach to young offenders became more humane and welfare-oriented, with the 1908 Children Act making punishments less physically severe and providing for separate courts for juveniles; the probation service's work with juveniles was developing around the same time. The 1902 Midwives Act, and the reforms in 1906 and 1907 relating to school meals and medical inspections, reflected the concern with child health, as did the permitting of the Poor Law authorities to relieve undernourished children in 1905, and the establishing of infant welfare centres after 1906, while maternity benefits began in 1911. These more universalistic provisions for child welfare may also be seen as consonant with the third value perspective, that is with an emphasis on supporting families and children in general, in order to improve child care.

The single dominating piece of legislation of the first twenty years of the century was the monumental 1908 Children Act, described as, for example,[49] 'a great and fundamental step in child protection'. It both consolidated and extended existing law and introduced some innovations – in the response to cruelty, neglect, juvenile health and juvenile crime. By 1914, according to one judgement,[50] 'it was clear beyond doubt that children had rights of their own, which were independent even of their own parents, and which the state would try to safeguard for them'. The standing of children was high relative to the previous century, and there was an awareness of the link between the condition of childhood and physical health and fitness in adulthood. The child welfare role of the state expanded.

In the inter-War period a somewhat Spartan regime in the upbringing of young children was favoured by the child care experts of the time, contrasting with the more child-centred, solicitous and indulgent approach characteristic of the pre-War years.[51] In keeping with received professional wisdom emphasising reduced attention to children at home and emotional independence, nursery schooling was favoured; there was also much interest in IQ, developmental stages, and the possibilities of a stimulating environment provided by trained teachers. A recognition of state intervention as legitimate continued, and there was a good deal of concern about particular groups of children, the illegitimate and young offenders for example. While better treatment was delivered to children in state care, the concept of replacing the child's original unsatisfactory environment with something better was still firmly established, so that substitute care was again largely seen as permanent. In a sense, state intervention with children may be seen as more sweeping and authoritarian than in some later periods. Family life in general apparently suffered a loss of status at this time,[52] and the task of rehabilitating families so that children in care could return to them was seen as too great for the legislation to encourage. In the years of recession there were few resources for the expansion of welfare provisions, and the major preoccupations of government social policy were unemployment and housing, not child care. Heywood (1978)[53] speaks of the concern about economic distress and unemployment being reflected in the 'impaired vitality of the progressive work with children which had been proceeding over the last seventy years', while Middleton (1971)[54] notes 'A general lack of interest in the public care of children'. However, specific child welfare issues did attract some attention, and these included illegitimacy, Poor Law children, young offenders and children in need of care and protection, as well as guardianship and adoption, and to a lesser extent private fostering and child health.

Illegitimate births increased, and emerged as a specific policy issue, during the First World War. There was a certain amount of effort among voluntary organisations in this field, and the illegitimate, traditionally heavily disadvantaged and stigmatised, were also helped by the coming of legal adoption in 1926; while a Legitimacy Act of the same year enabled their legitimation by subsequent marriage of their parents.[55] The care of the Poor Law child became more child-centred and constructive, although work to prevent the need for Poor Law care arising, or to restore the Poor Law child to his family of origin, was lacking. But the care of children under the Poor Law became less differentiated from that of *other* deprived, neglected and homeless groups of children. There was active interest in the treatment of young offenders, and a Departmental Committee on this topic reported in 1927.[56] This led to the 1933 Children and Young Persons Act, which may be seen as furthering the trend already established, of regarding young offenders as different from, and less culpable than adult offenders, and of some concern about their well-being. In this field there *was* some work done with the child's original family. The 1933 Act also widened protection against cruelty and neglect and extended the powers of the juvenile courts. They now, for example, covered young persons up to the age of 17. But, while a higher standard of welfare was set, the solution to neglect and cruelty was still seen as removal from adverse conditions and the provision of a permanent substitute home.

The Guardianship Act of 1925 stated the equality of the rights of mothers and fathers and the paramountcy of the child's welfare in custody disputes and decisions. It seemed that children were being seen less as possessions to which warring parents might or might not have a rightful entitlement, and more as persons with rights and claims of their own. The Adoption Act of 1926 followed concern about the problems of unregulated adoptions, and the reports of two committees which had considered legal provision for adoption. The Act made a legal transfer of rights from birth parents to adoptive parents possible for the first time. Another Act in 1939 regulated adoption further. Finally, private fostering and general child health were again a focus of interest and concern. The regulation of private fostering became more specialised; while school medical services and the raising of general standards of housing, health and cleanliness helped to reduce illness and death among children. Free milk was made available to needy children and expectant mothers.

The 1920s and 30s, then, were a time of harsher attitudes to children in some respects; children were not a major focus of government policy; yet state intervention did expand, and the notion of the autonomous family, impervious to outside interference, was weakened further. The treatment of the neglected, ill-treated or abandoned child by the state became less punitive as the influence of the Poor Law, or at least its harshest features, diminished. The period was again dominated by a huge consolidating statute, in this case the Children and Young Persons Act of 1933, which developed further the provisions for both young offenders and children in need of care and protection. As well as consolidation, the Act included some innovations, such as the extension of the powers of local education authorities and probation officers, and more emphasis on welfare.

The child care climate of these first forty years of the twentieth century in England is well-illustrated by Section 44(1) of the 1933 Act, which stated that the court, in dealing with those children and young persons brought before it, whether they were offenders or in need of care or protection, should: 'have regard to the welfare of the child or young person and shall in a proper case take steps for removing him from undesirable surroundings, and for securing that proper provision is made for his education and training'. This neatly encapsulates certain key features of the child care policy of the time: the common treatment, to some degree, of offending children and those in need of compulsory care for their own good; the emphasis on welfare; the emphasis on removal and training; and the rather moralistic orientation reflected in concepts of 'undesirable surroundings' and 'proper provision'.

Three main themes present in these first four decades of the century will be briefly outlined: the emphasis on the child's *physical* well-being; the downgrading of the birth family; and the elaboration of the powers and activities of the state.

Firstly, an emphasis on *physical* welfare, fitness, strength, and indeed on the prolongation of physical life, is found in the legislation and provisions of these years. Psychological well-being is distinctly secondary, if present as a factor at all. Where it is present, it is often embodied in a concern about cognitive development, training, socialisation and control. The measures of the earlier, pre-War years, in particular, were a response to fears about the population's declining capacity as a fighting force. There was anxiety that Britain would become a 'C3' nation, ie belonging to the lowest army medical classification. A moving force behind some of the child care reforms was an Interdepartmental Committee specifically on physical deterioration (1903–1904).[57] In the inter-War years, too, children's emotional needs were largely overlooked, or at least understood differently from more recent times, while there was still concern about their physical needs.

The insensitivity to psychological, as opposed to physical well-being, was reflected in the low priority given to the child's original family and his bonds with them. In the two main fields of child care work – the care of Poor Law children and children in need of care or protection – the intention was not to rehabilitate the child with his own parents but to provide him with a 'fresh start' in life; emigration to the colonies, used by both voluntary and statutory child care agencies, was an extreme manifestation of this approach. For other children legalised adoption enabled a permanent legal severance of the blood tie with the original parent. A limited exception to this emphasis was found in work with young offenders and others in 'approved schools'.[58] But in general the strength of original bonds, which might occur even in cases where the family and its surroundings might be deemed unsatisfactory and undesirable, was not fully appreciated. In Goldstein, Freud and Solnit's terms, psychological parenthood was not well understood in this early twentieth century form of paternalism. This shortcoming was also reflected in the substitute care provided, much of which was still poor quality institutional care.[59]

Thirdly, the period was marked by an increase and elaboration in the power and activity of state agencies in the child care field. Local authorities acquired more powers – acting as education authorities, to be 'fit persons' in respect of children who had appeared before the courts as needing compulsory care; and acting as health authorities, to carry out the regulation of private foster placements. The role of the probation service expanded. Foster and adoption placements were both heavily regulated by the state; for example, there were boarding out regulations governing the Poor Law children (revised in 1905, 1909, 1911 and 1933), powers to supervise and where necessary remove children in the private foster homes, and various prohibitions and controls surrounding adoption placements. There were restrictions on who could adopt and on the making of payments, while the court had to be satisfied that adoption was for the child's welfare. Adoption societies were regulated and some children placed for adoption were supervised.

In other words, the state had become heavily interventionist in the field of child care, and parental freedom was markedly more limited than in the nineteenth century. But differences from more recent forms of paternalism should be noted, in particular the lack of emphasis on the child's psychological welfare and emotional ties, the less sophisticated system of substitute care, the somewhat more punitive approach to the child's original parents where found to be inadequate, and correspondingly the more marked devaluing of the original family unit.

## PATERNALISM AND PROTECTION IN ENGLISH CHILD CARE LAW AND POLICY IN THE 1970S

In the 1970s, partly in response to well-publicised cases of child abuse, paternalism re-emerged in its modern form. The child abuse scandals produced a greater emphasis, as compared with the immediately preceding decades, on protecting children from their families, and on the use of substitute care. Greater use was made of local authorities' powers of compulsion with respect to children, and it became more likely that unsatisfactory parents would lose their children against their will. More was seen of the controlling state than in the previous decade; the family-oriented support work of the 1950s and 1960s was giving way to a greater readiness to focus on the child as a separate individual and to act, coercively if need be, on her behalf. Meanwhile foster care (as opposed to residential care) dropped, and then revived in popularity;[60] concern developed about its legal security, and legislation in 1975 in fact strengthened this. The tendency to emphasise security and permanence for the child in care was linked with a greater readiness to use legal powers against parents. And adoption was viewed increasingly favourably, although fewer of the traditional type of adopted children – illegitimate babies – became available. But older children with a history of being in care were more readily considered for adoption. At the same time, the proportion of all children in care rose.[61]

As the fate of Maria Colwell was so influential in this decade, and is so often referred to when the recent history of child care policy is discussed, a few details of this case will be given to illustrate the roots of the 1970s child abuse 'panic'.[62] Maria, born in 1965, was fostered from an early age (about six months) with an aunt and uncle, initially on a private and voluntary basis and later (after a short period with her mother) under a Care Order, altogether for about six years, but with the long-term plan being to return Maria to her mother. Contact with her mother continued irregularly, and her mother increasingly pressed to have her back. Maria, however, had a close relationship with her foster parents whom she called Mum and Dad, and she began to be distressed by contact with her birth mother and to fear a permanent return to her. By 1970 her mother was living with a new partner and had a number of children by him. Contact was increased, as the local authority Social Services Department's long-term plan was still for Maria to be integrated into her mother's family. Increasingly, though, Maria resisted the visits and showed signs of trauma as a result of them; in June 1971 she was diagnosed as depressed. Yet the Social Services Department decided not to oppose the mother's intended application for a revocation of the Care Order, despite the evident undesirability of moving Maria full-time to her mother's home at that stage. She *was* moved to her mother's in October 1971 and never saw her foster parents again. In November 1971 the mother's application to discharge the Care Order was heard, and was not opposed by the local authority, although a Supervision Order was recommended; both the discharge of the Care Order and the making of a Supervision Order were granted by the juvenile court. In the ensuing period (1972), despite the local authority's supervisory role, there was abundant evidence of neglect and abuse of Maria, including reports from neighbours and observations by teachers; but not all the relevant information was passed on, and the social worker supervising only saw Maria infrequently and failed to pick up the severity of the signs of ill-treatment. The report of the inquiry into the case comments: 'because of the fatal failure to pool the total knowledge of Maria's background, recent history and physical and mental condition the last real opportunity of removing her was missed', and Howells that: 'In the last nine months of her life, 30 complaints were made by 17 people or groups of people about the way she was cared for by her natural mother and stepfather. The complaints referred to loss of weight, neglect, injuries, scape-goating, and excessive physical demands.' In January 1973 Maria was taken to hospital by her 'parents' where she was found to be dead. She was found to be brain-damaged, severely bruised with internal injuries and severely underweight. Her mother's partner, the 'stepfather', was convicted of her manslaughter.

The history of Maria thus highlighted a number of crucial child care issues: the attachment of a child to long-term foster parents; the absence of a bond with the biological mother; the problems surrounding a 'stepfather' figure; the inadequate response of the agencies to signs of abuse; and the overlooking of a child's clearly expressed preferences (it had been obvious from Maria's behaviour that she did not wish to live with her mother). The inquiry report emphasised the role of the failure of the *system* in the case, particularly a failure of communication, but also implicated child care *policy*. The media, broadly, blamed the social worker involved.

A rapid outcome of the Colwell case was a proliferation of procedures and safeguards to ensure the early detection of, and action on, child abuse. The inquiry report had highlighted poor communication and co-ordination between the different professional groups involved. Corby[63] (1987) comments that the result 'was a swift reaction on the part of the Department of Health and Social Security which by means of a series of circulars issued between 1974 and 1976 established the framework of the administrative system for detecting, investigating and processing child abuse cases that currently exists'. The main features of the system were Area Review Committees, drawn from the higher levels of the agencies, which were to be involved with policy decisions; Case Conferences bringing together front-line practitioners to assess and make decisions about individual cases; registers to record children deemed to be at risk of abuse or further abuse, so that previous instances of recorded abuse were not overlooked; and child abuse manuals providing guidelines for cases of allegations of child abuse. Corby sees this response as largely a 'managerial' one: 'The focus was exclusively on how to recognise child abuse and manage cases, with particular emphasis on ensuring good interprofessional communication,' rather than on resources to be developed.

In line with the protectionist trend was the major piece of child care legislation of the 1970s, the 1975 Children Act, the form of which was influenced by the Colwell case, as well as by other cases of long-term foster children reclaimed by birth parents who retained their rights. Most of the Act followed the recommendations of the Houghton Committee Report 1972.[64] Broadly, the Act extended the powers of local authorities and foster parents over children in care and brought in certain measures which made adoption easier. To take the most significant changes in the order in which they occur in the Act: under Section 1 local authorities were obliged to establish an adoption agency service in their area, and under Section 3 the welfare of the child became the first consideration in all decisions relating to adoption; adoption was accordingly construed more definitely as a child welfare service. Section 12 widened the grounds for dispensing with parental consent (now termed agreement) to adoption, so that serious, as well as persistent, ill-treatment could enable an adoption against the parent's wishes, if rehabilitation with the parent seemed unlikely. Section 14 introduced a new procedure for 'freeing' a child for adoption before a specific placement was found; it was thought this would facilitate the adoption of some children. Section 26 contained an emphasis on genetic ties not found elsewhere in the Act in enabling adults adopted as children to obtain their original birth certificate, and therefore information about their parent(s) of origin. Under Section 29, those who had cared for a child for five years could apply to adopt and the child could not be removed before the court hearing. The five-year time limit did not apply if the parent had agreed to the application. Section 32 permitted the payment of allowances to adopters under approved schemes. Sections 33–55 of the Act set out a new form of guardianship termed custodianship; substitute parents could apply for this status if they had cared for a child for three years, or a shorter period with parental consent, and again the child could not be removed before the hearing. Other sections dealt with children in care. Section 56, for example, enabled the local authority, if a child had been in voluntary care for six months or more, to require the parent to give 28 days notice of reclaim of the child. (During that period, parental rights could be assumed by resolution if there were grounds for doing so; voluntary care would thus become compulsory.) Section 57 widened the grounds for assumptions of parental rights – most significantly, they could be passed solely on the grounds that the child had been in voluntary care for three years – and Section 59 applied the 'welfare principle' of Section 3 to decisions on children in care, that is, the child's welfare was the first consideration. In both Sections 3 and 59, it may be noted, the wishes and feelings of the *child* were to be ascertained where practicable. Sections 64–66 are worthy of note: they acknowledged the possibility of conflict of interest between parent and child and thus allowed for their separate representation in court in certain cases and under certain conditions. This could occur, for example, where the parent applied for a discharge of a Care Order and the local authority was not opposed to this step (which had been the situation of Maria Colwell). These sections, like the 'wishes and feelings' provisions in Sections 3 and 59, reflect more of a children's rights perspective. It is recognised that the child may have a viewpoint of her own. The Act, it should be noted, was implemented by stages in the late 1970s and early 1980s.

The Children Act, like several statutes before it, was described as a 'children's charter'; it was also hailed as a 'foster parents' charter', 'anti-mother', and 'anti-family'.[65] The latter epithets are too extreme but it is true that a significant extension of foster parents' and local authority powers took place.

As well as acquiring new powers, it seemed local authority Social Services Departments were also using the powers they had more widely. For example, the power to assume parental rights was more commonly used in the late 70s – 13.6 per cent of children in care were subject to these assumptions in 1972; 18.2 per cent by 1979.[66] There was apparently an increased use of Place of Safety Orders – for example, figures from Hallett and Stevenson (1980),[67] also quoted by Parton (1981),[68] show the number of Place of Safety Orders increasing from 204 in March 1972, to 353 in March 1974, to 759 in March 1976. Parton has also claimed an increase in children taken into care at birth. Furthermore the percentage of the under 18 population in care increased over the 1970s (eg from 0.65 per cent in 1971 to 0.75 per cent in 1976 to 0.77 per cent in 1980[69]). The numbers of those who were in care under Care Orders also increased. There were, for example, 38,200 Care Orders in England in March 1972, and 45,600 in 1977[70] an increase of nearly 20 per cent, and the percentage of all children in care in England who were under Care Orders increased from 44.6 per cent in 1975 to 47.5 per cent in 1980.[71] The use of wardship proceedings, another form of compulsory care, also rose sharply in the 1970s.[72] It may convincingly be argued that local authorities had greater resort to their legal powers in the child protectionist 1970s, although debate may arise about the significance of the figures. Practice became more defensive in response to anxiety about child abuse. Parton (1985)[73] comments: 'It is evident that the panic and subsequent procedures and practices developed to "manage" the problem of child abuse, have had far more wide ranging implications than simply work with children in physical danger. The more alert, anxious and decisive approach has been applied to children of all ages and very different circumstances.'

The 'permanency' movement in child care has already been referred to. In the context of a *laissez-faire* position, permanency means there is little tolerance of an uncertain situation; the child must remain securely in his original home, except in extreme cases, when he must be securely established at once in another one. State paternalism allows intervention in less extreme cases and is a little more tolerant of uncertainty; but still the ideal to be striven for is a single set of parents with legal security. The 1970s, broadly, saw local authorities increasingly seeking permanency for children either through rapid return to the family of origin, or through a substitute home placement secured by means of, for example, the assumption of parental rights or adoption. (This trend strengthened later; in the 1980s, although with a 'backlash' appearing, supporting parents' rights.)

It is of interest that in the 1970s, as in the inter-War years, the family as an institution experienced a certain loss of status. Critical views of the family emerged from at least two sources: feminism, which saw the family as particularly disadvantaging, even oppressive, to women, locking them into powerless and dependent positions; and the 'Anti-Psychiatry' movement associated with R. D. Laing, which construed many parent-child relationships as damaging to the child, and as implicated in much apparent psycho-pathology. In some quarters there was a quest for alternatives to the conventional family. Particular types of family also came under attack. Keith Joseph identified a 'cycle of deprivation' in which maladaptive behaviour forms were supposedly passed on in certain families.[74] There were other anxieties about the state of the family on the political right. As mentioned, Parton (1981 and 1985)[75] saw the preoccupation with child abuse and readiness to use legal powers as stemming from a deeper moral anxiety about the decline of the family as a socialising agent; this was linked with wider fears about the social order. Traditional values were felt to be under attack; violence and permissiveness were feared. There was also objective change in the family – an increase in marital break-up, as there had been in the 1920s and 30s;[76] a falling birth rate, also characteristic of the inter-War years;[77] and an increased movement of married women into the labour market.

It may be helpful to see child care developments in this context. The family's uncertain status may have contributed as a background factor to a greater willingness to break families up. On the other hand, it was with substitute *families* that children were, ideally, to be placed. It is hard to link state paternalism unequivocally with a rejection of the nuclear family form as such.

The changes in child care policy in the 1970s also took place against a background of increasing tough-mindedness towards certain groups and towards welfare policies in general. Within the field of juvenile justice, attitudes to offenders hardened somewhat; the 'treatment' or 'welfare' philosophy probably reached its peak in 1969 and thereafter declined, with magistrates seeking the power to send offenders away from home for specific periods, and a demand for more severe sentences. There was perhaps less tolerance of deviance in general. Welfare spending was begining to be cut back, and a 'crisis' in the legitimacy of the Welfare State began to be identified, ending years of apparent consensus when a major role for a high-spending Welfare State was widely accepted.[78] The social climate was becoming more utilitarian and less generous towards deprivation. Hence a search for cheaper solutions, in child care perhaps as in other areas of social policy. Growing attention to child abuse, however, made child care provisions difficult to ignore.

A number of general themes, then, may be drawn out of child care developments in the 1970s. Child abuse was a preoccupation; more positive child protection was the response. This took the form of new procedures, wider powers, more extensive use of the powers, more use of adoption and secure fostering for children in care, and generally a philosophy well-represented by the publications of BAAF in this era. Permanency was favoured; expensive 'preventive work', complex arrangements where children belonged to more than one family, or extensive efforts to rehabilitate them or keep original family contacts alive, less and less so. The standing of parents *qua* birth parents was at a low ebb, and the family itself seemed almost under seige, a situation which provoked a backlash which was already becoming apparent by the end of the 1970s.[79] Cuts in welfare services in response to public expenditure policies began to bite in these years, although they were not as extreme as in the decade which followed. The differences distinguishing 1970s state paternalism from inter-War paternalism should be remembered, and consist of less severe attitudes to parents (likely to be construed as inadequate rather than culpable), *some* regard for the birth family (which might, after all, prove a source of 'permanence'), better quality substitute care, and a more informed and sensitive approach to child psychology. Even so, the theme of the 'fresh start', albeit differently expressed, is common to both periods, as is the granting of increased powers to the state.

## SOME REFERENCES RELEVANT TO THIS PERSPECTIVE

Association of British Adoption and Fostering Agencies (ABAFA) 1976 *Practice Guide to the Children Act 1975*
ABAFA 1977 *Assumption of Parental Rights and Duties – Practice Guide*
ABAFA 1979 *Terminating Parental Contact*
L.J. Allen 1978 'Child Abuse: a critical review of the Research

and the Theory' *in* J.P. Martin (Ed) *Violence and the Family* Chichester, Wiley

G.K. Behlmer 1982 *Child abuse and moral reform in England 1870–1908* Stanford, California, Stanford University Press

British Agencies for Adoption and Fostering (BAAF) 1985 *Good Enough Parenting*

J.V. Cook and R.T. Bowles 1980 *Child Abuse: Commission and Omission* Toronto, Butterworths

R. Dingwall, J. Eekelaar and T. Murray 1983 *The Protection of Children: State Intervention and Family Life* Oxford, Blackwell

R. Dingwall, J. Eekelaar and T. Murray 1983 'Times change and we change with them?' *Community Care* 16 June 1983

L.M. Fox 1986 'Parental Rights Assumptions, The Passage of Time and "Natural Justice": The Use of Section 3 (1) (d) of the Child Care Act 1980' *British Journal of Social Work* 16(2) 161–80

A.W. Franklin 1982 'Child abuse in the 1980s' *Maternal and Child Health* 7 12–16

J.S. Heywood 1978 *Children in Care. The development of the service for the deprived child* London, Routledge Kegan Paul

Home Office/Scottish Education Department 1972 *Report of the Departmental Committee on the Adoption of Children* Cmnd. 5107 London, HMSO

J. Howells 1974 *Remember Maria* London, Butterworths

J. Lewis 1980 *The Politics of Motherhood, Child and Maternal Welfare in England 1900–1939* London, Croom Helm

N. Middleton 1971 *When Family Failed. The Treatment of Children in the Care of the Community during the First Half of the Twentieth Century* London, Victor Gollancz Ltd

S. Millham, R. Bullock, K. Hosie and M. Little 1985 'Maintaining Family Links of Children in Care' *Adoption and Fostering* 9(2) 12–16

J. Packman 1981 *The Child's Generation. Child Care Policy in Britain* Oxford, Basil Blackwell and Martin Robertson

N. Parton 1981 'Child Abuse, Social Anxiety and Welfare' *British Journal of Social Work* 11(4) 394–414

N. Parton 1985 *The Politics of Child Abuse* London, Macmillan

M. Kellmer Pringle 1974 *The Needs of Children* London, Hutchinson

M. Kellmer Pringle 1980 *A Fairer Future for Children* London, National Children's Bureau

M. Kellmer Pringle 1972 'Better Adoption' *New Society* 29 June 1972

M.K. Pringle 1967 *Adoption. Facts and Fallacies* London, Longman

J. Rowe and L. Lambert 1973 *Children Who Wait* ABAFA

A. Samuels 1976 'The Children Act 1975. A Critical Appraisal: The View of the Lawyer' *Family Law* 6(1) 5

J. Seglow, M.L.K. Pringle and P.J. Wedge 1972 *Growing up Adopted* Windsor, NFER

Carole R. Smith 1984 *Adoption and Fostering. Why and How?* London, BASW/Macmillan

B. Tizard 1977 *Adoption. A Second Chance* London, Open Books

J. Tunstill 1977 'In defence of parents' *New Society* 42(785) 20 October 1977

I. Vallender and K. Fogelman 1987 *Putting Children First. A Volume in Honour of Mia Kellmer Pringle* London, Falmer Press/National Children's Bureau

J. Walvin 1982 *A Child's World. A Social History of English Childhood 1800–1914* Harmondsworth, Penguin

# NOTES AND REFERENCES

1.  M. Kellmer Pringle 1974 *The Needs of Children* London, Hutchinson.
2.  M. Kellmer Pringle 1980 *A Fairer Future for Children* London, National Children's Bureau. Chapter 4.
3.  See, for example: Kellmer Pringle 1978 'A Ten Point Plan for Foster Care' *Concern* 30, republished in: I. Vallender and K. Fogelman (Eds) 1987 *Putting Children First. A Volume in Honour of Mia Kellmer Pringle* London, Falmer Press/National Children's Bureau.
4.  R. Dingwall, J. Eekelaar and T. Murray 1983 *The Protection of Children* Chapter 2, footnote 3.
5.  A. W. Franklin 1982 'Child abuse in the 1980s' *Maternal and Child Health* 7, 12–16, as quoted in R. Dingwall *et al.* 1983 Footnote 4.
6.  J. Howells 1974 *Remember Maria* London, Butterworths.
7.  D. G. Gil 1975 'Unravelling Child Abuse' *American Journal of Orthopsychiatry* 45(3), also in J. V. Cook and R. T. Bowles 1980 *Child Abuse: Commission and Omission* Toronto, Butterworths.
8.  N. Parton 1981 'Child Abuse, Social Anxiety and Welfare' Chapter 2, footnote 53.
9.  E. Lord and D. Weisfeld 1974 'The Abused Child' in A. R. Roberts (Ed) *Childhood Deprivation* Illinois, C. C. Thomas.
10. R. Dingwall, J. Eekelaar and T. Murray 1983 'Times change and we change with them?' *Community Care* 16 June 1983.
11. B. Tizard 1977 *Adoption. A Second Chance* London, Open Books.
12. L. Lambert and J. Streather 1980 *Children in Changing Families* London, National Children's Bureau/Macmillan.
13. S. Wolkind 1984 *Taking a stand: child psychiatrists in custody, access and disputed cases* British Agencies for Adoption and Fostering (BAAF) discussion series 5. Referred to in a review by M. Adcock 1986 'Children in families' *Adoption and Fostering* 10(4) 61.

14. J. Rowe and L. Lambert 1973 *Children Who Wait* Association of British Adoption and Fostering Agencies (ABAFA).
15. See, for example, editorial 1983 'BAAF and natural parents' *Adoption and Fostering* 7(3); and M. Adcock 1983 'Working with natural parents to prevent long-term care' *Adoption and Fostering* 7(3).
16. ABAFA 1976 *Practice Guide to the Children Act 1975*.
17. ABAFA 1977 *Assumption of Parental Rights and Duties – Practice Guide*.
18. J. Tunstill 1977 'In defence of parents' *New Society* 42(785) 20 October 1977 121–2.
19. ABAFA 1979 *Terminating Parental Contact*.
20. M. Adcock, R. White and O. Rowlands 1983 *The Administrative Parent* BAAF.
21. C. E. Cooper 1979 'Paediatric aspects' in ABAFA 1979 *Terminating Parental Contact* Footnote 19.
22. M. Freeman 1983 *The Rights and Wrongs of Children* Chapter 2, footnote 45.
23. For example, 1975 'Young Children Need Full-Time Mothers' republished in I. Vallender and K. Fogelman (Eds) 1987 *Putting Children First* This chapter, footnote 3.
24. C. Cooper 1985 '"Good-enough", border-line and "bad-enough" parenting' in BAAF *Good Enough Parenting*; Child abuse authors focusing on abusing parents' individual characteristics include: R. E. Helfer and C. H. Kempe (Eds) 1968 *The Battered Child* University of Chicago Press; R. E. Helfer and C. H. Kempe (Eds) 1976 *Child Abuse and Neglect* Cambridge, Massachussetts, Bullinger; R. S. Kempe and C. H. Kempe 1978 *Child Abuse* London, Fontana; A. W. Franklin (Ed) 1977 *The Challenge of Child Abuse* London, Academic Press; A. W. Franklin (Ed) 1975 *Concerning Child Abuse* London, Churchill Livingstone; See also: L. J. Allen 1978 'Child Abuse: a critical review of the Research and the Theory' in J. P. Martin (Ed) *Violence and the Family* Chichester, Wiley.
25. M. Loney 1987 'Pain in a Wider World' *Social Services Insight* 13 November 1987 20–2.
26. This is *not* however the case with Dingwall *et al.* 1983 *The Protection of Children* Chapter 2, footnote 3.
27. See: J. Seglow, M. L. K. Pringle and P. J. Wedge 1972 *Growing up Adopted* Windsor, NFER 140–1; M. Kellmer Pringle 1972 'Better Adoption' *New Society* 29 June 1972.
28. R. Holman 1978 'A class analysis of adoption reveals a disturbing picture' *Community Care* 26 April 1978 30.
    For a class analysis of children in care, see: B. R. Mandel 1973 *Where are the Children? A Class Analysis of Foster Care and Adoption* Lexington Books; A. L. Schoor (Ed) 1975 *Children and Decent People* London, Allen and Unwin; S. Jenkins and E. Norman 1972 *Filial Deprivation and Foster Care* Columbia University Press.
29. See B. Tizard (1977) *Adoption* 233–4. This chapter, footnote 11.
30. See L. M. Fox 1982 'Two Value Positions' Foreword, footnote 1. On adoption outcomes, see also: Carole R. Smith 1984 *Adoption and Fostering. Why and How?* London, BASW/Macmillan, Chapter 2.
31. See: M. K. Pringle 1967 Adoption. *Facts and Fallacies* London, Longman; Carole R. Smith 1984 *Adoption and Fostering* Footnote 30.

32. See, for example: S. Millham, R. Bullock, K. Hosie and M. Little 1985 'Maintaining Family Links of Children in Care' *Adoption and Fostering* 9(2) 12–16; S. Millham, R. Bullock, K. Hosie and M. Haak 1986 *Lost in Care: the problems of maintaining links between children in care and their families* Aldershot, Gower.

33. R. Thorpe 1974 'Mum and Mrs. So-and-So' *Social Work Today* 4(22) 7 February 1974 691–5.

34. The procedure for taking parental rights by a committee resolution was in fact abolished by the Children Act 1989.

35. Adoption allowances were enacted by the Children Act 1975, Section 32, implemented in February 1982.

36. Sir Walter Monckton 1945 *Report on the circumstances which led to the boarding out of Dennis and Terence O'Neill* Chapter 1, footnote 4.

37. For example, Shirley Woodcock 1982, Jason Plischkowsky 1986, Gavin Mabey 1987.

38. National Council for One Parent Families (NCOPF) 1982 *Against Natural Justice*; L. M. Fox 1986 'Parental Rights Assumptions, The Passage of Time and 'Natural Justice': The Use of Section 3 (1) (d) of the Child Care Act 1980' *British Journal of Social Work* 16(2) 161–80.

39. The proposals by Dingwall *et al.* resemble, in some respects, the Emergency Protection Orders and Child Assessment Orders enacted by the Children Act 1989.

40. The concept of likely harm is embodied in the new grounds for a Care Order in the Children Act 1989, which includes the words: 'that the child concerned is suffering, or is likely to suffer, significant harm.' (Section 31)

41. The Old Testament ten commandments, interestingly, themselves contained nothing on how parents should treat their children (although children were instructed to honour their parents).

42. Of interest here is: D. Quinton and M. Rutter 1988 *Parenting breakdown: the making and breaking of inter-generational links* – as reviewed by R. Parker 1989 *Adoption and Fostering* 13(1) 60–1.

43. G. K. Behlmer 1982 Child Abuse and Moral Reform in England Chapter 2, footnote 36.

44. M. Bruce 1961 *The Coming of the Welfare State London*, Batsford. However, the fear of physical deterioration was exaggerated by the type of recruit who tended to apply – the casual poor and ill-nourished.

45. Ibid 189.

46. For the emphasis on motherhood during this period, see J. Lewis 1980 *The Politics of Motherhood, Child and Maternal Welfare in England 1900–1939* London, Croom Helm.

47. J. Walvin 1982 *A Child's World. A Social History of English Childhood 1800–1914* Harmondsworth, Penguin.

48. 1909 *Report of the Royal Commission on the Poor Laws and the Relief of Distress* Cd. 4499 London, HMSO.

49. J. S. Heywood 1978 *Children in Care. The development of the service for the deprived child* London, Routledge Kegan Paul.

50. J. Walvin 1982 *A Child's World* This chapter, footnote 47.

51. C. Hardyment 1983 *Dream Babies. Child Care from Locke to Spock* London, Cape.

52. J. S. Heywood 1978 *Children in Care* 131 This chapter, footnote 49.

53. Ibid.
54. N. Middleton 1971 *When Family Failed. The Treatment of Children in the Care of the Community during the First Half of the Twentieth Century* London, Victor Gollancz Ltd.
55. But only if their parents were legally free to marry each other at the time of their birth.
56. Departmental Committee on Young Offenders 1927 *Treatment of Young Offenders* Cmd. 2831 London, HMSO.
57. 1904 *Report of the Royal Commission on Physical Deterioration* Cd. 2175 London, HMSO.
58. For example, the Children and Young Persons Act 1933 made provision for the after-care of young offenders and other approved school children/young persons (Section 74).
59. See N. Middleton 1971 *When Family Failed* This chapter, footnote 54.
60. The peak year for fostering was 1963, when the percentage of children in care who were fostered reached 52 per cent. By 1970 the percentage had declined to 42 per cent, and it declined further until 1975, when it had fallen to 32 per cent. The rate then rose again, reaching 37 per cent by 1980. (It continued to rise after 1980.) Sources: J. Packman 1981 *The Child's Generation. Child Care Policy in Britain* Oxford, Blackwell and Robertson; *BAAF Annual Review 1985–6*; CSO *Social Trends 1987*; DHSS *Children in Care of Local Authorities Year ending 31st March, England*, various years; DHSS *Health and Personal Social Services Statistics for England 1987* – all London, HMSO.
61. In 1971 0.65 per cent of the under 18 population were in care; by 1976 the percentage had risen to 0.75 per cent, and by 1980 to 0.77 per cent. Source: DHSS *Children in Care of Local Authorities Year ending 31st March, England*, various years. London, HMSO.
62. The sources drawn on in giving details of this case are: Secretary of State for Social Services 1974 *Report of the Committee of Inquiry* Chapter 1, footnote 2; J. Howells 1974 *Remember Maria* This chapter, footnote 6. For an account of the social reaction to the Colwell case as a 'moral panic', see N. Parton 1985 *The Politics of Child Abuse* Chapter 2, footnote 53.
63. B. Corby 1987 *Working with Child Abuse* Milton Keynes, Open University Press. Government Circulars after the Colwell case included: DHSS 1974 *Non-Accidental Injury to Children LASSL (74) (13)*; DHSS 1975 *Non-Accidental Injury to Children LASSL (75) (29)*; DHSS 1976 *Non-Accidental Injury to Children: Area Review Committees LASSL (76) (2)*.
64. Home Office/Scottish Education Department 1972 *Report of the Departmental Committee on the Adoption of Children* Cmnd. 5107 London, HMSO.
65. A. Samuels 1976 'The Children Act 1975. A Critical Appraisal: The View of the Lawyer' *Family Law* 6(1) 5.
66. Source: DHSS *Children in Care of Local Authorities Year ending 31st March, England*, various years. London, HMSO.
67. C. Hallett and O. Stevenson 1980 *Child Abuse. Aspects of Interprofessional Co-operation* Allen and Unwin.
68. N. Parton 1981 *Child Abuse, Social Anxiety and Welfare* Chapter 2, footnote 53.

69. See this chapter, footnote 61.
70. DHSS *Health and Personal Social Services Statistics for England 1978* London, HMSO. These were Care Orders under the Children and Young Persons Act 1969.
71. Calculated from DHSS *Health and Personal Social Services Statistics for England 1987* London, HMSO. See Chapter 7, footnote 56.
72. See N. V. Lowe and R. A. H. White 1979 *Wards of Court* Chapter 2, footnote 27.
73. N. Parton 1985 *The Politics of Child Abuse* Chapter 2, footnote 53.
74. Sir K. Joseph 1972 'The Cycle of Deprivation' reprinted from a speech given to a Pre-School Playgroups Association Conference 29 June 1972, in E. Butterworth and R. Holman (Eds) 1975 *Social Welfare in Modern Britain* Glasgow, Fontana/Collins.
75. N. Parton 1981 *Child Abuse, Social Anxiety and Welfare* and 1985 *The Politics of Child Abuse* Chapter 2, footnote 53.
76. For example, in 1970 there were 4.7 divorces per 1,000 married persons; by 1972 there were 95.; and by the end of the 1970s the figure was over 11 per 1,000 married persons. Sources: F. R. Elliot 1986 *The Family: Change or Continuity?* Basingstoke, Macmillan; G. Allan 1985 *Family Life. Domestic Roles and Social Organisation* Oxford, Blackwell, quoting CSO *Social Trends 1970; Annual Abstract of Statistics 1981*; OPCS *Monitor* FM 2 83/4. In the inter-War period, it seems that it was separation orders rather than divorces which increased. See J. S. Heywood 1978 *Children in Care* 131. This chapter, footnote 49.
77. There was a steep drop in the birth rate through the 1970s until 1977; then a plateau, followed by a rise in 1978 and the early part of 1979. Source: OPCS *Population Trends*.
78. See, for example: R. Mishra 1984 *The Welfare State in Crisis* Brighton, Wheatsheaf; M. Wicks 1987 *A Future for All. Do we need the Welfare State?* Harmondsworth, Penguin; M. Loney 1986 *The Politics of Greed*.
79. For example, in the late 1970s both main political parties declared themselves to be 'the party of the family' and there was a good deal of interest in 'family policy'.

# CHAPTER FOUR

# The modern defence of the birth family and parents' rights

## INTRODUCTION

The third, pro-birth family perspective encapsulates the idea that birth or biological families are important both for children and parents, and should be maintained wherever possible; where families have to be separated, links should usually be kept up. The role of the state is seen as, ideally, neither paternalist nor *laissez-faire*, but supportive of families, providing various services that they need to remain together. Class, poverty and deprivation are seen as important elements in child care, explaining much of what occurs in the child care field.

### (i) *The main elements of the perspective*

Two preliminary points should be made about this value perspective. Firstly, it is clearly distinguished from the state paternalist viewpoint just described. The latter position focuses strongly on the child as an entity distinct from his parents, seeing parenthood in terms of its service to the child's welfare. Parental *duties* are valued, not parental rights. Where high standards of parental care are not met, a strong role is envisaged for the state in transferring children, where necessary, to other adults who will parent them better. Early parent-child bonds are – relatively – de-emphasised. And much faith is placed in the power of the state and its agencies. On all these points – the emphasis on the child as a separate entity; the devaluing of the original parents; the view of the state – the second and third perspectives part company sharply, as will become apparent.

Secondly, and perhaps less obviously, the third perspective should also be firmly distinguished from the first, *laissez-faire*, position. It might seem that as both the first and third perspectives resist coercive state intervention and wish to keep families intact wherever possible, there is little to differentiate them. The proponents of both perspectives emphasise, broadly, the right of birth parents to care for their own children, and the right of children to live with their own parents. Nevertheless, important differences open up; again this will become more apparent as the third perspective is discussed. These differences are partly to do with concepts of the preferred role of the state and the nature of the state child care system; they also reflect differences over the relative importance of biological and psychological bonds between adults and children, and over the basis of effective parenthood.

To take the biological-psychological issue first, the modern defence of the birth family stresses the value of both *psychological* and *biological* bonds for individuals. The original, biological family is perceived as being of unique value and as being, for the vast majority of children, the optimum context for their growth, upbringing and development. Biological bonds are usually emotional ones as well, but even if they are not, knowledge of, and contact with, one's family of origin are thought to be important. It is not altogether clear to what degree the proponents of this perspective would want to maintain a link with biological parents who are in no sense the psychological parents as well – that is, how much they value the blood tie as such. It seems that in supporting the birth family they have mostly in mind cases where the original parents are also the *psychological* parents, albeit inadequate ones. Yet some value is seen in the birth tie and genetic links *per se*. Biological bonds are also emphasised from the parents' point of view; there is great sensitivity in this perspective to the needs of *parents* for their *children*, and to the sense of loss of parents whose children pass into the care of the state and to substitute families. There is an emphasis on the rights of parents as people in their own right; and alongside this an explanation of poor quality child care which is sympathetic to parental difficulties. Where parents fail to parent their children satisfactorily, this is often because they are oppressed by circumstances outside their control. Bad parenting is firmly linked with social deprivation and its concomitant pressures on families. The remedies focus on reducing deprivation and its pressures through measures such as increased daytime care for children and better financial and other kinds of support for parents. The basis for effective parenting is thus both biological and material (rather than, say, rooted in individual psychological history) – birth parents are (mostly) the best providers of care, but they need support from a materially favourable environment.

This point leads on to the issue of the child care role of the state in this perspective. The perspective prefers an extensive role for the state, not in separating children from parents and providing substitute care, but in providing support for families so that children do not *need* substitute care. This may take the form of intensive help directed to those families on the verge of breaking up, or of broader social policies to support *all* families with children. This, it should be noted, is very different from a 'minimalist' position on the role of the state. The state should be active in helping families. But actually putting children in substitute care is seen as generally (though not invariably) undesirable.

Where children do, almost as a last resort, have to come into state care, considerable intervention should be devoted to helping their families and maintaining links with them so that the children can return home again. This may mean the child relating to a number of parent figures at once. While the first two perspectives seem preoccupied with the necessity for certainty, permanence, security, and a stable bond with a *single* set of parent figures, defenders of the birth family find more acceptable a situation where, say, a child may maintain an active relationship with the birth parent(s) while living with foster parents. Indeed, the type of foster care which is preferred in this perspective is of the 'inclusive' kind where the birth parents remain positively involved in the child's life. 'Exclusive' fostering, where the foster parents tend to treat the child rather as though she were their own or they had adopted her, is thought to be damaging to the child's identity, as well as hindering restoration to the birth parents.[1]

State policies on child care tend in this perspective to be viewed critically for their insufficient emphasis on the prevention of children entering state care, or on work to reunite families separated in this way. There is also scepticism about the adequacy of courts and social service agencies as decision-makers on child placements and the child's interests and well-being, and about the quality and value of substitute care. Removing a child from an unsatisfactory home is no magic answer but may be damaging, resulting in, for example, placement in a series of unsuitable foster homes, and a cumulative experience of rejection and failure. Substitute care may be *worse* than care in the birth family – and child deaths in supposedly supervised foster homes are not unknown.[2]

It is also stressed that findings which apparently indicate the beneficial effects of adoption may have their root in a class effect. The birth parent perspective sees parents who come into contact with state child care agencies as in a weak power position. This is related to factors of social disadvantage, primarily social class. This perspective is much more conscious than the first two of the class element in state child care. It is pointed out that social workers, magistrates and judges – the state decision-makers in child care – are middle class, while the child care interventions of the state are not uniformly distributed among parents in society but are concentrated on those parents who come from particularly poor and disadvantaged groups – single parents, the unskilled, the unemployed, those from ethnic minorities and in bad housing and deprived neighbourhoods. The causes of their poor parenting, as already noted, are seen as lying largely in these external factors; yet the state, it is said, offering little tangible help, punishes them by too readily removing their children and making it extremely difficult for them to get them back. This perspective is highly conscious of this injustice; it does also value child welfare, but sees the child's interests as lying in remaining with the birth parents in the vast majority of cases.

To summarise, this viewpoint favours extensive state intervention but not of the coercive kind. Birth families should be supported in their caring role; children should not enter substitute care except as a last resort or on a 'shared care' basis; having entered care, most of them should be kept in touch with their original family and should wherever possible return to it. The state in its child care role pays insufficient attention to upholding birth families; it also operates in a discriminatory way on the basis of social class. Most of the child care problems to which the state responds are attributable to poverty and deprivation.

### (ii) *Some authors associated with the perspective*

The most notable author associated with this position is Holman, who has argued consistently for the defence of the natural or birth family. For example, in a pamphlet entitled *Inequality in Child Care* (1976 and 1980)[3] Holman argues that a good deal of the apparent need for substitute care for children is produced by social deprivation and its attendant pressures on families, rather than parental inadequacy or culpability. The ties between parents and children are strong; parents may be forced into, rather than willingly accepting of, separation from their children through substitute care; once separated, they may not want to make the final break via adoption. The response of the social services to poor standards of parenting should be the provision of more supportive services to enable birth families to cope better, rather than facilitating the removal of children to substitute care and the ultimate separation of adoption. Holman thus sees the major child care policy need as being a broad one – to provide the necessary environmental supports to prevent families breaking up because of poor child care, and to enable separated families to live together again. Prevention, at the broadest level, involves the amelioration of wider conditions that cause deprivation; this involves more general questions about how best to care for *all* children.

A major plank in Holman's argument is that the need for children to enter care is strongly associated with – indeed caused by – various forms of deprivation. Drawing on research, he identifies five features associated with social deprivation as conditions linked with children's admission to care. These five are: lone parenthood; large families; parents who are unskilled manual workers; low income; and inadequate housing. Generally there is evidence of a relationship between poverty and admission to care. Children coming into care also come disproportionately from geographical areas of social deprivation. Holman suggests that social deprivation has two relevant effects: firstly it affects parenting behaviour and child-rearing methods, and secondly it leads to a lack of child care resources in the home. So certain families among the socially deprived find it difficult to attain the child care standards set by societal norms (norms which they may share). A life of deprivation makes children vulnerable to separation through coming into care.

Parents who lose their children to public care are thus disproportionately poor and lower class. (The inference is that inadequate middle class parents suffer less visibility and have a wider range of child care options open to them.) Class, then, is significant in the child care actions of the state – a variable which is conspicuous by its absence in the first two perspectives discussed. Holman (1978) also carries a class analysis into the field of adoption,[4] noting the gross under-representation of Classes IV and V among adoptive parents. In other words, adoption is perhaps moving children up the social scale, or redistributing children from the worse-off to the better-off.

Holman speaks emotively in *Inequality in Child Care* of parents 'losing' their children, which suggests that he regards the wishes and feelings of parents as being of not insignificant importance alongside the needs of children. He sees most parents whose children enter care as in fact sharing the child care objectives of the middle class professionals who pass judgement on them – but as being prevented by circumstances from realising these objectives. Identifying emotionally with the parents, and calling on his readers to do likewise, Holman seeks help for parents which would directly or indirectly benefit their children also. Parents are subjects to be considered; indeed, in an earlier article on unmarried mothers and child separation (1975),[5] Holman specifically stated that the wishes of the mothers should be taken into consideration more strongly in the legislation concerning the future of the children.

In his pamphlet Holman is particularly critical of the 1975 Children Act for taking no cognisance of the link between child separation and poverty and for facilitating the placement of children in other, permanent homes while doing nothing to help parents struggling in the face of material difficulties. The 1975 Act as shown in Chapter 3 contained various provisions to limit parental rights, the effects of which were to increase the likelihood of parents losing touch with their children and to encourage quasi-adoptive fostering, while no extra resources were provided to prevent children having to leave their parents at all. The Act, in other words, encouraged permanence in the secure foster home or adoptive home but militated against prevention and rehabilitation. In Holman's view social work practice at that time tended *not* to encourage contact between parents and their children in care, or the reunification of separated families. In support of this he quotes research done by, for example, Thorpe (1974),[6] who found in a study of long-term foster children that only 27 per cent had contact with their parents every six months or more frequently, and that over 60 per cent of the parents did not know where their children were living, with only 21 per cent feeling encouraged by their social worker to maintain contact. In only 5 per cent of cases was rehabilitation considered by the social worker to be a possibility and in no case at all was there any definite plan for rehabilitation. Holman stresses that lack of contact did not necessarily reflect parental wishes (in fact nearly a half of the parents wanted their children back) but parents felt they were being tacitly excluded by the agency. Holman's conclusion from findings of this type is not – as supporters of the child protection perspective might infer – that the children should therefore be found secure substitute homes, but that more effort should be put into maintaining children's links with their original parents. This seems an equally defensible conclusion. Thoburn's research (1980),[7] for example, has shown that persistent social work can in fact bring about the return of children to birth parents who previously could not cope, while work by Millham *et al.* (1986)[8] confirms that absence of contact between children in care and their parents is more due to various structural barriers experienced by both children and parents, such as changes in the parents' situation and limited social work support, rather than just parental unwillingness or indifference. Millham *et al.* comment that the majority of parents initially 'seek access to their children and strive to make contact in other ways'. Indeed: 'the majority of children and parents *do* manage to remain in contact. It says something for the resilience of the blood-tie that . . . links are maintained.'

In an article in 1980[9] Holman reiterated his arguments. He suggested that the drop in children available for adoption in the 1970s led adoption pressure groups to advocate a form of fostering which was closer to adoption, with the birth parents being less involved in the foster placement. Holman saw a link here with Goldstein *et al.* whose doctrine, as shown in Chapter 2, stresses psychological rather than biological ties and the difficulty of children relating to more than one set of parent figures. In contrast, Holman finds the more desirable form of fostering to be that of the 'inclusive' kind where parents are actively included in the placement and therefore do not lose contact.[10] Children having more than one set of parent figures – living with foster parents while continuing to relate to birth parents – is not seen as problematic.

A more recent book by Holman, *Putting Families First. Prevention and Child Care* (1988),[11] restates the position, while giving considerable space to the role of voluntary bodies in preventive child care work. Reviewing the history of child care policy, Holman notes the case for prevention which was put in the 1950s and 1960s. This was partly an argument about costs – having children in local authority care was expensive; partly there was concern about foster home breakdown; then there was the theory (derived from Bowlby) that separation from the original parents, especially the mother, was damaging. So 'the conviction gained ground that a child's own family was, in most cases, the best place for him to be'. There was also research evidence that many admissions to care could have been avoided by earlier intervention. Holman broadly sees the 1960s as strongly preventionist, the 1970s as dominated by fear of child abuse and the permanency movement, and the 1980s, it seems, as mixed, with a further drive for prevention but also pressures against it, including the recession and financial curbs on services.

In his last chapter Holman restates the case for prevention under four headings. Under 'research and family separation' he refers to studies revealing the harmful effects of removing children from their birth families. The essential themes here are: that prolonged separations are likely to impair child development; that care placements are unstable, with many changes; that residential care in particular is damaging and does not prevent delinquency; and that separation has a negative impact on parents as well. Being in care is also stigmatised. Thus, the trauma of separation and entry to care should be prevented whenever possible. Under 'the family in society', Holman next argues that the case for prevention depends on the place of the family in society. The family of parents and children remains a major institution held in high esteem; here Holman refers to the family's functions – basically socialisation and the provision of individuals with an identity. And the fact of birth constitutes a powerful and special bond. The point here is that if children are taken from their families, they are deprived of 'what is considered the normal and rightful lot of most children'. In the next section Holman brings in his personal experiences as a wartime evacuee and child care worker, from which he draws five lessons, two relating to the family, two to care, and one, interestingly and significantly, to neighbourhoods. In the order that Holman gives them, these points are that:

> the family is the basic unit of our society;
> children and families may relate closely to their neighbourhoods;
> families rarely wish to be broken up;
> public care produces complications and sufferings;
> some admissions to care and custody could have been avoided.

Again, Holman's central themes of the importance of origins, and the dubious value of being in care, are present. Referring to his Christian and Socialist beliefs, Holman acknowledges his debt to R. H. Tawney. In his final section here, 'social action', Holman briefly addresses the role of the state, referring to the right-wing *laissez-faire* writer Mount,[12] with whom, predictably, he disagrees. Mount sees all forms of state welfare as threatening to the family by removing its privacy and self-responsibility. To refute this position, Holman refers back to Victorian times, when many families were destroyed by huge deprivation in a society where there was little collective welfare provision.

Holman, then, has consistently backed the integrity of the nuclear family and an extensive supportive role for the state. The title of his latest work, *Putting Families First*, may be usefully contrasted with that of a volume recently published in honour of Kellmer Pringle, who has been identified with the child protectionist stance: *Putting Children First*.[13] The titles neatly summarise the difference in emphasis. Finally, two quotations from Holman's writings highlight his perspective. In his pamphlet (1980) he says:

> By failing to tackle social deprivations, by refusing to strengthen
> effective preventive work and by legislation only for the separation of
> families, the government . . . casts the parents in the role of those who

are not to be helped but are to be punished . . . the fact of living with parents who conceived the child does usually create an affinity and should be the foundation on which socialisation and domestic life is based. The present social system appears to accept this premise for most families but its inequalities inhibit a minority of families from enjoying normal family life.

*Putting Families First* ends with a vision of the 'preventive neighbourhood' (not to be used as an excuse for avoiding structural reforms), which might lead to 'the reality of a society where far fewer children have to leave their homes and neighbourhoods, where few are subject to neglect and abuse, where all families are prevented from suffering gross social disadvantages, and where all parents are enabled to develop their parenting capacities to the fullest'.

Considerable space has been devoted to Holman as perhaps the most explicit proponent of this value perspective. Other writers who have put similar arguments may be referred to more briefly. Walton and Heywood (1975)[14] note a general social trend to separation and disengagement in relationships, and foresee a strong tendency in society to minimise the importance of the blood tie and kin relationships. They are struck by the attenuation of social attachments, and note the fragmentation of families and the diminution of parental rights accompanied by what they refer to as the 'hysterical grasping after the straw of greatly extended adoption of deprived children'. Like Holman, they argue for better community provision and for policies that would prevent families breaking up, rather than the provision of more substitute care. Tunstill (1977),[15] as mentioned in Chapter 3, attacks practice guides for social workers issued by the then ABAFA (later BAAF) for emphasising the removal of parental rights and placement of children for adoption and long-term fostering. Tunstill suggests that the guides take a hardline criterion against the birth parents which does not take account of social workers' failure to encourage regular contact between parents and children in care. In a later article (1985)[16] Tunstill analyses the extent to which the 1975 Children Act resembled elements of the old Poor Law legislation. Emphasising the link between poverty and entry to care, she is critical of the 1975 Act for doing nothing to alleviate poverty or facilitate preventive work. Other articles by Tunstill explore the field of prevention.[17]

Andrews (1980)[18] is another author who may be identified with the birth parent school. He notes that while in the 1970s social workers had been accused of blind allegiance to the principle of the blood tie, to the detriment of the child's welfare, the reality was somewhat different: social workers were in fact involved in protecting children from their parents and challenging the sanctity of the blood tie. Andrews argues that in general the blood tie is not a bad presumption for child care legislation. The birth family provides security, consistency of care and attachment. But for the family to work, the parents need to feel protected and free from undue interference; parental rights provide a framework for the responsible exercise of parental obligations, in which the child's right to his own family can be met. Andrews maintains that the assumption that a parent knows what is in the interests of his [sic] child is a reasonable one and holds for the vast majority of families. The arguments take place around the exceptions to the general rule. Andrews notes that the 1963 Children and Young Persons Act revived the blood tie philosophy, assuming that the long-term interests of children could best be secured within their own families, and that the 1969 CYPA similarly interpreted the child's welfare in terms of his own family. However, the 1970s witnessed another move (like that in the 1940s and – questionably – the 1950s) away from the blood tie philosophy, and the 1975 Children Act incorporated this shift, in the provisions giving additional powers to local authorities and foster parents over children in care. Andrews notes that the Act was passed in the wake of the Maria Colwell outcry and 'tug-of-love' incidents (involving birth parents and foster parents), which led to a search for greater security for those providing substitute care.

An account of the development of child care policy by MacLeod (1982)[19] also broadly takes a preventionist, pro-birth parent stance. MacLeod charts the movement in policy towards, and then away from, family based child care, seeing social work as being directed to the support of the family in the 1950s and 1960s, but moving away from family care in the 1970s. It is clear that MacLeod is critical of the latter move and broadly in favour of the former. She is also aware of the financial disadvantages experienced by many parents of children in care, and of their difficulties in staying in touch with their children. Interestingly, MacLeod comments on the changing view of the family in child care policy, that: 'It is as though the relationship aspects of family life now take second place to the caring/nursing aspects and the family is valued for its caring capacity, rather than being seen as a grouping of individuals linked by a network of relationships which locate and provide status for individuals in a complex society.' MacLeod is sceptical about the value of fostering and about changes in the 1970s which 'have driven social workers to look energetically for new homes rather than spend a great deal of energy enabling natural families to live together'. MacLeod favours general supportive services for families.

The House of Commons Social Services Committee Second Report *Children in Care* (1984)[20] shares to an extent this broadly preventive and rehabilitative emphasis. For example, under the heading 'Prevention' the Report recommended, *inter alia*, that the long-term rate of Supplementary Benefit be paid to unemployed families with children; that local authorities compare preventive expenditure under Section 1[21] with the actual cost of keeping a child in care 'in order to judge the potential effectiveness of a more constructive use of cash payments or loans' and that there be every effort by local authorities to improve co-operation between Housing and Social Services Departments to avert the reception of children into care because of homelessness. Under its 'Conclusions' the Report again has a section headed 'Prevention' which favours closer co-operation between Social Services Departments and Social Security offices, easier access to day care for pre-school children, more effort in the prevention of child abuse, and a co-ordinated approach to non-school attendance. Another section headed 'Rehabilitation' comments that the extension of the duty to seek rehabilitation to all children in care might be effective,[22] and referred this idea to a proposed review of child care law.[23] The Report was aware of the significance of social deprivation, and the Introduction to the Report had commented: 'It is often the adults concerned and not the children who are most in need of help.' However the Committee also thought that there was a danger of over-stating the potential for preventive strategies, and that the idea of 'preventing' care gave an unduly negative picture of it.

A more radical approach is taken by Parton (1981 and 1985).[24] Locating child abuse in its social and political context, Parton sees – and regrets – a growth in coercive interventions by social workers, based on a social anxiety about the decline of the family, as well as on the assumption that child abuse is rooted in individual pathology rather than in social inequality or social divisions. It is difficult to do justice to the sophistication of Parton's extensive work on this subject in a short resumé, but briefly, Parton regards the 'disease model' of abuse as fundamentally flawed. Abuse cannot be predicted and identified with precision; and the 'disease model' has been interpreted in an increasingly conservative way, with a strong emphasis on personal responsibility for abuse and the social control role of social workers. Shifts in child care policy in Britain in the 1970s and 1980s reflected these trends. Parton refers to 'panic' over child abuse, to a 'more alert, anxious and decisive approach' and a 'more resolute approach'. Local authorities used their statutory powers more, and were more unhappy about involving parents in child care. Such a 'rescue' approach 'has helped to deflect attention from the more serious deficiencies in welfare provision for all children and families and implies that help is only available in situations of extreme severity or crisis'. Parton sees this general trend as in line with Thatcherite political economy. By contrast, Parton himself views child abuse as strongly related to class, inequality and poverty, and favours preventive action in the broadest sense, tackling the wider conditions associated with abuse. The terms of the debate need to be recast, and 'It is not that we simply need an expanded role for the state but that the social relations which it reflects should be democratic and play an active and supportive role in bringing up children'. In a later article (1986)[25] which critically analyses the inquiry report on the case of the abused and murdered child Jasmine Beckford, Parton elaborates some of the same themes. He is critical of the 'disease model' of abuse adopted in the Report, and its assumptions about social work attitudes and practice – ie assumptions that social workers should make greater use of statutory power and authority, becoming controlling and more sceptical about how far parents can change.

Other relevant authors, Frost and Stein (1989),[26] present a structural analysis of child care issues, arguing that child welfare can only be fully understood as a political process reflecting social divisions. Through examination of 'the family' as the context for childhood, and the historical and political framework of child welfare, the authors set the context for a discussion of child abuse, juvenile justice, the care of separated children and the under-fives. Their basic premise is that these topics cannot be understood in isolation from broader social forces; and they argue that the fundamental theme of *inequality* provides an explanatory framework for child welfare. Inequality is manifest in class, gender, ethnicity, disability and generation differences. While wary of the dangers of idealising 'the family', and aware that children and young people have a separate identity and set of interests distinct from their parents, Frost and Stein share with Holman and other proponents of the birth parent school an emphasis on the link between class/poverty/deprivation and child care, and quote some of the relevant evidence; they also point to the increasing isolation of working class families; and to the over-representation of black and mixed race children in care, which seems to be due not just to social deprivation but to 'eurocentric' assumptions imposed on these families by white social workers. Seeking a response to child welfare which is firmly located in its social context, Frost and Stein favour policies of 'structural prevention', and a child welfare practice responsive to divisions of class, ethnicity, and gender. Progressive child welfare practice should embrace the key themes of empowerment of children and young people, and of challenging models which are based only on individual and family pathology. However, Frost and Stein distance themselves from the more extreme manifestations of the children's rights approach. Day care for children under five is seen as crucial, the struggle for this being 'a struggle over the definition of the public and the private, the dispute over whether parents should be left to care for their children, a struggle over the construction of gender and of whether child care is properly a public concern'.

A final group of authors who can be mentioned are Beresford, Kemmis and Tunstill (1987)[27] who in *In Care in North Battersea* report on a study of children in care, and point to the relationship between the social-economic structure and the percentage of children in care. Beresford *et al.* found a high proportion of black and mixed race children in care; that single parents and those dependent on state benefits were most likely to have their children in care; and that a high proportion of children in care had unemployed parents. Generally, there was evidence for an association between reception into care and social deprivation. The authors emphasise the importance of prevention, and the lack of it in practice; the need to give special attention to the needs of black families; and the need for resources to combat poverty, unemployment and poor housing.

Mention must be made of the pressure group the Family Rights Group, which has worked with numerous parents who have felt unfairly deprived of custody of, or access to, their children by local authority Social Services Departments; this group has issued publications arguing the value of the birth family, and contact with it, for the child. For example, *Fostering Parental Contact* (1982)[28] in a series of papers puts forward arguments for preserving contact between children in care and the birth family. One paper in the pamphlet by Benians[29] argues for the psychological significance of parents in terms of attachment, reciprocal and continuous relationship, example of how to care for self and others, models with whom to identify, and knowledge of origins. A later pamphlet *Permanent Substitute Families. Security or Severance* (1984)[30] questions the trend to the severing of contact between children in care and their families, rather than encouraging and enabling families to share in their children's care. One of the papers in the pamphlet by Kelly[31] concludes that the new conventional wisdom sprang from pressures on social work rather than from research, practice or theory; the other by Atherton,[32] *inter alia*, describes barriers to contact between families and children in care and the lack of commitment in Social Services Departments to enabling children to return home. Atherton questions the philosophy of permanence, seeing over-rigid planning and neglect of partnership with parents as particular defects. She points out that permanence in the foster or adoptive home cannot anyway be guaranteed, and comments: 'Children do not see family separations as an end to relationships, and clean breaks reflect the concerns of the adults, not the children, about these relationships.'

The National Council for One Parent Families has taken a similar approach to the Family Rights Group, defending birth parents and arguing in particular (1982)[33] that the use of the local authority power to assume parental rights by resolution could constitute a breach of natural justice. There is evidence that single parents are more likely than others to lose their children to local authority care.[34] These parents are seen as being in a weak power position *vis-à-vis the state, finding difficulty in defending their rights. In a small study of 40 (nearly all single) parents who had had their parental rights removed by means of a resolution,[35] the NCOPF found that:*

> The majority of the parents were poor, on Supplementary Benefit and under emotional stress. Voluntary care was often the only immediate solution to their problems because other alternatives and resources did not exist. But the act of accepting this solution was often later interpreted as evidence of a parent's weakness and failure. . . . many were deeply shocked where resolutions were taken or access curtailed.

## (iii) *Rationale and underlying values*

In the first two perspectives on child care policy, one element of the underlying rationale which was identified was the emphasis on *psychological* rather than *biological* parenthood. For both the *laissez-faire* school of the Goldstein *et al.* type, and the state paternalists, the psychological bonds formed between children and their primary caretakers are overwhelmingly more important than any notion of a blood tie, a bond which is based on genetic and birth links alone. For the proponents of the third perspective – the pro-birth family or pro-birth parent view – links with original *biological* parents are crucial. Yet the rationale for taking this position is somewhat ambiguous. In so far as these links are important *because* birth parents cared for the child in the early stages of his life, the third perspective does not part company very sharply with the first two. Here the third perspective can draw on the work of authorities such as Bowlby,[36] who showed that separation in the early years from a maternal figure (not necessarily the biological mother) to whom the child had become attached, or deprivation of loving, continuous maternal care, could be extremely damaging. Holman in fact invokes Bowlby's work, referring, for example, under 'The Case for Prevention', to Bowlby's conclusions that normal development required an intimate, continuous relationship with a mother or permanent mother substitute, that separation could have permanent adverse effects, and that adoptions needed to start in the child's first two months to facilitate success. Here the emphasis seems to be mainly on early psychological bonds. There is also the point that children, it is thought, suffer particularly if there is secrecy about their family of origin, experiencing feelings of shame and inferiority. They may also experience feelings of disloyalty if they become too fond of foster parents, or may develop an idealisation of an absent parent. Children, then, may retain a sense of identification with their origins.

However, it seems that proponents of this perspective do, at least, implicitly, go beyond this to support the importance of biological bonds *per se*. It would seem. for example, that Holman values knowledge of, as well as contact with, the birth family as a source of the individual's identity. Andrews explicitly defends the blood tie. The field of sociobiology might provide one legitimating theory to support the view that individuals feel a deep bond with those who share some of their genes, even in the absence of a history of interaction. However, Holman and the other authors cited here do not explore this. Another possible way of thinking about the issue, mentioned in Chapter 2, is to point out that families are *socially* defined, but that society defines them in biological terms. Therefore to have lost some of one's nearest biological relatives is to be socially defined as having something missing. And as Holman (1988) says, 'in a society where living at home with natural parents is the norm, stigma against those who do otherwise is very deeply entrenched'. Holman is here supporting biological ties because they are defined as normal. Another point that may be mentioned here is the importance of *ethnic* origins and identity, raising particular issues for black children with white substitute parents.

Further suppport for the view is found in the evidence that some individuals do strenuously seek information about, and possibly meetings with, a biological parent who has always been a stranger to them. The main categories here are people adopted early in life and those who never knew their biological father (including some conceived by artificial insemination). Of interest here is Section 26 of the 1975 Children Act which made it possible for adopted adults to gain access to their original birth certificate, and therefore possibly to trace their original parents. Only a minority of those eligible have taken up this opportunity, however.[37] Nevertheless, it is clear from anecdotal and autobiographical evidence that some individuals do become involved in a passionate quest for a totally unknown biological parent.[38] And one supporter of the pro-birth parent school interviewed by Fox[39] did speak of children 'having intense feelings for their own parents even if they've never seen them'.

What is also clearly an underlying value in this third child care perspective is the importance to *parents* of having conceived and given birth to a child. Unlike the second perspective, the third does not disregard parents' needs and interests or treat parents only as a means to the end of child welfare. The emotional importance to a parent of a biological bond is identified and given some weight in its own right. And there is considerable sympathy for the 'vulnerable' parent – the parent who is poor, single, living in adverse conditions – who may lose a child about whom they do care.

This concern for parents links with two other elements in the underlying values supporting the third perspective – a focus on the family unit rather than the child as a separate individual, and a particular view of society and social problems. To take the first point, the focus on the family unit, it is clear that in this perspective the interests of parents and children are seen (in the vast majority of cases) as a relatively undifferentiated area, so that help to the parents, broadly, equals help to the family, equals help to the children. The family of parents and children is perceived as an interacting unit whose members' welfare is closely linked and interdependent. Proponents of this perspective might convincingly argue (along the lines of the Seebohm Committee Report of 1968[40]) that different family members' problems, symptoms or stresses interact with each other in a complex and inseparable way. For example, mental or physical illness in a parent may have severe implications for the standard of child care. Conversely, extra demands generated by a child's illness or disability may create great stress for the parent. Abuse or neglect may be seen as a problem of family circumstances or relationships. Furthermore, problems such as inadequate income or poor or unhealthy housing conditions affect the *whole* family. It is artificial to separate out children's well-being from that of their parents. At the same time, children positively *need* their own parents. Thus the focus in policy and social work practice should be the nuclear family as a unit. This is seen as the most effective path to enhancing child welfare. While the emphasis is mainly on the nuclear family, wider kinship links beyond the parent–child unit may also be seen as valuable to the child.

The next point concerns the underlying view of society and social problems held by most proponents of this perspective. As has already been shown, the social institutions which respond to child care problems are seen as shaped by social class, in that they embody largely middle (and upper?) class decision-makers acting against the most deprived members of the working class. The concept of society is thus characterised by social divisions and inequalities of resources and power. Part of the reason why the state is able to remove certain children from their parents, to override those parents' rights, and to keep the children away permanently, is to do with the powerlessness of poor people. Middle-class people, it may be argued, are less likely to come under the kinds of surveillance which lead to an identification of poor child care, neglect or abuse; less likely to have their child care actions labelled in these terms; and, should their children in fact be taken from them, are more capable of agitating effectively to get them back. When better-off parents do encounter child care problems, they are less likely to involve social workers from child care agencies, and more likely to use their resources to obtain private forms of help such as nannies, boarding schools, or therapy. An essentially class-bound society produces a particular pattern of child care policy which is strongly influenced by social class. Similarly, an essentially racist society produces racist child care policies independently, it seems, of the factor of social class.

Thus social problems, including those of poor child care or troublesome child behaviour, are seen as derived from a divided society. As indicated, the child care actions of the state are partly governed by differences in surveillance, labelling, and the power to resist in different groups; but in addition there may indeed *be* problematic standards of child care to a greater extent among certain groups. In so far as this occurs, however, it is thought to be due to pressures of social deprivation. It has been shown how Holman argues, for example, that social deprivation affects parenting behaviour and child-rearing methods, and leads to a lack of child care resources in the home. While socially deprived families may share generally-held child care norms, they find it more difficult to attain them. Hence the child care actions of the state tend to remove their children to a slightly 'higher' class, to homes which do not experience deprivation to the same degree.

The political assumptions of the third perspective, then, imply a society which is divided by class and power. Child care policies are seen as part of a structure of unequal political and economic relations in which dominant groups control subordinate and, in particular, deviant groups by a range of sanctions. It is mostly these weaker groups who are interfered with by state child care agencies, with the objectives of upholding dominant values about child-rearing, maintaining particular sorts of socialisation, and, to some degree, redistributing deprived children to members of somewhat more powerful social groups who wish to care for them.

The underlying view of the state in the third perspective is not entirely negative, however. While it might be thought from the preceding arguments that the state acts, and can act, only in a wholly oppressive way towards the most deprived groups, the supporters of the third child care perspective do not on the whole take a Marxist-type view of a capitalist state fundamentally opposed to the welfare of the working class. They tend to take an optimistic – perhaps a naive? – approach to what *can* be achieved even by a capitalist state, acting in a more enlightened way. The preferred approach is basically more redistribution and an extension of the 'Welfare State'. Holman, for example, advocates better financial benefits for all families and more child day care. Tackling social deprivation and doing effective preventive work *are* seen as possible within the framework of the capitalist state.

So in this perspective an extended role for the state could achieve much. Those who argue the birth parent view are concerned about the *direction* of much state intervention in family life, but would not want to see this intervention withdrawn from the family arena altogether. State intervention, basically, should be supportive rather than coercive, punitive or intrusive. Extensive help should be offered to families but on a voluntary basis. Even temporary removal of a child should (in the vast majority of cases) be undertaken in this spirit, with the objective being return of the child when the family's problems have eased. So while the state in its more controlling aspect is certainly seen as threatening to the liberties of poorer families, the state is also seen as *potentially* benign if prepared to commit more resources to a more appropriate form of intervention, ie acting against social deprivation, and helping parents to keep and care for their own children, and to regain them if they are temporarily relinquished to other forms of care. Thus the welfare role of the state is strongly supported – a very different position from *laissez-faire* and more identifiable with a moderately left-wing perspective on the expansion of state welfare and the reduction of social inequalities in general.

This faith in the *potential* ability of the state to extend effective help to poorer parents and children is complemented in Holman's case by a faith in voluntary action and in working class self-help and self-determination in finding solutions to family problems, for example through community action by groups of parents. [41]

Finally, it may be noted that in this perspective what is good for children is again attributed to them by adults. In this respect the third perspective falls into line with the first two. In the *laissez-faire* approach, it will be remembered, the child's *own* viewpoint is not strongly present. Childen's interests are largely imputed to them by others. The paternalists of the second perspective see children as fundamentally different from adults, with different needs and rights; children are unable to care for themselves and need adult protection and guidance. In the third perspective the relevant adults who make decisions about children are (mostly) their parents. Parents, it may be safely assumed in the vast majority of cases, care about their children's welfare and are aware of what it consists of. Again, children's autonomy has a low profile; but the mantle of paternalism is assumed by *parents* rather than *the state*.

## (iv) *Criticisms of the modern defence of the birth family and parents' rights*

### (a) *Empirical support*

In general, this value perspective seems relatively well supported by empirical data. Holman, for example, cites a wealth of studies on children in care to support his position. However, one major aspect of the empirical backing for this perspective must be considered critically, and that is the claim that the causes of poor parenting lie largely in material rather than in individual psychological factors. Two subsidiary aspects which will be discussed are the overlooking of the evidence of the extent of child abuse, and the difficulty of comparing the adverse effects of being in care with what *would* have happened to the children if not admitted to care. Lastly, the force of individual cases in supporting this value perspective will be considered briefly, as it was in examining the paternalist perspective.

An important claim of the proponents of the third perspective is that the roots of poor parenting and poor child care, and hence of the need for the state and other agencies to take full-time care of some children, lie largely in social deprivation and its ramifications rather than in the personal and psychological characteristics of parents. There is research work which does not altogether support this claim. For example, a study by Isaac *et al.* (1986)[42] of families of children in care and parental mental health found a high rate of past and current psychiatric disorder in the sample of parents which appeared to be an important factor influencing children's admissions into, and discharge from, care; concluding that the study confirmed other recent work which had found 'that families of children who enter care are characterised not only by material and social deprivation but also by considerable personal problems in the parents'. The other recent work quoted is that by Quinton and Rutter (1984)[43] which compared families with children multiply admitted to care with a comparison group from the same area. Nearly two-thirds of the in-care group mothers had been under psychiatric treatment at some time; two-fifths had been in-patients. These proportions were very much higher than for the comparison group. And the rate of current psychiatric disorder was four times that of the comparison group. Certainly the in-care group also had material problems, but Quinton and Rutter concluded that while 'the parenting difficulties of the families might be interpreted as being either a direct reaction to social disadvantage or secondary to the resulting stress and psychiatric problems experienced by the parents', nevertheless 'it is not possible to conclude that current social disadvantages are a sufficient explanation for the differences between the groups with respect to either parenting problems or psychiatric disorder. Questions remain as to why some disadvantaged families have children taken into care whereas others do not, and on why families come to be in poor social circumstances.' Studies of children in care whose parents' rights have been assumed by resolution have also shown rather high rates of parental psychopathology. The present author (under the name of Fox (1986)[44]) found that just over 40 per cent of a small sample of children whose parents' rights had been assumed after three years in care, had at least one parent who had shown marked psychological problems at some stage (although material problems were also common); Lambert and Rowe (1974),[45] studying parental rights assumptions on all grounds, also found a relatively high rate of parental mental illness; while a similar study in Strathclyde (1980)[46] found that mental ill-health affected the ability of a third of the mothers to care for their children. More strikingly, Adcock *et al.* (1983),[47] also studying parental rights assumptions, found that social workers thought that only 16 per cent of mothers were severely limited in their parenting capacity by housing problems, and only 9 per cent by economic problems, while many of the parents 'were not thought by their social workers to be overwhelmed by material problems'. The emphasis was on personal or behaviour problems or parental rejection of the children. In Packman's study (1986)[48] of children seriously considered for care (some of whom were admitted and some not) 30 per cent of mothers were said by social workers to suffer from some form of mental disorder; there were also high levels of family disruption; although low social class, unemployment and low income were also distinguishing features of the families.

Two questions immediately arise, however, in response to findings that parents of children in care tend to have personal and psychological problems as well as material ones. The first concerns the way in which such personal and psychological problems are identified – to what extent, for example, the findings are reliant on the judgements of social workers; and the second, to what extent mental illness and psychopathology are themselves linked with poverty and deprivation.

Two subsidiary aspects of the question of empirical support for this perspective concern the evidence of the extent of child abuse, and the problem of making hypothetical comparisons. On child abuse, NSPCC estimates[49] suggest that 8,044 physical abuse victims were newly registered in England and Wales in 1987, and 7,119 sexual abuse cases. The total number of children estimated by the NSPCC as registered as abused or at risk by the end of 1987 was 43,985. According to the first national DHSS statistics published on this question (1988),[50] almost 40,000 were on child protection registers in England, this being three per 1,000 of those under 18; 23 per cent were registered because of physical abuse, 13 per cent because of sexual abuse, and 11 per cent because of neglect.

It should be remembered that doubts always arise about the meaning of figures for *reported* cases – the real figures are likely to be higher. While it may be argued that the figures only represent a small proportion of the child population (eg less than 0.3 per cent), nevertheless levels in the tens of thousands suggest a serious problem of abuse and undermine idealised pictures of family life. The severity of abuse is another aspect of the question: NSPCC figures for 1986[51] showed that of children physically injured, 11 per cent of injuries were serious or fatal. It is suggested here that the pro-birth parent perspective tends to de-emphasise the extent and seriousness of child abuse as an actual problem, as opposed to a problem of social response or 'moral panic'. For example, Parton (1979, 1981 and 1985),[52] while acknowledging that official figures are underestimates, concentrates on the process of discovery and definition of child abuse and the link between concern over child abuse and wider social anxiety. The *actual* abuse of children and its effects are somewhat marginalised. This orientation is linked with the relative neglect of the need for the state to have coercive powers, which is discussed below.

On the question of hypothetical comparisons between entry to care and remaining with the birth parent(s) (or, having entered care, *remaining* in care or a substitute home, and *returning* to the birth parent(s)), one argument is that, while being in care may well be an adverse experience for the child, the valid comparison to be made in these cases is not between experiences in care and children's experiences in 'normal', unstressed families where their welfare is well-catered for, but between care and the family situations the children *would* have been in, had they not entered care. Tizard (1977)[53] makes this point in her work on adoption quoted when discussing the second, paternalist perspective. She asks: 'With whom is one to compare the adopted children?

One obvious comparison group would be the natural children of parents of the same social class and general background as the adoptive parents. But, from the viewpoint of social policy, such a comparison would be both unrealistic and irrelevant.' The alternatives actually available to the adopted children in Tizard's study were institutional care or a return home to birth mothers who were usually living in difficult circumstances. Similarly with children who come into care, or may come into care, the alternatives to care may be very unfavourable. It may be that the picture of birth family life in these cases held by the proponents of the third perspective is idealised and inaccurate. The reality may be more disturbing. Millham *et al.* (1986),[54] for example, have shown that the families of children in care tend to be subject to many changes, with partnerships and households fragmenting and re-forming. Packman's research (1986)[55] found that 26 per cent of children seriously considered for care came from reconstituted families where one parent was 'step', and that the most striking feature of the families studied was the degree to which they were incomplete, disrupted or restructured. The 'family' life which is the alternative to being in care is, then, for many children, unstable and volatile. The problems of their being in care need to be seen in this context.

In discussing the state paternalist perspective, individual cases of horrific child abuse were mentioned as constituting apparent empirical support for the position. Such cases tend to give rise to a feeling that *any* action must be contemplated, *any* policy disadvantage born, to prevent such cruelty occurring again. On the other side, the birth parent school of thought also have their catalogue of horror stories – cases of anguished parents who have been apparently maltreated by the authorities and deprived of their children unjustly and against their will – sometimes losing them altogether to adoption. Cases of parents who desperately want their children back but are forcibly deprived of them have been dealt with by pressure groups; some have been highlighted by the media; and a few have reached the European Court of Human Rights.[56] But a reservation about the strength of this 'empirical support' arises over and above even the reservations held about individual cases of child abuse. There is a sense in which, say, post-mortem findings of child injuries and extreme malnutrition have a factual nature; by contrast, the wounds of parents are emotional rather than physical. Parents, when putting their case to an advocate, pressure group or the media, will inevitably give *their* view of events – or the view they wish to project. This sounds hard on parents, but it is suggested that individual cases cannot be used to provide evidence for this perspective in the way that child abuse cases can (within limits) be used to support the second perspective. An example of the sort of problem of distortion that can arise is the book by the M.P. Stuart Bell on the Cleveland child sex abuse scandal of 1987, *When Salem came to the Boro'* (1988).[57] This book has been criticised by Campbell (1988)[58] for only recounting one side of the case (the fathers') – for not mentioning, for example, when dealing sympathetically with the sufferings of the men accused of sexually abusing their children, that the children had indeed made allegations of abuse, or that the wife believed that abuse was in fact taking place.

### (b) *Problems with the implications for policy*
It is clear that the implications for policy of the pro-birth parent position are that the state should do *more* for parents and children in a supportive sense, but *less* in a coercive sense. For example, the state in this view should increase family benefits via the social security system, and extend payments to vulnerable families via local authorities to prevent children coming into care; and should expand day care provision for children, and other services in kind for children and families, again through local authorities.

An obvious first objection is the cost of such programmes. Depending on how wide the net of supportive programmes is cast, and on the levels of provision, the cost could be moderately high to astronomical. An increase in Child Benefit in Britain of 45p, for example, merely enough to keep pace with inflation in April 1989, would have resulted in a net cost of nearly £203 million at that time,[59] therefore a *real* increase of a mere 45p would presumably have cost over £400 million, and a real increase of only 90p over £600 million. In other words, rather large amounts are involved in creating only modest increases. The average cost of a local authority day nursery place per child day was £16 in 1986/7,[60] while the total number of under-fives in the United Kingdom was 3.7 million in 1987;[61] merely providing day care for 2 million (54 per cent) of these would, then, presumably cost in the region of £32 million per day (1986/7 prices). The costs of social work and other forms of practical support to families are difficult to quantify and highly variable according to the level of intensity, but could, perhaps, be more expensive than an ordinary foster placement for a child. Intensive social work activity to help rehabilitate a child could also be relatively costly. Tackling all family problems of housing and homelessness, which can cause children to come into care, would also be an expensive project to carry out effectively, although it may justly be pointed out that the cost of a Council house or flat may well be less than maintaining a homeless family in a bed-and-breakfast hotel, as has been done increasingly frequently in the 1970s and 80s.[62]

The detailed costs of such policy proposals are not characteristically worked through by the supporters of the pro-birth parent perspective.[63] It has to be remembered that state welfare expenditure in Britain, and local authority expenditure in particular, was held under severe restraint from the mid-1970s, initially under the Labour government, and later, with increasing stringency, under the 1980s Conservative governments. Local authority expenditure was held down by a series of devices, including expenditure limits, withdrawal of government grant, prohibition of supplementary rates, and statutory limits on the amounts that could be raised in rates ('rate capping') imposed on some authorities. Local authorities by the end of the 1980s therefore seemed to have little scope for extending their services to families without cutting back elsewhere. And, notwithstanding *apparently* greater provision for prevention under the Children Act 1989 (to be discussed further in Chapter 7), there was little support for the kinds of policies favoured by the pro-birth parent supporters at *central* government level in the 1980s. Conservative ideology favoured the *reduction* of state welfare expenditure rather than its expansion; housing subsidies were progressively withdrawn; and in social security the government preferred means-testing or 'targeting' to universal benefits, so that Child Benefit, for example, was significantly reduced in real terms.[64] Even so, better means-tested benefits for families with children might have provided a way of channelling resources to those families who are most vulnerable to losing their children to substitute care; however, while the effects of British government social security changes were mixed – and often

127

unclear – no significant improvement in the living standards of families on benefits seemed likely by the late 1980s.[65]

To be realistic, then, the policy implications of the third pro-family value perspective seemed unlikely to be followed through while local authority expenditure was curtailed, and while central government ideology militated strongly against welfare expenditure and perceived 'dependency' on the Welfare State, and firmly favoured privatised and individual solutions to need. While government may indeed in its rhetoric have strongly supported 'the family', this was done mainly from a *laissez-faire* stance – it was the family's autonomy and internal responsibilities which were stressed, not its claim to state material support.[66]

However, it may be said that this is only a pragmatic objection to the policy implications of the third perspective, and that the proposals are still worthy of support as *ideals* (furthermore the political and economic climate is subject to change). Are there then any further objections that would still hold even should the proposals be capable of early implementation from a government ideological and public expenditure point of view? Three aspects will be explored: the issue of whether the notion of 'prevention' is valid and can be relied upon to work; the neglect in this perspective of the need to use coercive powers when children are at risk; and a rather more specific point about the role of foster care and the difficulties of ensuring the type of foster placement that Holman, for one, would prefer.

A fundamental objection arises over whether 'prevention' 'works', about its effectiveness, and indeed its moral appropriateness. A philosophical objection to any kind of broad preventive policy can be derived from Popper. For example, Magee (1973)[67] states that in Popper's work *The Open Society* (1966)[68] the general guiding principle for public policy is: '"Minimize avoidable suffering." Characteristically, this has the immediate effect of drawing attention to *problems*.' The Popperian approach, Magee argues, instead of encouraging one to think about Utopia 'makes one seek out, and try to remove, the specific social evils under which human beings are suffering'. Lait (1979)[69] has applied Popper's work to the personal social services field, arguing that preventive work is based on the dubious proposition that social workers should be involved in making life 'better' rather than making it 'less bad'. Speaking of 'a transformation in my thinking achieved by studying the works of Sir Karl Popper', Lait argues that preventive work embodies the idea of 'better' rather than 'less worse'; thus: 'those who seek to do preventive work have not merely a sense of what constitutes a family so bad that it cannot care for its children, but that they also have a version of a "good" family and their work is focused on helping the family to attain a state of goodness.' Lait goes on to assert that there is no evidence to convince a sceptic 'that the intervention of a social worker, professionally trained or not, has averted a single case of baby battering unless the social worker has physically removed the child from the threatening environment, or interposed his body between the child and the aggressor'. Preventive work also tends to lack clearly defined objectives, and to be based – as indicated above – on notions of what is a desirable condition. Furthermore, intervention by 'officials' to enhance well-being risks interfering with liberty. And, 'Since wellbeing is a quality difficult to define, and highly idiosyncratic in its manifestations, such intervention is in any case unlikely to attain its objectives.' The main points of a Popperian objection to a preventive approach in child care, then, would appear to be: that the notion of enhancing well-being and making life in families 'better' for children (as opposed to acting on specific problems) is dubious and based on imprecise objectives; that preventive action does not necessarily have the intended effect; and that it is potentially authoritarian. It is not possible in a short space to do justice to the complexity of Popperian analysis of public policy, or indeed even to the ideas in Lait's brief article; but it seems worth making the point that there are some fundamental reservations about the very concept of policies designed to make life better for children and families with the aim of averting the need for substitute care.

The second aspect of the policy implications where serious doubts arise, is the relative neglect of the need for coercive action, that is the use of power backed up by the law, in some cases where children are at risk. While it is not being claimed that the supporters of the birth-parent position entirely deny the need for local authorities and courts to have *some* powers, to be exercised in *some* cases, however, where attention is given to the question of legal powers in child care policy, it usually takes the form of criticism of the extent of these powers and the extent of their use. Holman criticised the 1975 Act from this sort of viewpoint, and Parton the increasing use of, for example, Place of Safety Orders. Clearly, the supporters of the birth family perspective feel that the implementation of the other measures they favour would reduce the *need* for the use of statutory powers. Yet there must be some unease about their attack on this important aspect of the state's child care role, and about a possible overconfidence that such compulsory cases could only constitute a small residual minority. This is linked with their relative neglect of the extent of child abuse, referred to earlier. The problem is one of emphasis – it is not that the supporters of the third perspective overlook abuse and the need for legal powers of compulsion *altogether*. As Holman (1980)[70] says of the 1975 Act: 'It is not disputed that legislation was required to raise the standard of adoption services and to clarify the relationship between substitute parents and the children in their care.' Nevertheless, the emphasis on *help* to families leads the pro-birth parent school to direct their attention away from the need for *legal powers* to be held by courts and local authorities. It must be said that the National Council for One Parent Families are something of an exception to this; their concern with the taking of parental rights by resolution led them to look in detail at this area, and to recommend a court hearing in every case, a more legalistic solution.

The final point concerns the feasibility of ensuring the 'inclusive' type of foster placement which the supporters of this perspective would favour as being most conducive to the maintenance of the parent-child link and the eventual return home of the child. In this type of placement the foster parents do not wholly assume the parental role, and the birth parents (and the social worker) remain actively involved in the child's life. It is of interest that one of the supporters of this perspective, Tunstill, herself concluded from a small study of foster parents (1980)[71] that:

> they appear to be firmly in favour of the 'exclusive' model: . . .
> As a group the foster parents overwhelmingly agreed with the intentions and provisions of the [1975] Act. . . . they defined that well-being [of the child] in terms of the present security of the child, taking no account of security which might depend on knowledge of, and identification with, natural parents.

They saw their main task as being to incorporate the child in a caring family which he could regard as his own. Tunstill also quotes earlier research by, for example, George (1970)[72] and Adamson (1973)[73] which showed that over half of foster parents saw themselves as a natural rather than a foster parent. Rowe (1977),[74] quoted by Tunstill, talks of the gap 'between social work emphasis on the need for foster parents to avoid possessiveness and not become too emotionally involved with the child, and foster parents' persistence in considering themselves as substitute parents'. And Kelly (1981),[75] in an article on foster child contact with birth parents, says: 'All the major studies in the UK report that a majority of foster parents prefer to regard the children as their own and do not see themselves in the role of foster parent but would rather be seen as the child's own or adoptive parent.' The problem, then, is that the kind of substitute care seen as preferable in this third perspective may not be easily attainable while children are placed in foster homes. In so far as foster parents' motivation is bound up with a desire to 'parent' the child in a full sense, attempts to impose an 'inclusive' model may cause a reduction in the supply of foster homes. Alternatively, foster parents may be explicitly regarded more as 'professionals' than parents, and paid accordingly, but this is an expensive option. Another alternative is greater use of residential homes, but these are also found undesirable on a number of counts, and have not been in favour in the 1980s.

### (c) *Problems of rationale and underlying values*
The ambiguity of the rationale given by the proponents of this perspective for supporting birth parent-child links has already been commented on under (iii). It is not clear to what extent these bonds are defended solely *because* they constitute early psychological links, or to what extent, and why, the blood tie itself is being valued and protected. It is suggested that the way in which this rationale is not fully worked through is a rather serious deficiency in this perspective, and contrasts with Goldstein *et al.*'s fuller exposition of why it is that *psychological* bonds should be respected. A clearer understanding of *why* the birth family should be important to the child's welfare would at least perhaps enable distinctions to be made between, say, situations where the birth parents have never been known to the child; where there was interaction but there are now no conscious memories; and where the child has conscious memories of the parents. A further distinction which needs to be taken on board, and which is perhaps not entirely faced by the supporters of this position, is between different types of relationship between parents and children, positive and negative experiences, happy and unhappy memories. Not all parent-child relationships are good, and children may reject their parents as well as *vice-versa*. Would it, for example, still be held that the blood tie is good for the child if the child himself denies it?

This leads on to the second point which may be criticised, one which the third perspective shares with the first two, and that is the implicit devaluation, in much of the writing, of the child's right to self-determination. Again, it seems, decisions and judgements are made *for* the child. As was noted in discussing the first and second perspectives, the child's *own* wishes and viewpoint are overlooked. In the first perspective, children's interests are generally imputed to them by others, and conflict is seen as lying between *parents* and the state. The child's *wishes* are neglected. In the second, the psychological differentiation of children led to the conclusion that their rights are *different* from those of adults: children have rights to proper care, not to freedom to choose. Neither perspective is uniformly supportive of the idea of separate representation for the child in court.[76] With the third perspective, the neglect of children's independent rights arises basically from a high degree of trust in parents' ability to act in their children's interests. The child's voice is therefore effectively unheard. Most proponents of the third perspective tend to be non-committal about the idea of separate representation for the child; they would not throw it out but do not positively support it either.

Supporters of the fourth perspective to be discussed, the children's rights school, would be particularly critical of this overlooking of the child's independent view.

A further and related problem with the underlying rationale is a relative lack of differentiation of the interests, feelings and welfare of different family members. For the purposes of this discussion, it is the lack of differentiation of *children* as separate individuals which is important. Whether or not children's *rights* to self-determination and autonomy are supported, it is still possible to differentiate children's needs and interests from those of other members of their families. Many proponents of the pro-birth parent perspective tend not to do this. There is a recognition of the family as an interacting system, but less recognition that each individual's life may also be seen as a system in its own right, although linked to other systems.[77] Reference is made to the family as the target of child care (and broader social) policy. Yet the family is a group in which power and resources tend to be distributed unequally. There is simply no guarantee, for example, that an increased child allowance or other income paid to a parent will indeed find its way to benefiting the children. Even in affluent family households, women and/or children may be, in fact, poor.[78] Social work help may come to focus on the parents' needs and problems, and overlook the children's.[79] To take another example, there is a certain ambiguity in recommending child day care to free a stressed and poverty-stricken single parent to go out to work. It *may* be reasonable to conflate the parent's and the child's well-being in this situation, but it needs to be made clear that this is what is being done. Some insight into this problem may be gained by translating the parent-child issue into male-female terms. The unacceptability, for many, of such an approach to women, would be apparent in a view which neglected to differentiate the two partners to a marriage in terms of needs, interests, feelings and welfare, so that husband and wife were not considered as individuals but conflated, with references persistently made to the need to uphold and support 'the marriage'.

Lastly, a major underpinning value characteristic of the third perspective which must be looked at critically is its broader political viewpoint. It will be remembered that poor child care and the state bodies which respond to it are seen as shaped by social divisions, primarily class; that social inequality is a crucial issue in the approach; and that social problems are accounted for in these terms. Three critical points will be made here. Firstly, the view of the state is inconsistent. Secondly, a related point, if the analysis of a class-divided society is correct, it seems little can be achieved in the child care field without major political structural change. Thirdly, and again a connected point, the Welfare State whose extension advocates of this perspective broadly support, itself ran into major problems from the late 1970s.

Firstly, the view of the state held in this perspective seems inconsistent. On the one hand its actual interventions in the child care field are seen as excessively authoritarian and intrusive while its public expenditure policies limit the development of a truly preventive strategy; on the other hand the emergence of an effective preventive policy is seen as capable of creation by the same state. Parton, perhaps, goes some way to recognising that we may be talking about a different kind of state, but in Holman's work the disjuncture is more apparent. However, Holman does acknowledge that he is envisaging a different kind of *society*, a more equal one, where 'as the costs of public services are largely raised through central and local government taxation, it is likely that the more affluent sections of society would find their own disposable income somewhat reduced'. The power of the more affluent sections to resist, through the state as well as through other institutions, is perhaps overlooked here.

The second objection is that if the class analysis of child care policy is substantially accurate, then child care policy is unlikely to change its fundamental (class-biased) nature unless and until the class nature of society is itself changed. That is, the ending of social deprivation, of a system where middle class decision-makers pass judgement on and punish the poor, and of processes which separate parents and children instead of helping them to remain together, is unlikely – perhaps impossible – while capitalism perpetuates social inequalities and creates victims. The root causes of poor child care – and inappropriately coercive state responses – seem to lie embedded within capitalism, in this perspective. Holman (1988)[80] in fact attempts to side-step the logic of this by saying that the argument is *not* that no progress can be made without fundamental changes, and that piecemeal gains *can* be achieved; and Parton takes a similar position; but Holman's statement follows a plea for: 'an increase in public expenditure on the social services, an acceptance of greater equality, and a shift in values on the side of the belief that the "good" family life should be extended to all families.' A little later Holman notes: 'During this present century the state has gradually extended its commitment towards the well-being of socially deprived families and, indeed, the welfare state was brought into existence.' Holman here appears to overlook the fact that in the 1980s in Britain such policies went into reverse. The third critical point, then, is the pragmatic one that, whether or not the expectations held of the state in this perspective are contradictory, whether or not the class nature of society means that a satisfactory (from this perspective) child care policy cannot actually be achieved, the Welfare State which the proponents of this perspective support and require, in fact ran into a serious ideological and fiscal crisis in the late 1970s and 1980s, not only in Britain but in other western countries. Reference may be made to the extensive literature on this topic.[81] The point to note here is that a key assumption in the underlying values and rationale of the third perspective, is that the Welfare State as it has been known *will* continue and *can* expand. This assumption is questionable.

## (v) *The perspective in practice*

Following the model of the previous chapters, the discussion has covered the main elements of the value perspective, some authors associated with it, the rationale and underlying values, and criticisms relating to empirical support, implications for policy, and underlying values. The perspective will now be illustrated by reference to child care law and policy in particular periods and places. The first illustration is English child care policy in the 1950s and 1960s. This was a period when 'preventive' policies were increasingly favoured. The second example concerns Australian policy in the 1970s. Here also policy apparently moved from an emphasis on protection to prevention.

## THE DEFENCE OF THE BIRTH FAMILY IN ENGLISH CHILD CARE LAW AND POLICY IN THE 1950S AND 1960S[82]

Chapter 3 showed how the earlier part of the twentieth century in England was marked by a rather crude form of paternalism in child care policy, in which there was greater interest in children and more state intervention to protect their welfare than had been the case, but the emphasis in policy was more on children's physical welfare than their psychological welfare; the bonds with early caretakers were not well understood; and children in need of care or protection were given a 'fresh start' rather than rehabilitated with their families. In the inter-War period family life seemed to suffer a loss of status, and in some ways developments paralleled later ones in the 1970s (also discussed in Chapter 3).

The atmosphere in child care policy in the early post-Second World War period was very different, with higher standards for the welfare and care of the child and a greater awareness of the importance of families. Although some *general* child welfare provisions had appeared in the early years of the century, provisions which might be seen as helping parents to care for their own children appropriately, it was not really until this post-War period that the modern defence of the birth parent perspective became clearly influential, at least in the statutory sector. (It was present earlier in parts of the voluntary sector; for example, the National Council for the Unmarried Mother and her Child, which in modern times became the National Council for One Parent Families,[83] from its early days after the First World War worked to enable mother and child to stay together.)

The 1950s and 1960s cannot be fully understood without reference to the late 1940s. The Second World War had engendered much greater awareness of the strength of the bonds between children and their original parents, and sympathy for the family. This was mainly due to two factors. Firstly, the wartime evacuation of children from urban areas served to reveal to many of the middle class just how severe were the conditions experienced by some children.[84] The fact that it was the poorest and most congested areas that had to be evacuated exacerbated the impact. The revelations produced greater support for the family as an institution: while some blamed parents for their children's deprivation, others saw it as aggravated by lack of support for families and particularly mothers, and by policies which had failed to look at underlying problems. Social legislation had mostly focused on the treatment of problems *outside* the family – individuals tended to be removed from their family background and treated in institutions or substitute homes; and the strength of the family as a social and psychological unit was seemingly not fully appreciated until the wartime disruptions highlighted it. Many families in fact resisted the separation brought about by the evacuation and re-united.

Another factor helping to underline the importance of family ties was the widespread provision of day and residential nurseries, set up mainly to release women into the wartime labour force. Studies of children separated from their families in the nurseries showed the psychological dangers of sudden separation from parent figures, and led to a greater understanding of the need for emotional attachment, security and continuity, and therefore an emphasis on the original parents. It was at this time that Bowlby's work first became influential.

The first major piece of post-War legislation in the child care field, the Children Act 1948, therefore needs to be seen against this background. The specific child care issues which were of concern in the 1950s were mostly linked with the sweeping changes in the organisation of state child care which came about with this Act. The changes included the setting up of local authority Children's Departments; an emphasis on boarding out as a method of child care; restoration of children in care to their original family; more emphasis on adoption, including the adoption of children in care; and the involvement of Children's Departments with young offenders.

The Children Act reflected an entirely new ethos. With the Poor Law, including its child care role, now finally abolished,[85] the Act set new and higher standards of welfare for children in care. Instead of 'less eligibility' – the Poor Law principle that those cared for and maintained by the state should always be *worse* off than others – there was a notion of positive discrimination to compensate the deprived child for her deprivation. Partly in response to the findings of the Curtis Committee on the care of children (1946),[86] and partly reflecting the general emphasis on welfare and collectivism of the times, the 1948 Act emphasised better treatment for children deprived of their home life, stating in Section 12 the local authority's duty to exercise its powers towards the child 'so as to further his best interests, and to afford him opportunity for the proper development of his character and abilities'.

Most significant organisationally was the setting up, under the Children Act, of separate local authority Children's Departments to specialise in child care work. These Departments were the responsibility of a single local authority committee and a single chief officer, the Children's Officer. Specialisation was intended to raise standards of care, as was the training and professionalisation of the new occupaton of Child Care Officer. The system of public child care now became more sophisticated and demanded greater resources. An important element in this new system was the emphasis on fostering or 'boarding out'. The Curtis Committee had made some disturbing discoveries about institutional care, but had been generally impressed by the system of boarding out. In the years following the 1948 Act boarding out was strongly preferred to the use of residential homes, and the Home Office issued an annual 'league table' showing the percentages of children in care in different local authorities who were in foster homes. Foster care was seen as more in tune with the new individualised and child-centred approach, although the boarding out system itself had a long history. The average boarding out rate rose from, for example, 35 per cent in 1949, to 44 per cent in 1954, to 48 per cent in 1960, with a peak of 52 per cent being reached in 1963, after which there was a decline.[87]

Perhaps not entirely consonant with the trend to put children in care into foster homes whenever possible was the emphasis, again stemming from the 1948 Act, on restoration of the child to her original birth family. Restoration and foster placement might conflict if the foster parents regarded themselves as effectively the child's parents. (Interestingly, the Curtis Committee had noted that some foster mothers seemed too possessive.) While the emphasis in the post-1948 child care world was on good quality substitute care, children were to be in care only as long as their welfare required it. The Children's Department had to strive to discharge the child from care to a parent, friend or relative wherever this was consistent with his welfare.[88] This constituted a break with pre-War practice. The official policy was thus now for most children in care to return to their original family, and the Children's Departments had a duty to help families to resume care. Certainly the *ideology* of the time emphasised that being in care should not be construed as permanent (even if, in practice, it was).

What was not present in the 1948 Act was a remit to work with children and families to prevent the need for substitute care arising. There was *some* awareness of the problems of children still in their own homes, however. A Women's Group on Public Welfare produced a report on neglected children and the family in 1948,[89] and a Home Office circular also in 1948 stressed the importance of prevention, while another in 1950 proposed co-ordinating machinery to prevent entry into care.[90] However, local authorities' responses to the call for co-ordination were not uniform and there was some difficulty in getting the machinery to work successfully. Feeling also developed in the child care service in the 1950s that its remit was too narrow and its activities were unduly restricted by being confined to children deprived of a normal home life, and thus excluding work with cases where the need for substitute care might have been avoided. While a few local authorities may have informally undertaken 'preventive work' – for example, Oxfordshire appointed a preventive case worker in the early 1950s[91] – there was no statutory base for spending money in this way, and the authorities were perhaps acting *ultra vires* in doing so. At the same time, emphasis in child care work moved more towards the family and its problems rather than the child taken in isolation. A further factor providing impetus for change at the time was the question of cost: there was concern at the rising expenditure on the child care service, and a belief that extra work undertaken to keep children in their own homes would – in the long term – prove cheaper. Both child neglect and juvenile delinquency were seen as originating in the same type of family, and from a malfunctioning of the family as a socialising agent. The prevention of *both* problems was seen as involving a focusing on the *family* rather than the individual child as the target for intervention.

Another element of child care policy in the 1950s, which may, like the emphasis on foster care, be seen as somewhat dissonant with the objective of care by the birth family, was the increased attention given to adoption. This was seen as the best form of care for children who could not be cared for by their own families, and Children's Departments were given powers to place children in care with prospective adopters and to act as adoption agencies,[92] while adoption was further regulated and controlled.[93] The permanence of adoption, its closeness to the norm of the birth family, constituted an attraction when children faced substitute care for many years. It was also seen as a solution to the increasing problem of illegitimate births. And adoption usually signified the end of the local authority's involvement and thus averted the need for further expenditure. However, the focus on the adoption of children already *in care* should be seen in relation to the emphasis on rehabilitation. Adoption was in fact still primarily concerned with placing young babies, rather than older children with a history in care.

A further element in 1950s child care was the involvement of Children's Departments with young offenders. When the specialist child care service was set up, the groups of children in state care included some young offenders, as well as non-offending children who had been before the courts.[94] Under the 1948 Act local authorities had a duty to act as fit persons where Fit Person Orders (the predecessors of Care Orders) were made; they were also empowered to admit to care children released from approved schools; and from 1952[95] they were empowered to do approved school after-care in the community. Juvenile offending was a field where there had long been work on rehabilitating the child with his original family. As indicated, a belief now grew that neglect and juvenile delinquency were rooted in similar causes, factors to do with a malfunctioning of the family. Delinquency was also thought to be due to the 'maternal deprivation' outlined by Bowlby.

Developments in the 1950s also need to be set in their general welfare context. There were enormous legislative changes in the field of welfare in the mid-late 1940s – the Education Act 1944, the Family Allowances Act 1945, The National Health Service Act 1946, the National Assistance Act 1948 – legislation which is generally construed as the foundation stone of the modern 'Welfare State' in Britain. The child care changes thus occurred in a context where there were more generous state provisions for the general health and welfare of the population, including children – universal health care, better social security benefits, an improved education system, and so on. These changes continued to form the background to child care policy in the 1950s. The improved general provisions may be seen as having a broadly preventive role, supporting the family in its care and socialisation functions.

In the 1960s the swing towards favouring 'preventive work' intensified. Indeed, the 1960s may be seen as the high point of the emphasis on prevention and the natural family. There was greater state activity and involvement with families and children generally. It has been mentioned that in the 1950s the co-ordinating machinery concerned with child welfare was found wanting; the child care service itself experienced its remit as too narrow; and there was concern about the cost of substitute care. Most importantly, the Ingleby Committee on children and young persons, set up in 1956, reported in 1960.[96] It had been felt that there was a need for an inquiry into social services concerned with the family, to look at the issue of child neglect at home and its prevention, and at juvenile delinquency, which was an increasing problem. The Committee's main concerns were the prevention of delinquency, neglect and children entering care; children at risk of these fates and how to provide support for their families; treatment facilities for those who came before the juvenile courts; and the courts themselves. While stressing that parents still had the prime responsibility for their children, which was not to be taken over by the state, the Report emphasised better co-ordination between agencies, skilled intensive casework with families, and the power to give material aid; and it recommended that local authorities should therefore have a duty to prevent child neglect at home, and powers to give material help to achieve this.

The 1963 Children and Young Persons Act embodied these proposals: the local authorities – in effect their Children's Departments

– were given preventive functions in the duty laid on them by Section 1 to give advice, guidance and assistance in order to diminish the need for reception into care or for bringing a child before a court. Assistance in cash or kind was possible, but cash was only to be given in exceptional circumstances. As a result of this change Children's Departments now began officially to use resources on preventive work with families, with the Child Care Officer's role becoming more that of a family caseworker; yet the Act had not mentioned extra resources, indeed it was hoped that successful preventive work would save money. Various types of preventive work were undertaken: family casework and family advice work, children's holidays, group and community work, for example, with material assistance being used sparingly at first but growing in scale over the 1960s.[97] Social workers began to have more contact with other agencies, to specialise in 'welfare rights' work more, and to act as advocates on their clients' behalf; they had more dealings with families whose chief or only problems were material rather than psychological.

The 1960s, like the 1950s, were marked by a concern for problems at the family level – the 'problem family', or even the 'multi-problem family' was widely discussed. A concern with the less immediate social environment, with the wider social structure and its implications for child deprivation, developed more strongly from the later 1960s and early 1970s, with the appearance of 'radical social work'. This approach stressed the structural origins of many client problems, the inadequacy of other systems within the Welfare State, and a social activist and advocate role for the social worker. More doubt about the effectiveness of preventive programmes also came later; but the early and mid-1960s were a time of relative confidence about what such programmes could achieve (although the proportion of children in care in fact remained stable after the 1963 Act – at approximately 0.5 per cent of the population under 18 – and then began to rise[98]). Parton (1985)[99] speaks of the optimism in child care in the 1950s and 1960s, and the confidence in Child Care Officers, who, it was believed, could bring about change in families through casework and counselling.

Other issues of importance in the 1960s which can be mentioned more briefly include fostering and adoption, and young offenders. Fostering and adoption of deprived children became increasingly linked in child care thinking. Initially, fostering was much favoured, as it had been in the 1950s, and, as mentioned, the highest boarding out rate was achieved in 1963, when it was 52 per cent; by 1970, however, the rate was down to 42 per cent (reaching its lowest point in 1975).[100] Fostering was becoming less popular as its problems were increasingly appreciated; thinking swung more to seeing an equal balance between the merits of care with foster parents and care in a residential home, and to determining the best solution for each child rather than assuming that foster care was an *a priori* good for all. This might have rendered contact with the birth parent, and eventual return to the parent, easier to achieve. But by the late 1960s, another kind of concern was developing: for the security of foster placements when birth parents retained their rights. This was influential in the deliberations of the Houghton Committee, set up in 1969, whose report of 1972[101] ultimately led to the Children Act of 1975. These evelopments reversed the 1950s' and 1960s' practice of holding open the door to eventual return to the birth family for most children in foster care.

In the field of adoption, the early 1960s saw an increasing number of local authorities making use of their powers to act as adoption agencies, and an increase in adoptions generally. One trend that appeared in the later 1960s, however – which intensified later and was influential in developments in the 1970s – was the drop in the number of *babies* available for adoption, due to a number of factors such as more widely available contraception and abortion and a changed social climate with regard to illegitimacy and unmarried motherhood. At the same time there was an increased number of children with particular difficulties and needs, including a long history in care, who were now seen as suitable for adoption. Again, a shift was beginning away from keeping open the option of rehabilitation indefinitely, and this also intensified in the 1970s.

On the question of juvenile offending, the Ingleby Committee's role has already been referred to. The rise in juvenile crime was causing concern, and the Committee addressed itself to the roots of delinquent behaviour and the treatment of delinquency. As with neglect, prevention was seen as involving a focusing on the family, although not to the point of taking over its functions entirely. The Ingleby Report commented: 'It is the parents' duty to help their children become effective and law-abiding citizens by example and training and by providing a stable and secure family background in which they can develop satisfactorily.'

The 1963 Act which followed Ingleby gave the Children's Departments duties and powers to avert children appearing before the juvenile court, whether as offenders or as in need of protection. The later 1969 Children and Young Persons Act owed much to a family-oriented approach and perhaps marked the high point of the 'treatment' model in responding to juvenile crime. Preceded by two

141

*Perspectives in child care policy*

White Papers in 1965 and 1968 (the first of which was more radical than the second),[102] it embodied a further movement away from the concept of punishment of an offence and a conventional criminal justice approach in dealing with young offenders. Children in trouble with the law were to be treated in almost the same way as non-offending children in trouble. Wherever possible offending children were to be kept in their own home, and to be spared the stigma of prosecution and/or punitive sentences. It should be noted, however, that the Act was never fully implemented, and in the 1970s, this trend went into reverse.

1960s child care policy should also be viewed in the general welfare context of the decade. The 1960s were a time when the general consensus on welfare policies continued to hold, and the later 1960s may even be seen as a high point for the Welfare State. Mishra (1984)[103] describes the 'high tide of legitimacy' of the Welfare State, when 'the correction of social imbalance through social programmes and services became almost a bipartisan policy'. It was a general climate, then, which was favourable to the policy preferences of the pro-birth family perspective for widespread welfare services to support and help families with children generally.

In summarising these two very important decades, certain themes in keeping with the pro-birth parent perspective should first be referred to. Two characteristics of the 1950s were an enhanced emphasis on child welfare *and* a recognition of the importance of the birth family. The specialisation of the children's service, and the incorporation of knowledge of child psychology, raised standards of substitute care; but the importance of the original family, and of restoration to it, was also a prominent feature of policy and practice. Improved general provisions for child health, welfare and education may be seen as having a broadly preventive function at this time. And the early post-War period was in general a relatively child-centred time, with notions of a more 'permissive' and indulgent style of child upbringing becoming apparent. In the 1960s the concern with birth families and the prevention of children entering substitute care found legislative expression, while towards the end of this decade, a greater awareness developed in social work of the relevance of structural factors and social deprivation to the situations to which social workers had to respond. A generally permissive and child-centred approach to children continued to flourish, although with some signs of retraction towards the end of the period;[104] the family was in favour; and the legitimacy of state welfare expenditure remained well supported.

Other themes of the 1950s and 1960s are not entirely in harmony with the preventive school of thought: the stress on foster care, and later on *secure* foster care; and the high valuation of adoption and its extension to somewhat older children who had been in care. Nevertheless, in general these two decades provide a good illustration of a broadly preventive, pro-birth family approach at work – more so than any other period in recent English history. The second example to be considered involves another country – Australia.


## THE DEFENCE OF THE BIRTH FAMILY IN CHILD WELFARE POLICY IN AUSTRALIA IN THE 1970S

A report by Carter (1983)[105] entitled *Protection to Prevention: Child Welfare Policies* charts developments in this field in Australia over the 1970s, and will be the main source drawn on in showing how Australian trends in that decade approximated to the preventive and birth parent perspective, in contrast to trends in the 1970s in England and Wales and the United States. The report collates data on various aspects of child welfare policy in Australia over the 1970s, making comparisons with similar data on the United States and England and Wales.

In Carter's report, 'protection' is used to mean the rescue or supervision of a child using compulsory intervention, while 'prevention' refers to the use of a range of non-compulsory services 'to reinforce and enhance the caring capacity of the family for the child'. Carter's main finding is set out in her Preface; it is that: 'In the past decade, the numbers of children under the guardianship of the State and cared for by agencies other than their own families has diminished considerably in Australia. By contrast, in England and Wales and in the United States, the number of children in the care of the state has grown.' Yet, as Carter says, there have been similar pressures on governments in all of these three countries – for example, to increase protection against child abuse. Applying a useful framework, Carter classifies child welfare services into: **substitute** (standing in for the family after child and family have been separated); **supervision** (oversight *within* the family); **supplementary** (services on a voluntary basis to back up a needy or limited family); and **supportive** (services to *all* families to help them bring up their child more effectively). These types of intervention can be ranged on a protection-to-prevention spectrum, and it will be apparent that the first two would find greater favour with the paternalist/protection school of thought, and the latter two with the third, pro-family perspective. As Carter says, a central matter here is 'the type of relationship; past, present and future, between the family and the state'.

Commenting on Australian child welfare policies in the past, Carter says: 'child and family policies were not linked together. Rather, they were discontinuous, for public policies for children came into operation only after policy for families had broken down.' However, a new recognition came about – in the 1960s, it seems – that it was not sufficient merely to provide substitute care after family breakdown: breakdown itself should be resisted. And family policy itself has attracted rather more political attention in Australia than in either the United States or England, while such policy has been defined in Australia to include policies for adults caring for children.

Carter's approach was to seek information from eight child welfare administrations in six Australian States and two territories, and from the Office of Child Care within the Department of Social Security of the Australian *Commonwealth* Government. Annual reports for the years 1972–81 were used to investigate interventions in the fields of protection and prevention. From these sources Carter found considerable changes in the philosophy and operation of child welfare departments over the period studied, characterised as a 'moving out', a shift in emphasis from picking up social problems to a broader model, with the departments taking initiatives, in response to change and increased demand, becoming more accessible, and emphasising preventive services. However, another theme was to improve child protection services, and all States increased the scope and scale of their work here after 1975.

Drawing on her four-fold classification, Carter first considers **Substitute Interventions**, and finds a considerable reduction in the numbers of children under State guardianship, that is in State care, in Australia over the 1970s. For example, the estimated rate was 5.9 children per '000 population under 18 in 1972; by 1980 the ratio had dropped to 4.2 per '000, with a further reduction to 3.8 in 1981; so 'the number in guardianship had reduced by over a third in a decade'. In contrast, as Carter notes, the ratio in England and Wales rose during the same period, and in 1980 the ratio in Australia was less than half the ratio in England and Wales, and possibly half the United States rate. In both Australia and England and Wales there were considerable internal geographical variations, but whereas the range was 1.1–7.2 children per '000 in Australia in 1980, in England and Wales the range was 1.7–19.9 In fact, each Australian State had *increased* the overall numbers of children in guardianship during the *first* part of the 1970s, but reaching a peak year after which the numbers began to drop. The peak years were mostly in the earlier half of the 1970s.

As well as fewer children being placed under guardianship in Australia than in England and Wales, a higher proportion of children under Australian guardianship were found to be placed with their biological families than were children in care in England and Wales (for example 25 per cent in 1980 in Australia, as compared with 18 per cent in England and Wales). This implies a greater emphasis on maintaining children in their own families in Australian policy. Carter suggests that such a preference for maintaining the biological family can also be seen in the adoption figures – while at the beginning of the 1970s the States' role was to redistribute children from their natural family to others, by 1980 half of the adoptions were by couples where at least one adopter was a biological parent; this trend in the second half of the 1970s was in the opposite direction to that in England and Wales. Nevertheless, Carter's figures show a greater percentage of adoptions within biological families for England and Wales than for Australia (68 per cent in England and Wales in 1975 and 58 per cent in 1980, as compared with only 33 per cent and 49 per cent in Australia). It may also be noted here that in England specific measures to limit step-parent adoptions were instituted in the 1975 Children Act.[106]

Looking at **Supervision Interventions**, Carter concludes that, given certain qualifications 'there appears to have been an overall decline in the numbers of supervision and allied orders'. She suggests, however, that as a large number of children under guardianship were placed in their own homes, new resources were required to oversee the care of children at home, and the major new resource here was field workers, who increased in numbers in most States during the 1970s (in some cases, dramatically). Carter goes on to ask, in the light of these trends: 'Have Australian departments over the seventies increased their capacity to work with children without requiring the compulsory powers of legal orders? If so, how can the non-statutory workload of departments be quantified?' Unfortunately, no real answer was found to this question, as a lot of non-statutory work was officially unrecorded. Carter summarises this section by saying, however, that the numbers of children under supervision – along with those in guardianship – appeared to have declined, but a new workload had appeared which required intervention without coercive, legal back-up.

Carter next turns to **Supplementary Interventions**, commenting first that assessing services as belonging to this category 'is bedevilled by the problem of what services *mean* to providers and recipients. Whereas substitution and supervision revolve around the presence or absence of legal definitions, supplementary services are more ambiguous'. Looking back first to the late 1960s, Carter found that the States concentrated almost exclusively on substitute interventions; the initial emphasis on supervisory interventions was often expressed as a need for field services to work with families before children entered formal care; but 'there was little analysis of the role of such services, nor was it envisaged that practical resources were required to back up field services'. There were no formal supplementary interventions at the end of the 1960s apart from day care for children. But by 1975 'a new pattern of services had commenced'. Carter shows the range of services in a table, classifying services into socialisation and development (for example, holidays and playgroups), help, rehabilitation, therapy and protection (for example, counselling, family day care, housekeeper services, and material and financial aid), access, information and advice, and social action (for example, community development). She comments that if the table were redrawn for 1980, the States would offer a wider range of supplementary services at the preventative end of the continuum. These would include playgroups, day care, homemaker services, centres of various kinds, family support and crisis services. The Commonwealth Family Support programme 1978–84 is worth particular mention. This assisted 170 low cost projects aimed to support families in their child-rearing responsibilities, including services of housing referral, emergency accommodation, counselling and homemaker assistance. Carter contrasts the Commonwealth government's promotion of supplementary interventions here with its substitute intervention role with other client groups such as the elderly. The Commonwealth's emphasis on supplementary interventions with children is also in marked contrast to the central government's role in the United Kingdom in the later 1970s, which focused on child protection rather than prevention.

Carter deals very briefly with her fourth category, **Support Interventions**, commenting that aside from family allowances it was difficult to find other measures supporting all families; although the universal provision of a subsidised pre-school year in some States came close to a universalist support intervention.

In her final chapter, Carter concludes: 'One thing is clear: in Australia there has been a decline in the use of protective interventions (particularly substitution) and an increase in the use of preventative interventions (at least of the supplementary variety).' Comparing Australia with England and Wales, she notes that: 'Australian government interventions into children's lives have become altogether less coercive and more persuasive, less remedial and more developmental. And even although more resources remain in the substitute sector, the pattern suggests that Australian governments take a more favourable view of the family as a child rearing institution than their British counterparts.' The contrast is drawn again a few pages later, when Carter says: 'While the Australian government has sponsored preventative services, central government in England and Wales has supported protective regulations,' by means of Area Review Committees for child abuse, the sponsorship of enquiries into individual abuse cases, the distribution of formal guidelines, and the promotion of registers for suspected abuse cases; and: 'Of the two countries, it appears that Australian policies work to enhance the child rearing role of the natural family; British policies and outcomes endorse the role of the family in child rearing with less vigour. A greater (and increasing) prominence has been given to coercive interventions . . . in England and Wales . . .' Carter suggests that Australia may have learned from one significant child welfare failure, that is, mass removal of Aborigine children from their families. This 'may have made Australian child welfare experts more cautious about substituting the "society as parent" ideology over and above primacy of kinship'.

**In summary**, Carter's research showed that Australian child welfare policy had in general over the 1970s moved from the substitute, or protectionist, or coercive, end of the intervention continuum, to the supplementary, or preventative, or voluntary, end, with fewer children in care and a greater emphasis on the biological family, although there were some qualifications to this picture. However, it should be noted that another writer in this field, Sweeney (1983),[107] takes the view that 'guardianship and/or substitute care remain the focus of State Government intervention' and that resources were more readily available to remove a child from home than to support him in his own home. The Commonwealth Government is seen as having created some supportive services in the early 1970s – child care centres, pre-school, family day care – but the situation changed in 1975–6, with the services suffering funding cuts and being re-orientated away from pre-school and day care to other forms of family services. Sweeney comments that the Government 'has been selective in defining which children had a need for services'. Help was focused on particular groups of the disadvantaged, but relatively little success was achieved, in Sweeney's view, with 'a degree of disparity between the stated aims and the reality'. The programme was essentially selective and discriminatory, in contrast to the universalist policies earlier in the 1970s. Nonetheless, support for remedial and rehabilitative services designed to keep children out of substitute care did increase, and Sweeney sees the Commonwealth services as preventative (though not, as she would prefer, developmental).

## SOME REFERENCES RELEVANT TO THIS PERSPECTIVE

C. Andrews 1980 'Is blood thicker than local authorities?' *Social Work Today* 2 September 1980 12(1) 19–21

P. Beresford, J. Kemmis and J. Tunstill 1987 *In Care in North Battersea* London, North Battersea Research Group

J. Carter 1983 *Protection to Prevention: Child Welfare Policies* Social Welfare Research Centre, University of New South Wales, Australia

Family Rights Group 1982 *Fostering Parental Contact*

Family Rights Group 1984 *Permanent Substitute Families. Security or Severance*

Family Rights Group 1986 *Promoting Links – Keeping Children and Families in Touch*

N. Frost and M. Stein 1989 *The Politics of Child Welfare: Inequality, Power and Change* Hemel Hempstead, Harvester/Wheatsheaf

J. S. Heywood 1978 *Children in Care. The development of the service for the deprived child* London, Routledge Kegan Paul

R. Holman 1975 'The Place of Fostering in Social Work' *British Journal of Social Work* 5(1) 3–29

R. Holman 1975 'Unmarried Mothers, Social Deprivation and Child Separation' *Policy and Politics* 3 1974–5 25–41

R. Holman 1976 and 1980 *Inequality in Child Care* London, Child Poverty Action Group Poverty Pamphlet 26

R. Holman 1978 'A class analysis of adoption reveals a disturbing picture' *Community Care* 26 April 1978 30

R. Holman 1980 'A *real* child care policy for the future' *Community Care* 18/25 December 1980 340 16–17

R. Holman 1982 'Exclusive and inclusive fostering' in Family Rights Group *Fostering Parental Contact*

B. Holman 1988 *Putting Families First. Prevention and Child Care* Basingstoke, Macmillan Education

House of Commons 1984 *Second Report from the Social Services Committee* (Session 1983–4) *Children in Care* (The Short Report) London, HMSO

Ingleby Committee 1960 *Report of the Committee on Children and Young Persons* Cmnd. 1190 London, HMSO

B. C. Isaac, E.B. Minty and R.M. Morrison 1986 'Children in Care – the Association with Mental Disorder in the Parents' *British Journal of Social Work* 16(4) 325–39

J. Lait 1979 'Is less worse better than better?' *Community Care* 14 June 1979 24

V. MacLeod 1982 *Whose Child? The Family in Child Care Legislation and Social Work Practice* Study Commission on the Family Occasional Paper no. 11

B. R. Mandel 1973 *Where are the Children? A Class Analysis of Foster Care and Adoption* Lexington Books

S. Millham, R. Bullock, K. Hosie and M. Haak 1986 *Lost in Care: the problems of maintaining links between children in care and their families* Aldershot, Gower

National Council for One Parent Families (NCOPF) 1982 *Against Natural Justice*

J. Packman 1981 *The Child's Generation. Child Care Policy in Britain* Oxford, Blackwell and Robertson

J. Packman 1986 *Who Needs Care? Social Work Decisions about Children* Oxford, Blackwell

N. Parton 1979 'The Natural History of Child Abuse: A Study in Social Problem Definition' *British Journal of Social Work* 9(4) 431–46

N. Parton 1981 'Child Abuse, Social Anxiety and Welfare' *British Journal of Social Work* 11(4) 394–414

N. Parton 1985 *The Politics of Child Abuse* London, Macmillan

N. Parton 1985 'Politics and practice' *Community Care* 26 September 1985 22–4

N. Parton 1986 'The Beckford Report: A Critical Appraisal' *British Journal of Social Work* 16(5) 511–31

J. Thoburn 1980 *Captive Clients: Social Work with Families of Children Home on Trial* London, Routledge Kegan Paul

R. Thorpe 1974 'Mum and Mrs. So-and-So' *Social Work Today* 4(22) 7 February 1974 691–5

J. Tunstill 1977 'In Defence of Parents' *New Society* 42(785) 20 October 1977 121–2

J. Tunstill 1980 *Fostering Policy and the 1975 Children Act* Brunel University Papers in Social Policy and Administration No. 2

J. Tunstill 1985 'Aiming to prevent misunderstanding' *Social Work Today* 17 June 1985

J. Tunstill 1985 'Laying the Poor Law to rest?' *Community* Care 20 June 1985 16–18

R. Walton and M. Heywood 1975 'Child care, culture and Social Services Departments' *Yearbook of Social Policy 1974* London, Routledge Kegan Paul

## NOTES AND REFERENCES

1. R. Holman 1975 'The Place of Fostering in Social Work' Chapter 2, footnote 23; R. Holman 1982 'Exclusive and inclusive fostering' Chapter 2, footnote 23.
2. See Chapter 3, footnote 37.
3. R. Holman 1976 *Inequality in Child Care* Chapter 2, footnote 17. Also a second edition, 1980.
4. R. Holman 1978 'A class analysis of adoption' Chapter 3, footnote 28; and other sources given in Chapter 3, footnote 28.
5. R. Holman 1975 'Unmarried Mothers, Social Deprivation and Child Separation' *Policy and Politics* 3 1974–5 25–41.
6. R. Thorpe 1974 'Mum and Mrs. So-and-So' Chapter 3, footnote 33. Other relevant research on long-term foster children includes: J. Rowe, H. Cain, M. Hundleby and A. Kearne 1984 *Long Term Foster Care* London, Batsford/British Agencies for Adoption and Fostering (BAAF).
7. J. Thoburn 1980 *Captive Clients: Social Work with Families of Children Home on Trial* London, Routledge Kegan Paul.
8. S. Millham *et al*. 1986 *Lost in Care* Chapter 3, footnote 32.
9. R. Holman 1980 'A *real* child care policy for the future' *Community Care* 18/25 December 1980 340 16–17.
10. R. Holman 1975 'The Place of Fostering in Social Work' Chapter 2, footnote 23; R. Holman 1982 'Exclusive and inclusive fostering' Chapter 2, footnote 23.
11. B. Holman 1988 *Putting Families First. Prevention and Child Care* Basingstoke, Macmillan Education.
12. F. Mount 1982 *The Subversive Family* Chapter 2, footnote 1.
13. I. Vallender and K. Fogelman (Eds) 1987 *Putting* **Children** *First* [my italics] Chapter 3, footnote 3.
14. R. Walton and M. Heywood 1975 'Child care, culture and Social Services Departments' *Yearbook of Social Policy 1974* London, Routledge Kegan Paul.
15. J. Tunstill 1977 'In Defence of Parents' Chapter 3, footnote 18.
16. J. Tunstill 1985 'Laying the Poor Law to rest?' *Community Care* 20 June 1985 16–18.
17. For example, J. Tunstill 1985 'Aiming to prevent misunderstanding' *Social Work Today* 17 June 1985.
18. C. Andrews 1980 'Is blood thicker than local authorities?' *Social Work Today* 2 September 1980 12(1) 19–21.

19. V. MacLeod 1982 *Whose Child? The Family in Child Care Legislation and Social Work Practice* Study Commission on the Family. Occasional Paper no. 11.

20. House of Commons 1984 *Second Report from the Social Services Committee* (Session 1983–4) *Children in Care* (The Short Report) London, HMSO.

21. Section 1 of the Child Care Act 1980, previously Section 1 of the Children and Young Persons Act 1963.

22. The duty to seek rehabilitation did not apply to children in compulsory care.

23. Subsequently a joint inter-departmental and Law Commission review was undertaken, resulting in consultation documents in 1985: DHSS 1985 *Review of Child Care Law: Report to Ministers of an Inter-Departmental Working Party* London, HMSO; and a White Paper: 1987 *The law on Child Care and Family Services* Cm. 62 London, HMSO. The Children Act 1989 was mostly based on these documents.

24. N. Parton 1981 'Child Abuse, Social Anxiety and Welfare', 1985 *The Politics of Child Abuse*, and 1985 'Politics and practice' Chapter 2, footnote 53.

25. N. Parton 1986 'The Beckford Report: A Critical Appraisal' *British Journal of Social Work* 16(5) 511–31.

26. N. Frost and M. Stein 1989 *The Politics of Child Welfare: Inequality, Power and Change* Hemel Hempstead, Harvester/Wheatsheaf

27. P. Beresford, J. Kemmis and J. Tunstill 1987 *In Care in North Battersea* London, North Battersea Research Group.

28. Family Rights Group 1982 *Fostering Parental Contact* Chapter 2, footnote 23.

29. R. Benians 1982 'Preserving parental contact' Chapter 2, footnote 24.

30. Family Rights Group 1984 *Permanent Substitute Families. Security or Severance*

31. G. Kelly 1984 'Natural parent contact – a theory in search of practice' in Ibid, footnote 30.

32. C. Atherton 1984 'Permanency planning for children in care – philosophy and practice' in Ibid, footnote 30. Also see other Family Rights Group publications such as: 1986 *Promoting Links – Keeping Children and Families in Touch*.

33. NCOPF 1982 *Against Natural Justice* Chapter 3, footnote 38.

34. For example, see: R. Parker 1977 'One Parent Families and Children in Care' Speech to NCOPF AGM; London, NCOPF. Also see: P. Beresford *et al.* 1987 *In Care in North Battersea* This Chapter, footnote 27.

35. NCOPF 1982 *Against Natural Justice* Chapter 3, footnote 38.

36. The most well-known sources here are J. Bowlby 1951 *Maternal Care and Mental Health* World Health Organisation; J. Bowlby 1953 *Child Care and the Growth of Love* Harmondsworth, Penguin.

37. See Chapter 2, footnote 21.

38. See Chapter 2, footnote 21.

39. L. M. Fox 1982 'Two Value Positions' Foreword, footnote 1.

40. 1968 *Report of the Committee on Local Authority and Allied Personal Social Services* (Seebohm Report) Cmnd. 3703 London, HMSO.

41. R. Holman 1976 and 1980 *Inequality in Child Care* This chapter, footnote 3; Chapter 2, footnote 17.

42. B. C. Isaac, E. B. Minty and R. M. Morrison 1986 'Children in Care – the Association with Mental Disorder in the Parents' *British Journal of Social Work* 16(4) 325–39.

43. D. Quinton and M. Rutter 1984 'Parents with children in care – 1. Current circumstances and parenting' *Psychology and Psychiatry* 25 211–29.

44. L. M. Fox 1986 'Parental Rights Assumptions' Chapter 3, footnote 38.

45. L. Lambert and J. Rowe 1974 'Children in Care and the Assumption of Parental Rights by Local Authorities' *Child Adoption* 78.

46. Strathclyde Social Work Department 1980 *Strathclyde's Children. 111 Children Whose Parents are the Regional Council.*

47. M. Adcock, R. White and O. Rowlands 1983 *The Administrative Parent* Chapter 3, footnote 20.

48. J. Packman 1986 *Who Needs Care? Social Work Decisions about Children* Oxford, Blackwell.

49. See also Chapter 1, footnote 1.

50. See Chapter 1, footnote 1.

51. These NSPCC figures from: National Children's Bureau (1988) *Highlight 80* 'Child Abuse' April 1988.

52. N. Parton 1979 'The Natural History of Child Abuse: A Study in Social Problem Definition' *British Journal of Social Work* 9(4) 431–46; N. Parton 1981 'Child Abuse, Social Anxiety and Welfare' Chapter 2, footnote 53; N. Parton 1985 *The Politics of Child Abuse* Chapter 2, footnote 53.

53. B. Tizard 1977 *Adoption* Chapter 3, footnote 11.

54. S. Millham 1986 *Lost in Care* Chapter 3, footnote 32.

55. J. Packman 1986 *Who Needs Care?* This chapter, footnote 48.

56. See, for example: L. Eaton 1986 'Parents' rights on trial' *Social Work Today* 17 November 1986 3; M. Fogarty 1986 'Whose son is it anyway?' *The Guardian* 26 November 1986.

57. S. Bell 1988 *When Salem came to the Boro'* London, Pan.

58. B. Campbell 1988 *Unofficial Secrets. Child Sexual Abuse: The Cleveland Case* London, Virago Press.

59. See *Poverty* No. 71, Winter 1988/9, 23. Child Poverty Action Group.

60. Chartered Institute of Public Finance and Accountancy *Personal Social Services Statistics 1986–7 Actuals* 49. The figure relates to the gross cost per child day excluding capital charges.

61. CSO *Social Trends 19, 1989* London, HMSO.

62. In London, the cost of bed and breakfast hotels for the homeless in 1986 was £7,670 per case p.a. (J. Campling 1988 Social Policy Digest, *Journal of Social Policy* 17(3) 387). In April 1989, a Salvation Army survey found almost 25,000 in bed and breakfast hotels in London ('Sally Army finds 75,000 homeless' *The Guardian* 28 July 1989).

63. Although Holman 1980 (*Inequality in Child Care* This chapter, footnote 3) does give a figure of £11.8m p.a. to provide 12,000 additional day care places.

64. For example, Child Benefit was increased by an amount less than the rate of inflation in the 1980s, and was frozen at its existing cash level in 1988, 1989 and 1990.

65. For the effects of the social security changes in the 1980s, see, for

example: Social Security Consortium 1986 *Of Little Benefit. A Critical Guide to the Social Security Act 1986*; National Association of Citizens' Advice Bureaux 1989 *The Social Security Act: First Impressions* London, NACAB; J. Roll 1986 *Family Impact: 1986 Social Security Bill* London, Family Policy Studies Centre; J. Roll 1986 *Family Trends and Social Security Reform* London, Family Policy Studies Centre; Various publications by the Child Poverty Action Group, including the journal *Poverty*.

66. The general tenor of Conservative government policy in the 1980s was towards an emphasis on 'family responsibility', for example in caring for dependent groups such as the young and the old. This appeared to mean at times a withdrawal of *state* support on the assumption that families could and would do more. However, such objectives were not always followed in a straightforward way.

67. B. Magee 1973 *Popper* Glasgow, Fontana/Collins.

68. K. Popper 1966 *The Open Society and its Enemies* London, Routledge Kegan Paul.

69. J. Lait 1979 'Is less worse better than better?' *Community Care* 14 June 1979 24. See also: C. Brewer and J. Lait 1980 *Can Social Work Survive?* Temple Smith.

70. R. Holman 1976 and 1980 *Inequality in Child Care* This chapter, footnote 3; Chapter 2, footnote 17.

71. J. Tunstill 1980 *Fostering Policy and the 1975 Children Act* Brunel University Papers in Social Policy and Administration 2.

72. V. George 1970 *Foster Care: Theory and Practice* London, Routledge Kegan Paul.

73. G. Adamson 1973 *The Care-Takers* Bookstall Publications.

74. J. Rowe 1977 *Fostering in the Seventies* London, ABAFA.

75. G. Kelly 1981 'The lost cord' *Social Work Today* 13(12) 24 November 1981.

76. It was noted in Chapter 2 that, among the supporters of the first, *laissez-faire* perspective, Goldstein *et al.* retreated from their initial support for separate representation. Morris *et al.* and Taylor *et al.*, however, did support it.

77. For families as social systems, see for example: S. Zimmerman 1988 *Understanding Family Policy. Theoretical Approaches* Chapter 5. California, Sage Publications.

78. See for example: J. Pahl 1989 *Money and Marriage* Basingstoke, Macmillan Education; J. Brannen and G. Wilson 1987 *Give and Take in Families* Chapter 2, footnote 2; H. Land 1983 'Poverty and gender: the distribution of resources within families' in M. Brown (Ed) *The Structure of Disadvantage* London, Heinemann. C. Glendinning and J. Millar (Eds) 1987 *Women and Poverty in Britain* Brighton, Wheatsheaf; M. Henwood, L. Rimmer and M. Wicks 1988 *Inside the Family: changing roles of men and women* London, Family Policy Studies Centre.

79. This criticism was put, for example, of the social worker responsible for the Jasmine Beckford case. See the Beckford Report, London Borough of Brent 1985 *A Child in Trust* Chapter 1, footnote 2.

80. B. Holman 1988 *Putting Families First* This chapter, footnote 11.

81. See for example: R. Mishra 1984 *The Welfare State in Crisis* Chapter 3, footnote 78; M. Wicks 1987 *A Future for All* Chapter 3, footnote 78.

82. For a more detailed account of the 1950s and 1960s, see: J. S. Heywood 1978 *Children in Care* Chapter 3, footnote 49; J. Packman 1981 *The Child's Generation* Chapter 3, footnote 60.

83. The National Council for the Unmarried Mother and her Child became the National Council for One Parent Families in 1973.

84. See: J. S. Heywood 1978 *Children in Care* Chapter 3, footnote 49; R. Titmuss 1950 'Problems of Social Policy' *History of the Second World War* London, Longmans Green.

85. By the National Assistance Act 1948.

86. Curtis Committee 1946 *Report of the Care of Children Committee* Cmd. 6922 London, HMSO.

87. Source: J. Packman 1981 *The Child's Generation* Chapter 3, footnote 60.

88. Section 1 (3).

89. Women's Group on Public Welfare 1948 *The Neglected Child and his Family* Oxford University Press.

90. Home Office Circular No. 160/1948; Joint circular from the Home Office (No. 157/50), the Ministry of Health (No. 78/50) and the Ministry of Education (No. 225/50) 31 July 1950.

91. J. S. Heywood 1978 *Children in Care* Chapter 3, footnote 49.

92. Adoption Act 1949.

93. Children Act 1958.

94. Under the care and protection grounds in the Children and Young Persons Act 1933.

95. Children and Young Persons Act 1952.

96. Ingleby Committee 1960 *Report of the Committee on Children and Young Persons* Cmnd. 1190 London, HMSO.

97. For example, according to J. Packman 1981 *The Child's Generation* Chapter 3, footnote 60, expenditure nationally (ie England and Wales) under Section 1 increased from £88,000 in 1966 to £202,900 in 1969. Jackson and Valencia 1979 give a figure of £66,600 in England 1965–6, and £377,000 in 1969–70. Source: M.P. Jackson and B. Valencia 1979 *Financial Aid through Social Work* London, Routledge Kegan Paul.

98. Source: Home Office *Children Act 1948. Summary of Local Authorities' Returns of Children in Care at 31st March*, various years. London, HMSO. The basis for the figures changes after 1970.

99. N. Parton 1985 *The Politics of Child Abuse* Chapter 2, footnote 53.

100. See Chapter 3, footnote 60.

101. Home Office/Scottish Education Department 1972 *Report of the Departmental Committee* Chapter 3, footnote 64.

102. Home Office 1965 *The Child, the Family and the Young Offender* Cmnd. 2742 London, HMSO; Home Office 1968 *Children in Trouble* Cmnd. 3601 London, HMSO.

103. R. Mishra 1984 *The Welfare State in Crisis* Chapter 3, footnote 78.

104. See C. Hardyment 1983 *Dream Babies* Chapter 3, footnote 51.

105. Welfare Research Centre, University of New South Wales, Australia.

106. Section 10(3).

107. T. Sweeney 1983 'Child Welfare and Child Care Policies' in A. Graycar (Ed) *Retreat from the Welfare State. Australian Social Policy in the 1980s* Sydney, London, Allen and Unwin.

# CHAPTER FIVE

# Children's rights and child liberation

## INTRODUCTION

The terms 'children's rights and child liberation' are used here for a perspective which emphasises the importance of the child's own viewpoint and wishes, seeing the child as a separate entity with rights to autonomy and freedom, rather like adults. The idea of control of children through the state or by adults individually is called into question, as therefore are notions of custody and parental rights. The strength of children, and their similarity to adults, are emphasised, rather than their vulnerability; but it is not clear how far children would be expected to carry the burdens and duties of adult status as well. A less extreme position would emphasise that children should at least have more say in what happens to them.

### (i) *The main elements of the perspective*

This value perspective may be regarded as somewhat more marginal to actual child care law and policy, certainly in its more extreme manifestations. Nevertheless it is of interest for its very different approach from the others; is of relevance to certain actual developments; and may be more strongly adhered to and expressed in law, policy and practice in the future. The distinguishing characteristic of this perspective, which marks it out from all of the other three, is that the emphasis is on the *child's* own viewpoint, feelings, wishes, definitions, freedoms and choices, rather than on the attribution by adults of what is best for the child – and therefore, it might be inferred, the very existence of a child care 'system', with the function of making *decisions about* children, is called into question. The child is seen very much as a separate entity in her own right – in this the fourth perspective resembles the second; but the emphasis is on the child's right to autonomy, self-determination, and to do the things that adults do, rather than – as in the second perspective – on the right to proper nurturance and care as this is interpreted by others, be they birth parents, substitute parents, courts or social workers. The child in the fourth perspective is seen as subject rather than object of others' actions and choices, as an actor with the ability to define his situation and arrive at independent decisions. The difference from the *laissez-faire*, paternalist and pro-parent viewpoints is fundamental. *Laissez-faire* basically sees children as appropriately under the control of their parents unless things go badly wrong, when they are put under the control of substitutes; for the paternalists, the state should have more control; while for the birth parent school, parents again should control their children, but with extensive support from the state. The fourth perspective questions the very *idea of control* itself – or certainly of control that is specifically directed towards the young just because they are young. Such an approach carried to its logical conclusion goes well beyond merely supporting, say, separate representation for the child in court, an issue about which the three other perspectives tend to be unenthusiastic or divided.[1] It embraces a whole field of issues in which, if the implications of this perspective are followed through, children should have a status more like that of adults. The need for *any* kind of tutelage of children – whether it emanates from state agencies, parents, or adults in general – is fundamentally challenged, even denied. The effects of such an approach are potentially far-reaching.

Underlying this fourth value perspective is a concept of childhood which is radically different from the concepts underlying the other three. The first and third perspectives see children as in great emotional need of their parents, and the second stresses the general vulnerability and dependence of children. But writers who support the children's rights perspective tend to emphasise the *competence* and *strength* of children, who are often seen as unfairly treated as inferiors by the adult world. Holt (1975),[2] for example, describes older people's perception of children as 'a mixture of expensive nuisance, slave and super-pet'. Holt, as will be shown later, is critical of this, emphasising both the degree of adults' misperception and what children can in fact achieve independently. Indeed, it seems that in diminishing or even denying the idea of the *weakness* of childhood, the proponents of this perspective are, at least implicitly, denying that childhood is a special developmental state with needs and rights which are important but different from the needs and rights of adulthood. In so far as it is being argued that children should have rights and freedoms similar to those of adults, it seems that there is an underlying assumption that children are not so very different from adults – in terms of behaviour, feelings, ideas, attitudes, competence, knowledge and skills.

But in so far as children should have similar rights to adults, should they also carry similar responsibilities? If their freedom should not be limited specifically because they are children, then it might be thought they should not be granted any special privileges on these grounds either. Such implications are not always fully worked through by the supporters of this perspective, however; similarly, the concept of childhood on which their position rests may be implied rather than explicit. The underlying notion of childhood is crucial, however, for where it is being argued that discrimination on the basis of age constitutes a kind of injustice, what is being implied is that in certain important respects, age should make no difference.

The basic approach of the children's rights school has considerable implications for the role of the state. The guardian role of the state, even in the residual form which is allowed under *laissez-faire*, is called into question by the insistence on children's liberties. In an extreme version of the perspective, what the state should do is to enable children to gain their freedom from their parents and other adults, by bestowing on them all the normal rights of citizenship, to vote, to work, to live where and with whom they wish, and so on. It thus seems that the protective role of the state to children as individuals in need of special safeguarding and care, would be drastically diminished or even abolished. The state would not distinguish between its citizens on grounds of age, and children would thus be allowed to do whatever adults could legally do. Presumably, neither the state nor individual adults, parents or not, would have significant special rights and powers over children, and there would therefore be no question of formal custody or the legal rights of parents, substitute parents, courts or social work agencies, over children, although there might still be parental *responsibilities*. Such a situation would require certain legal changes by the state, but once these were made, the state's role could be characterised as *laissez-faire* to a far greater extent than in the first perspective. The state – if this perspective is carried to its logical conclusion – would take *no* action to provide for the special needs of children, as this would be to curtail their liberties in a way not done for adults; however children would have the normal protection of the criminal and civil law like anyone else. Parenthood appears to be reduced to a very subordinate role here, that of enabling the child to achieve his goals; parents would have to accept that their children might decide to leave them and live elsewhere.

It is only fair, however, to distinguish between what the proponents of the fourth perspective spell out, and what they do not fully work through but which seems to be logically implied by the direction of their arguments. What they actually say, broadly, is that children should have more freedom from adult authority and control, and a greater degree of self-determination; at the extreme, children should have *as much* freedom as adults, and possibly even more. Children should not incur particular disadvantages or restrictions just because they are young. These authors see children as affected *adversely* by the commonly-held notion of childhood as a weak, dependent, and less responsible state. Abolition of childhood as generally understood would thus be a liberation. The children's rights authors envisage the *benefits* of adulthood as being conferred on children, and the more *oppressive* aspects of adult-child relationships and the social position of children being removed.

Yet adulthood has its disadvantages and childhood as presently construed some privileges. What the authors do not always appear to tackle fully is whether, for example, in the regime they anticipate, child offenders would be treated exactly in the same way as adult offenders; whether children would carry exactly the same resonsibilities and liabilities as adults under the civil law; whether they would, when earning, be liable for tax, and for maintaining certain members of their families; whether they would be liable for military service; whether they could expect no special protection or dispensation in any circumstances; and whether, in general, they would be expected to carry the full duties, burdens and responsibilities of citizenship as well as its rights and freedoms. While such notions do seem to be implied by the very libertarian concepts of childhood and adult-child relationships underlying the fourth perspective, it may be that in fact even the more extreme proponents of the perspective would *not* altogether welcome the prospect of children and young persons being burdened with the full liabilities, and the more negative aspects, of adult citizenship; but would prefer that children should be granted greater power, without necessarily commensurate responsibility. Such a notion carries its own problems, however, which will be referred to again later.

It should also be stressed that a much more moderate version of the perspective can be adopted, which is less aggressively libertarian while still emphasising children's rights in a rather more limited sense. Broadly consonant with the less extreme children's rights position is the argument that children should, in all spheres, at least have a greater independent say in what happens to them; and that the provisions of the state should allow for this, in child care law and policy, education, health care, and any other relevant areas. Decisions should not (on the whole) be made over the child's head. Thus the child's welfare is (at least partly) for the child herself to define.

## (ii) *Some authors associated with the perspective*

A fairly colourful exponent of a more extreme version of this perspective is Holt (1975)[3] in *Escape from Childhood. The Needs and Rights of Children*. This book is said by the author to be about young people and their place or lack of place in modern society; about the ways in which modern childhood is bad for most of those who live within it; and about how it might be changed. Being a child, according to Holt, means 'being wholly subservient and dependent . . . being seen by older people as a mixture of expensive nuisance, slave and super-pet' and this situation does harm to most young people. Holt proposes that the rights, privileges, duties and responsibilities of adulthood be made available to any young person who wants to use them, including the right to vote and participate in politics, to work and be financially independent, to receive the state minimum income, live away from home and seek their own choice of guardian, drive, use drugs, control their own sex lives, and generally do what any adult may legally do. He also advocates the 'right' to equal treatment at the hands of the law, and to be legally responsible for one's life and acts. Holt does not propose any lower age limit on these rights, and states that the young person should be able to pick and choose which he wants to assume.

Holt is critical of the social institution of childhood which he sees as meaning attitudes, feelings, customs and laws which put a great gulf or barrier between the young and their elders, making it difficult for the young to make contact with the larger society or to play an active, responsible part in it. He notes that the concept of childhood evolved with the modern family, but does not work well for many people. Tackling the argument that giving children greater independence could 'weaken the family', Holt argues that 'Any institution that really works is immune to attack, however severe', and that the family was an institution where some people were owned by others – men owned women and children. The family may be seen as a miniature dictatorship – 'a training for slavery'. Also, children need a larger network to relate to than the small nuclear family which can be destructive, over-intense and fragile. Children need adult friends other than their parents, as in extended families, so 'we need to allow, encourage, and help young people create extended families of their own'. According to Holt, adults resent and dislike children, and bringing them up is an endless worry and an emotional and financial burden. Nevertheless the institution of childhood has the function of benefiting *adults*, giving them someone to boss, someone to 'help', someone to love. Holt is also critical of the notion of 'help' to others, which as he sees it thrives on and creates helplessness. Another argument is that adults grossly underestimate the competence of the young, and therefore their capacities are not fully used. Children are capable of more than we give them credit for, he believes. A further problem that Holt perceives is the treatment of the child as love object, rather as men use women as sex objects. He comments: 'We treat someone as an object when we use him for our purposes, to achieve our ends, to get things for ourselves, without considering or caring what this does to him or how he feels about it, without asking what he gets out of it or whether he gets anything at all.' With children 'We think we have a right, or even a duty, to bestow on them "love" . . . whenever we want, however we want, and whether they like it or not'. This is exploitative, serving adults' needs.

Central to the argument of the children's rights school is the similarity of children to adults, and this is reflected in the title of Holt's Chapter 15, 'What Children Need, we all Need'. Here Holt claims that when we see children's needs as belonging only to children, we trivialise and invalidate them; we also ensure that they will not be met. Seeing childhood as a separate world means that adults decide what is good for children. Commenting on the use of the word 'rights', Holt says that he means by the term what is generally meant when we speak of the rights of adults. His argument is that the law should guarantee to the young the freedom it grants to adults. Of particular relevance to child care policy is Holt's view of the 'right' to a good home and family. The state cannot guarantee this, he says, in the way it can guarantee an income, but should leave to the child the right to decide how good his home is, and to choose something else if he doesn't like it. The state should not make alternatives compulsory, but should allow children to make other choices. Holt further notes that while some rights can be used relatively independently of others, some depend on other, linked rights being available, to be effective.

Holt's ensuing chapters discuss the recommended rights for children one by one: the right to vote; the right to work; the right to own property; the right to travel; the right to choose one's guardian; the right to a guaranteed income; the right to legal and financial responsibility; the right to control one's learning; the right to use drugs; the right to drive; and sexual rights. A few of the arguments which Holt puts forward in defence of these rights will be outlined here.

The right to vote, one of the most important, should not depend on any condition and should extend to people of any age. It is a matter of justice, Holt argues, that those who are affected by laws and decisions should have a say in them, and that 'Given real choices, people will choose for themselves better than others will choose for them'. Holt considers that it is particularly unjust to deny the vote to the young, because they will have to live longer with the effects of government decisions. While younger children would probably not want to vote, they should have the right to; childhood ignorance is not a justification for their exclusion, as many adult voters are ill-informed also. On the right to work, it is argued that children need their own money, want to be useful, and find work stimulating. However, working should be children's own choice – not forced upon them. Some dangers in children having wider access to the world of work are conceded. Also beneficial to children would be the right to travel without parental permission – this is an enjoyable way of learning about the world and becoming independent. In defence of the right to choose a guardian, Holt stresses the child's choice and the benefits of voluntarily undertaken relationships, saying: 'There is no *necessary* reason why parents should like their own children best, or like them at all; they might prefer someone else's.' Parents would *not* be free to end their relationship with their children, however – although the child would be free to move about. The right to a guaranteed income is again defended in terms of independence. The rights to travel, seek other guardians, and so on, cannot be meaningful if children cannot get money in their own right. Holt argues that families should not be treated as a single economic unit; in practice this often means that property and income belongs to the head and others have to bargain and beg.

In defending the right to legal and financial responsibility, Holt argues that the law (at the time he wrote) treated children *worse* than adults, for example by holding them in 'jails' (ie institutions) for reasons that would not apply if they were adults. Children should have 'the right to a fair trial, to all the protection of due process, and the right to bring suit'. Holt accepts here that the child would be accountable to fellow citizens and the law for what he did, and could be sued as well as being able to sue. What Holt has in mind is a means by which children could take a formal step to become independent citizens with full legal responsibility. Children would not have this status automatically, and would also have the right to opt back to 'dependent' status.

The right of the child to control his own learning is seen as fundamental because it is a part of freedom of thought; deciding what all young people are to learn is highly authoritarian, and compulsory education a gross violation of civil liberties. On the question of drugs (in the broadest sense) existing prohibitions are seen as counterproductive; driving is seen as ideally dependent on skill, not age; and young people living as independent citizens should have the same sexual rights as anyone else – although Holt is aware of more problems and dilemmas in this field.

Finally, under 'Steps to take', Holt suggests that in the interim adults should treat children as they would want to see them treated in the society here aspired to; that children should take greater financial responsibility, have more adult friends, be freer from dependence generally, acquire work experience, and not be punished more severely than adults. It is symptomatic of Holt's general view that he sees young people without families currently living as wards of the state, as 'prisoners of the state'.

Other authors from the 1970s who may be classed as belonging broadly to the children's rights school of thought, are Foster and Freed (1972),[4] Worsfold (1974)[5] and Farson (1978).[6] Foster and Freed in an article on 'A Bill of Rights for Children' claim that 'The status of minority is the last legal relic of feudalism', arguing for checks on adult authority and for children to be seen as persons entitled to assert their individual interests in their own right; paternalism they see as discredited. Their Bill of Rights contains ten proposed moral and legal rights for children; examples are, to receive parental love, to be maintained and educated, to be regarded as a *person*, to receive fair treatment from authority, to earn and keep his own earnings, to emancipation from the parent–child relationship when that relationship has broken down, and to be free of unnecessary legal disabilities. It is of interest, however, that the tenth right is to receive special care, consideration and protection in law so that the child's best interests are a paramount factor. From this and other points it is clear that Foster and Freed do not go quite as far as Holt in arguing that children's rights are or should be like those of adults; some concession is made to the idea of children having special needs and rights, and being vulnerable. Nevertheless, the general tone of their writing is very similar to Holt's.

Worsfold explores a philosophical justification for children's rights. Pointing out that paternalist views do not guarantee the acceptable treatment of children, Worsfold argues that Rawls' theory of justice[7] provides a justification for according children rights to fair treatment. As Worsfold sees it, in Rawls' model children should receive the full protection of the principles of justice because they have the capacity (even if not yet fully developed) for accepting the principle of fairness. Worsfold concludes: 'The justification of children's rights under Rawls's theory has one major emphasis: children have a right to make just claims, and adults must be responsive to those claims.'

Farson, like Holt, emphasises the child's right to self-determination, saying: 'The issue of self-determination is at the heart of children's liberation. It is, in fact, the only issue, a definition of the entire concept. The acceptance of the child's right to self-determination is fundamental to all the rights to which children are entitled.' Farson's 'Bill of Rights' for children contains many of the same ideas as Holt. Farson argues that children should have the right to alternative home environments, to design responsive to their needs, to information, to design their own education, to freedom from physical punishment, to sexual freedom, to economic and political power, and justice. These are seen as 'birthrights'. Like Holt, Farson would abolish virtually all age-related disabilities.

A more recent book edited by Bob Franklin (1986),[8] *The Rights of Children*, considers children's rights in various different spheres – in the political sphere, at school, in care and the juvenile justice system, at work, and in the area of sexuality. Franklin's introduction to the book shows a clear liberationist orientation. Claiming that the 'irrationality and immorality of systematic and institutionalised discrimination against individuals on the basis of their gender or race has, to some degree, been established', he argues that '*equivalent* [my italics] discrimination against people on the basis of their age has proven more resilient to change'. A consensus that children have suffered and been discriminated against is absent; yet because of their age children are denied rights which adults consider to be basic human rights. Their freedom is limited in ways which range from the significant to the relatively insignificant; and children 'form a large, long-suffering and oppressed grouping in society' with a forgotten and excluded status. For example, they are disenfranchised, economically disadvantaged, are considered the property of their parents, are obliged to attend educational institutions, and are subjected to the power and punishment of both teachers and parents. While children are a heterogeneous group, they *all* suffer political, economic, legal, educational and domestic restrictions.

Franklin goes on to elaborate the problems of the adult, idealised perception of childhood which denies that children are real people. Myths operate about the way adults treat children; an idealised adult concern, Franklin thinks, has informed much legislation relating to children; such legislation can, however, result in further unjust treatment. Because adult-child relationships are idealised, severe cases of child abuse tend to be greeted with incredulity, as an aberration. Another myth is of childhood as a 'golden age', a special time of innocence and happiness. This myth does not correspond to some of the known data about childhood; and Franklin brings forward evidence supporting a more negative view such as facts concerning child employment, poverty, children in care and child abuse. Acknowledging that the issue of children's rights is complex, Franklin then goes on to consider two aspects in particular: what is a child? and some of the complexities of the term 'rights'.

In brief, he says that childhood is not fixed but a historically shifting cultural construction, subject to wide variations by time and place. The division between childhood and adulthood is arbitrary and incoherent – different rights are allowed at different ages. The diversity found *within* the 'childhood' age range is clouded by the definition of all young people as 'non-adults'. And the term 'child' specifies a power relationship rather than chronological age as such. Then, historical evidence of the development of the concept of 'childhood' is cited, this being seen as a European invention of the last few centuries. Prior to this childhood was not seen as a special phase in life. Franklin here refers to the work of Aries (1962)[9] on the history of childhood, work which emphasises the absence of the concept of 'childhood' in the modern sense, in mediaeval times. The progressive differentiation of the child state is related to industrialisation and capitalism. This historical evidence challenges the common sense view of childhood as immutable.

On 'rights', Franklin makes the familiar distinction between legal rights (enforceable by law) and moral rights (based on an appeal to principle); nevertheless the two categories overlap – morality can inform and support law. It can also be a source of criticism of it. Franklin also discusses a four-fold classification of children's rights proposed by Freeman (1983) which will be discussed below. However it is worth noting at this point Franklin's statement that: 'Enhancing children's rights to protection from abuse, at least in the British context, has tended to diminish their autonomy.' Franklin discusses a broader two-fold classification of children's rights termed the 'liberationist versus protectionist orientation', noting that children require an expansion of both kinds of rights: there is not necessarily a tension between self-determination and protection.

As Franklin acknowledges, the chapters in his edited collection express both liberationist and protectionist positions. But his own chapter on the extension of the suffrage to children is, in his own words, 'clearly cast in the liberationist mould', and this chapter will be considered briefly before moving on. Entitled 'Children's Political Rights', the chapter examines, and finds ultimately unconvincing, the arguments used to exclude the young from political rights. For example, Franklin says that the case for children's political rights gets dismissed on the basis of implicit assumptions rather than reasoned argument. The 'commonsense' exclusion of children from political rights is rooted partly in an uncritical acceptance of paternalism. Franklin next examines paternalism, arguing that it 'offers no cogent grounds upon which to deny young people political rights . . . but simply provides a justification for political elites'. A detailed critique is put forward, of which only a few points will be mentioned here. One concerns individuals' rationality. Interference with an individual's freedom on the grounds of *her* own good (not somebody else's) is often justified, with regard to young people, in terms of their lack of rationality. Yet rationality is a difficult concept to pin down and use as a criterion distinguishing children from adults. Adults themselves are not fully rational, yet do not normally expect or accept the paternalistic interventions of others foisted upon them; indeed, any such paternalistic interveners and decision-makers cannot be considered fully rational either. One aspect of children's supposed lack of rationality is their propensity to make mistakes which are damaging to themselves. Again, adults also do this – sometimes horrific mistakes; while children need to make some mistakes as part of their learning process. These criteria do not justify the exclusion of children from political rights, in Franklin's view.

Franklin's solution, which has its root in Holt's work, is that children should have the right to vote when their interest and knowledge are sufficient to motivate them to do so. It is suggested that children have greater political maturity than is generally believed; and that younger children who are politically immature would not choose to vote, because they would not be interested. However political capacities might develop more rapidly if they were acknowledged by the adult world. Franklin further argues that extending the franchise to children would not significantly alter the pattern of voting for particular political parties. In defending Holt's proposal against likely objections, Franklin goes on to say that ignorance is not and should not be a criterion for the franchise; nor the ability to vote responsibly; the same applies to the tendency to vote for personalities rather than policies; and none of these three factors differentiates children in general from adults in general. Fourthly, there is the question of parental influence and coercion. Broadly, Franklin's response is that while this factor cannot be dismissed in the case of anyone, adult or child, however in a society where children had more autonomy in general, parental influence would be less significant. Franklin concludes that the denial of the franchise to the young offends fundamental democratic principles, and that its granting would help to ensure a higher profile for children's interests in various institutional contexts – to a degree that paternalism cannot achieve.

An author who can be identified with a much more moderate children's rights approach is Freeman (1980 and 1983).[10] Firstly, in an article in 1980 Freeman distanced himself from the more radical of the children's rights spokespersons, seeing their arguments as 'politically naive, philosophically faulty and psychologically wrong'. Freeman's view was that it should be obvious that age *is* a relevant differentiating factor in legal status, in a way that race and sex are not. He highlights the inconsistency of Holt and Farson in requiring the same freedom for children as adults, while assuming that parents would still have the obligation to nurture and maintain their children, and of bestowing rights on children but not expecting reciprocal responsibilities. Self-determination, in Freeman's view, is a capacity to be developed, rather than a right to be expressed. Freeman was also sceptical of Worsfold's attempt to justify children's rights with reference to Rawls' theory of justice, though finding Rawls useful in suggesting that decisions in the child's interest should be guided by what the child would rationally want. Finally, Freeman offers cautions on the limitations of rights in practice, concluding 'We need to change childhood but this need not involve ignoring its existence'.

Freeman's book *The Rights and Wrongs of Children* (1983) aims for a more considered insight into the issue of children's rights, reflecting an awareness of its complexity. As early as the Prologue to the book Freeman comments: 'it takes but a moment's reflection to realise that the position of children is not strictly comparable with that of women or blacks.' Freeman goes much further than the extreme child liberationists in acknowledging the differences between children and adults, although he *is* concerned with what happens to children and their rights in a broader sense. For example, 'sentimentality', he says 'is no substitute for the recognition of a child's entitlement to the right to equal concern and respect'. Children's capacities should be acknowledged, and they should be given a say in the decision-making process concerning them whenever feasible; their interests should be taken into account in policy-making. But, as Freeman sees it, protecting *children* and protecting their *rights* are not incompatible as aims.

Freeman's four-fold classification of children's rights has already been referred to briefly in discussing Franklin's work. This framework of Freeman's can be found in Chapter 2 of his book, where he elaborates his view of rights (having, in Chapter 1, traced the historical evolution of the concepts of children's rights and, more broadly, childhood). Having examined the importance of rights as a concept, and the nature of legal and moral rights, claims, demands, needs, the 'manifesto' use of the term 'rights', and obligations, Freeman goes on to set out his four categories of children's rights. The **first** category consists of 'generalised claims on behalf of all children. They can be described as welfare rights.' A clear statement of rights in this sense can be found in the 1959 United Nations Declaration of the Rights of the Child. This includes principles such as adequate nutrition, housing and medical treatment, education and care, love and protection; these can be seen as fundamental human rights, but they are not in general easily enforceable by law, or at least not by courts, and are somewhat vague. These rights are far from those envisaged by the child liberationist school. Freeman's **second** category is concerned with child protection and stresses child vulnerability and parental and adult responsibility. Freeman says that this is a view 'against which those who espouse children's liberation react with hostility'. This view of rights is broadly in line with the second, state paternalist perspective outlined in this book. A **third** class of children's rights *does* correspond closely to the preferred scenario of the liberationists. This is where the rights of adults are largely extended to children, either by abolishing age-related disabilities or by proceeding on a case-by-case basis, while any extant age limits should be constantly re-examined. A **fourth** type of rights is classed as 'rights against parents'; again, this is to do with autonomy and would find favour with the child liberation supporters. Children should have the freedom to act independently. At the very least, they should be able to challenge parental decisions through some other agent or decision-maker. The main focus here, according to Freeman, should be on adolescents, and on major, rather than trivial, decisions.

Freeman next outlines a theory of 'liberal paternalism' to justify children's rights, which represents his own position. He states that:

'Paternalism in its classical form does not acknowledge the existence of children's rights. Liberal paternalism, I believe, compels their recognition.' Drawing on Rawls' principles of equality and justice, Freeman asks: 'what sort of action or conduct would we wish, as children, to be shielded against on the assumption that we would want to mature to a rationally autonomous adulthood . . .?' The answer is that 'We would choose principles that would enable children to mature to independent adulthood. Our definition of irrationality would be such as to preclude action and conduct which would frustrate such a goal; within the constraints of such a definition we would defend a version of paternalism.' Constraints must be exercised in such a way as to enable children to develop their capacities. On these grounds Freeman would defend, for example, compulsory education. Robbed of this the young person would be less prepared to become a rationally autonomous person. But a limit on the exercise of paternalism stems from the prospect of the child's eventually seeing the correctness of the intervention. And certain current restrictions require re-examination, Freeman argues. It is clear that Freeman seeks to balance protection and autonomy in a way that would give greater emphasis to protection than the extreme child liberationists would allow, but would support more autonomy than would be favoured in the writings of the child protectionist/paternalist school. Freeman's book should be consulted for his detailed theoretical arguments. His subsequent chapters focus on specific problem areas such as children in care and children in divorce.

The work of the voluntary organisation the Children's Legal Centre may also be mentioned in the context of the children's rights approach. The Centre was formed in 1979 and aims 'to promote the recognition of children and young persons as individuals participating fully in all the decisions which affect their lives' through advice and information work, the pursuit of selected cases, research, training and responding to policies. The Centre has since 1983 published a monthly bulletin, *Childright*. According to a brief article by Wilson (1988)[11] on the Centre, in various fields – education, welfare rights, employment, criminal law and many others – children and young people are rarely recognised as a group with the right to have their views considered or their interests represented independently. A member of the Centre's staff was quoted as saying that the problem was due to the way society perceived and defined children. Children's rights may be defined as parents' rights – in questions of parental access, for example – and decisions rarely make the child's wishes a major consideration. Among the Centre's campaigns was the issue of corporal punishment; it was pointed out that children alone in society were unprotected from physical assault.[12]

The content of issues of *Childright* also reflects the Centre's concerns. One major focus of the magazine has been the law enforcement machinery as it affects children – for example, treatment by the police and the treatment of the young in custody. An overlapping area of concern is that of children in care – issues such as locking up children in care, the use of drugs to control them, the general treatment of children in care and opportunities for them to complain. Another concern, as indicated, is corporal punishment, whether in care, in schools, or in the parental home. A further prominent issue in *Childright* has been education in its many aspects, but with a children's rights emphasis, for example in highlighting pupil power in schools and complaints. Articles have also covered a wide variety of other issues – custody, adoption, race, disability, homosexuality, the UN Convention on children's rights, legal aid, medical treatment and contraception, access to records, illegitimacy, age limits, employment, homelessness, political participation, and children's evidence in court, to mention a selection. It will be clear that many issues can be examined within a children's rights framework. The magazine has an international orientation, and looks at the position of children in other countries, as well as immigration issues. It monitors current legislation and policy as it affects children, partly by the useful device of setting out Child Impact Statements for new Acts. It also deals with cuts in benefits and services affecting children, and with issues relating to children's health and safety – that is, it includes content which reflects a more protectionist and welfare orientation, alongside its generally liberationist apoproach.

The Children's Legal Centre has also played an important role in initiating and organising two Children's Congresses, one in 1984 and one in 1986. These congresses aimed to bring together relevant agencies and groupings, to focus expertise on children, and to improve children's influence and participation.

## (iii) *Rationale and underlying values*

Two themes which seem to be central to the more extreme child liberationist perspective are the perception of children as fundamentally no different from adults, and the emphasis on freedom from adult control as children's primary need and right. Both themes give the perspective much in common with other liberationist writing focusing on, for example, the freeing of women, and oppressed ethnic

169

groups, from the control of men and dominant ethnic groups. It can be argued that discrimination against children, and the allocation of a different legal status on the basis of age, is no more justified than discrimination on grounds of gender or ethnicity. 'Childhood' is seen as essentially a *social* construction, not inherent to the condition of children themselves – to the extent that the physical, psychological and social characteristics which self-evidently (or from a common sense viewpoint) seem to differentiate children from adults, tend to be denied. It may be claimed, for example, as it is by Holt, that children have a far greater capacity to survive unaided in society than adults give them credit for.

The general approach of the children's rights school seems to be that childhood is not so much a developmental process through which children gradually become socialised to take their place in the adult world – learn, in fact, *to be* adults – as an oppressed state in which individuals who are essentially no different from anyone else have become unjustly trapped. If it is indeed the case that children are essentially adults who happen to occupy a smaller body and to have been alive for a shorter span of years than others, such a critique of childhood would have great force – denying children the vote, for example, would seem equally unjust as denying the vote to adults under five foot, or with black skins, or with red hair. The questions of the *differences* between children and adults, their significance, and the degree to which proponents of this fourth perspective may overlook and deny real and relevant differences between different developmental stages (between older and younger children as well as between children and adults) will be explored further in examining criticisms of this perspective.

What the children's rights perspective does usefully highlight by questioning the very concept of childhood is the arbitrary and inconsistent nature of the formal age limits which society sets between childhood or minority and adulthood in its various contexts – for example, in England, the right to marry with parental consent and work full-time at 16, to drive at 17, to purchase alcohol and vote at 18. It may be pointed out that such limits can be – and have been – varied by law, and are clearly a social and legal construction imposed upon young persons, rather than a biological dividing line relating to any objective differences suddenly occurring at any of these ages. A similar objection may be raised to age limits at the other end of the age scale – for example, a fixed retirement age of 65 is an arbitrary boundary which makes 'old age' a social construction imposed on people who happen to have passed a certain age.[13] In so far as age limits cause resentment because they entail arbitrary discrimination, and are an entirely socially created barrier bearing little or no relation to people's actual capacities, it seems reasonable to argue for their complete removal. Problems with this approach will also be discussed in considering criticisms of this perspective.

Childhood, then, in this view, is a social construction subjected to arbitrary limits. The artificial construction of childhood allocates to children an essentially passive status in which they cannot exercise the normal rights, or receive the normal respect, of citizenship. In general adult-controlled and adult-defined society does not take seriously what children think, feel, say or do, but attributes different meanings to the actions of children solely because they are children. Linked with this perspective's view of the imposed passivity of childhood is its perception of the primary need and right of children as being to freedom from adult power. What children need is not, as in the second perspective, good quality care, but autonomy. Their primary problem is the restrictions which adults have imposed on them, and what would benefit children most would be to break free, to make their own decisions, and to lead their own lives. This is the most fundamental difference between the second and fourth value perspectives. Both tend to make children an absolute priority and to disregard, relatively, the interests of adults (which children will eventually become), but while for the second school of thought the obligation placed on adults with regard to children is essentially to care and protect (and indeed, to a degree, to control), for the fourth school the adult obligation is largely to let children go, to listen to what they say, and to respect what they want (rather than – according to an adult view – what they 'need'). The distinction corresponds broadly to Rogers and Wrightsman's (1978)[14] dichotomy between 'nurturance' and 'self-determination' orientations. Here nurturance stresses the provision of beneficial environments and experiences for children and is essentially a paternalistic approach, while self-determination emphasises potential rights which would allow children to exercise control over their environments and make decisions, that is, autonomy. The difference is also similar to Farson's distinction between protecting *children* and protecting children's *rights*. Little credit is given by the child liberationists to adults for their nurturance role, for their ability to care for and make appropriate decisions on behalf of children; in fact the idea that adult attitudes to children are generally benign is explicitly challenged. It is the more sinister and exploitative aspects of adult-child relationships which tend to be highlighted in the children's rights perspective. Even parental 'love' has its suspect side.

While the perspective suggests a particular idea of childhood, then, it also implies a particular notion of what *adulthood* means from the viewpoint of children. Adults are perceived rather negatively; their approach to children is chiefly determined by their wish and need to use children for their own ends. Thus children are used to gratify adult needs for power, love, sex, amusement, achievement, and social status. Adults, in fact, are not to be trusted, being the dominant side in a power relationship. This general cynicism about adults in their relations with children can be contrasted with the previous three perspectives discussed where at least *some* adults (parents in the first and third, various professionals, state agents and substitute parents in the second) are credited with understanding and acting on childen's interests and welfare.

The concept of rights is clearly also crucial to the rationale underlying this fourth perspective. The kinds of child rights with which proponents of the fourth perspective are characteristically concerned are, as shown, those rights which are to do with freedom, self-determination, autonomy etc., rather than to do with protection and welfare. Such rights of self-determination are claimed as moral rights which should be embodied in the law. Partly, the enforcement of these rights involves legislative action to remove age-related disabilities and parental and other adult power over children. Such action could create for the young, rights in the sense of freedoms: no legal bar would stand in the way of their exercising their rights, but no *specific* obligation or duty would fall on other parties. In the case of certain rights, however, it would seem that particular duties would also have to be created or maintained. It would seem, for example, that at least some adults would have to have an obligation to provide homes for children, if children are to be free to decide where they would live. If children are to be free to work but not to be forced to, some persons or some body must have the obligation to support them financially. Education must be provided for those children who do choose it. Freeman suggests that the right not to be subjected to corporal punishment requires the imposition of a duty on parents, teachers and others not to use it – however, this is a duty not to do something, rather than to do it. A better example might be Holt's right to a guaranteed income – which imposes an obligation somewhere to pay it; or Farson's right to alternative home environments – someone would have to provide them. Where a right involves a particular duty falling on another person or body, different problems of enforcement arise from the case where a right is merely a legal freedom to act in a certain way, such as to travel unimpeded by others. Problems of enforcement constitute one difficulty with the notion of rights in relation to children; another is the overemphasis on rights and duties in the construction of adult–child relationships, to the detriment of other values. These problems will be considered further in discussing criticisms of this value perspective.

Another point about rights is that those who hold them are usually held to incur a general duty to respect and safeguard other people's rights as well – that is, at least not to impede others in the exercise of their rights. Rights and duties are two complementary aspects of the notion of citizenship, of membership of a community where freedoms can be exercised but freedom itself is curtailed by the rights of others. It is noticeable, however, that Holt and the other liberationist writers say much about children's rights in the ideal they aim for, but very little about their proposed duties. The position of children aspired to seems to be more favourable in some ways than the current position of adults. This inconsistency will be looked at further later.

Two other underlying aspects of the children's rights perspective concern the view of the family, and of the state. Broadly, there is a *low* valuation of the family unit as conventionally understood, and a *negative* perspective on the state which, while it is adult-controlled, is not perceived as generally benign in its treatment of children. On the family first: this institution tends not to be discussed at length, but in its existing form is seen – at least by Holt – to be oppressive to children. (There is a parallel here with some feminist views of the family as a key site of *women's* oppression.) For example, Holt is dismissive of arguments that his proposals would weaken the family, seeing the family as often a locus of oppression and of power held by some over others, as claustrophobic and overburdened with feelings. Parents and children are not necessarily happy in their roles towards each other, and children need other adults besides parents. Holt also draws attention to the historical specificity of the modern nuclear family. But his comment: 'Basically the family was and is a tiny kingdom, an absolute monarchy' captures the flavour of his view; although he also thinks that strong and healthy families could not be threatened by his proposals for children's rights. Holt also suggests loose groups and communities as alternatives for some children; and he favours children having 'extended families' (in a broad sense) of their own.

There are, of course, a number of aspects of the modern family to which children's rights protagonists can point, as being unsatisfactory for children – violence, sexual abuse, family instability and breakdown and so on. As Macdougall (1985)[15] comments: 'Some will consider the children's rights movement as a necessary response to the failure of the modern family to meet the needs of children.'

The state, like the family, has a generally poor image in this perspective, and, at the extreme, being actually in the care of the state is likened to imprisonment. Holt refers to children in 'jails' and children as 'prisoners' of the state, apparently glossing over distinctions such as those between being in care for an offence, and being in care for the child's own good and to meet her need for care; or between being held in secure accommodation, and living in an ordinary children's home or foster home. Other authors writing from the children's rights perspective are much less simplistic than Holt, but their approach to the state systems which respond, for example, to juvenile offenders and children in need of substitute care, is a critical one. In Franklin's book a chapter by Lavery[16] on the rights of children in care sets out 'to highlight some of the ways in which the rights of children in care are violated'. Lavery is critical, for example, of some forms of residential care and fostering, and particularly of the denial of a children's say in decision-making – for example their exclusion from reviews of their progress in care. The right to privacy in children's homes, the use of corporal punishment and drugs, and locking up children in secure accommodation, are other issues highlighted by Lavery. It should be noted that Lavery is broadly supportive of the principle of parental contact for children in care and of preventive policies. In his conclusion Lavery comments that 'the state behaves in some strange, if not positively harmful, ways and, invariably, with paternalism as its hallmark. Its target always seems to be the poor.' A subsequent chapter by Adams[17] on juvenile justice also criticises the overriding of children's rights in specific parts of the system.

The journal *Childright* also reflects a concern about the more oppressive aspects of the state's dealings with children. Using drugs to control children in care would be one striking example; locking them up another; the police and the criminal justice system generally are also a target of interest and concern. For example, the first issue of *Childright* reported on young girls in care being forcibly injected with major tranquillisers while in a 'lock-up' (a secure unit); and on solitary confinement as a form of punishment in secure units.

The moderate children's rights author Freeman is also critical of the way children are treated by the state, as offenders, as being in need of care, and when their parents divorce. He comments, for example: 'One of the most unsatisfactory features of juvenile justice is that in reality there is very little justice. Neither pre-trial procedures nor the court processes themselves observe the sort of elementary natural justice requirements that are taken for granted in a court dealing with adult offenders.'

While not all criticisms of the state put forward by the proponents of the fourth perspective fall strictly into line with a children's rights viewpoint (for example, some of Freeman's criticisms of the response to child abuse resemble Holman's), in general what are emphasised are the areas where the state overrides the rights of children and treats them more unjustly, and more unfavourably, than it treats adults. Those areas where the state treats, or attempts to treat, children *better* than adults are de-emphasised, or interpreted as having the *effect* of *worse* treatment despite the intention – most obviously in the field of juvenile justice. The empowerment of children, for example through the franchise, would, it is argued, induce the state to be more receptive to their needs.

## (iv) *Criticisms of the children's rights and child liberation perspective*

### (a) *Empirical support*

Holt's manifesto for children's rights is not strongly supported by empirical studies relating to childhood and child care, but draws mainly on individual cases, press stories and anecdotes for backing. Foster and Freed's position depends mainly on argument and criticism of the present state of the law (in this case in an American context), while Worsfold bases his case on argument and theoretical discussion, mainly, as indicated, centred on the work of Rawls on justice. Farson does not even attempt this sort of justification. Franklin brings forward some evidence supporting a rather negative view of the condition of childhood, to counter the myth of childhood as a 'golden age', for example facts concerning child employment, poverty, children in care, and child abuse. Historical evidence on the development of childhood is also cited, to underline its socially constructed nature. There is a reference to research on childhood political socialisation in Franklin's chapter on political rights, research which suggests that the development of political knowledge and attitudes can be traced in three phases in childhood/adolescence. Chapters by the other authors bring forward some factual data relating to, for example, school behaviour, children in care, youthful offending, child employment and the enforcement of the child labour laws, child sexual behaviour and schoolgirl pregnancy, girls' educational performance and attitudes, and black children and young people in Britain (including their achievement and under-achievement at school and their employment situation). Much of the thrust of the book, however, would seem to depend on a particular *interpretation* of the evidence, on critical discussion of existing systems for dealing with children, and on the setting out of various arguments surrounding the question of children's rights. Freeman's book, similarly, is supported by theoretical argument and by critical discussion of state systems which affect children's lives − when children offend, are victims of abuse and neglect, are actually in care, or are involved in divorce. Data of various kinds are offered on situations affecting children and the state's response.

Two main problems seem to arise with the empirical backing for the fourth perspective (or certainly the more radical version of it). One is the degree to which evidence on developmental growth through childhood is ignored, and the other is how evidence which *is* offered is perceived and interpreted. On the first point, the argument that children should have virtually the same rights and freedoms as adults clashes, not only with the world of 'common sense', but with the findings of developmental psychology on how children are *different* from adults (and older children from younger children) − in other words, what growth through chronological age *means*. As Macdougall (1985)[18] comments: 'Psychological research raises significant questions about the decision-making capacity of children − including adolescents.' He quotes Teitelbaum (1980)[19] who noted an apparent conflict between the need to socialise an individual and the demand for individual autonomy: a healthy society will attempt to achieve both. That is, on the one hand children should learn cultural values and conform to social rules; at the same time they need to develop the capacity for choice and autonomous action. Failure to learn social values and rules means that the person cannot join the society; but a person without the capacity for choice cannot usefully participate in it. Freeman in his 1980 article commented:

> Although psychological theories of personality and moral development which reflect universal developmental assumptions may be readily challenged as ignoring socio-cultural history and not squaring with

anthropological evidence, it cannot be denied that a child matures
through a succession of stages and gradually increases his competence,
cognitive abilities and moral capacities. That children at an early stage
are egocentric is generally acknowledged.

Freeman goes on to say that while a child of seven is arguably capable
of exercising self-determination in relation to sleeping, eating or
dressing, he is hardly able to decide on long-term life goals.
Self-determination is a capacity that develops rather than a right to
be expressed at any age.

The volume of psychological literature on the various aspects of
child development – cognitive, emotional, social, moral and so on
– bears witness to the fact that it is not just in that world of
'common sense' that some liberationists deplore, that childhood is
seen as a special stage (or, to be more accurate, a series of special
stages) where patterns of perception, thought, feeling and behaviour
are to some extent different from those of adulthood. Central to human
development is the process of learning – and it is in the early stages
of life that learning is most rapid and influential. There is a very
basic point here emphasised in social science, which is that human
beings are not born, but *learn* to be, members of their society; can
learn vastly different things in different cultures; and without human
contact (for example if reared by animals) are not recognisably human.
It is not suggested that the liberationists would dispute this, but they
do perhaps overlook the obvious implications – that as children are
not born ready-socialised, there must be some doubt about the validity
of extending to them immediately the rights of full members of
the society.

However the children's rights authors correctly point to the
absurdity, in a logical sense, of distinct ages or cut-off points
below which certain rights cannot be exercised by young people.
How can their powerful arguments here ever be reconciled with the
findings of developmental psychology on how children are different?
One possible way out of the impasse is to point out that evidence of
growth and development through age relates to *general* or *statistical*
truth rather than telling us anything categorically about any given
individual. Of course *some* individuals below, say, the age of 18, the
age of majority in Britain, will be more rational, competent, aware,
considerate, independent, morally, socially and emotionally mature
and so on than *some* individuals above this age. But *in general* a
person of 16 will have less of these qualities than a person of 20, a
person of seven less than a person of 16, a person of two less than
one of seven and so on. Chronological age tells us something about

the *probability* that a person will possess a greater or lesser degree of certain qualities which we might subsume under the heading 'maturity'. Similarly, at the other end of the age spectrum, it is *statistically* the case that being over the age of, say, 75, indicates reduced mental capacity. The liberationists might respond that no one is proposing to disenfranchise all those who reach their 75th birthday. In reply, it may be said that it is emotionally more distressing and therefore politically more difficult – and indeed, perhaps more unjust – to deprive an individual permanently of something they have had all their adult life, than it is to defer (only) their receiving it initially.

An ironic twist to this issue of the evidence on development and difference is that Holt, in what was perhaps an unintended lapse, *does* acknowledge the different and asocial nature of children in saying that they are 'animals and sensualists: to them what feels good *is* good. They are self-absorbed and selfish . . . They are barbarians, primitives . . . have very little ability to put themselves in another person's shoes, to imagine how someone else feels', while Farson appears to become totally hoist on his own petard in admitting that children may not want rights; that 'the greatest resistance to the prospect of children's liberation will predictably come from those who are closest to the problem: parents, teachers and children themselves'. Does this not demolish the whole argument, for was not its central plank self-determination, giving children what they *want*? Furthermore, it is those who know children best who are anticipated to be the strongest opponents of their 'liberation' – why? Because their knowledge of children makes them sceptical of the underlying assumptions, perhaps.

Evidence on what children are like, then, which does not support the liberationist argument about their competence and similarity to adults, is ignored or not adequately incorporated into their viewpoint. There is an overlap between this problem of apparently ignoring contradictory evidence, and the interpretation of the evidence which *is* acknowledged. Franklin, for example, gives considerable space to the evidence for the historical specificity of childhood, drawing mainly on the work of Aries (1962),[20] but also that of Plumb (1972).[21] It is argued that childhood emerged as a special phase in life only about 400 years ago in Europe; prior to this there was little differentiation of children from adults, and children were very much a part of the adult world. The relevance of this is to the argument that there is nothing immutable or 'natural' about childhood; it is the product of social definition. Children have been closer to the adult world and therefore could be so again.

While Franklin does acknowledge that some criticism of Aries' work has been put forward, his own approach to Aries is still, it is suggested, too uncritical. For example, he does not fully take on board the arguments of Pollock (1983)[22] who also studied childhood in earlier centuries, using contemporary sources. Pollock attacks the theory that there was no concept of childhood as a separate state before the sixteenth century, suggesting that there has been considerable homogeneity and continuity in methods of child discipline over time, and that there *was* a concept of childhood in the Middle Ages – making the useful point that the fact that past societies may have had a *different* concept of childhood does not mean they had *no* concept of it at all as a separate stage of life. And parents were concerned about their children's welfare and education, Pollock claims. She says of the historical thesis of authors like Aries, DeMause[23] and Stone:[24] 'The sources upon which the received view is founded are obviously suspect and are certainly not a sound enough base to warrant the grand theories which have been derived from them. Aspects of the thesis, especially the assertion that there was no concept of childhood, have been shown by later research to be completely unjustified.'

A second criticism of Franklin's use of Aries' work is that, while he traces the appearance of 'modern' childhood in Aries' account to the development of capitalism and industrialisation, he offers no clear reasoning as to how we could, in Aries' terms, now revert to a 'mediaeval' incorporation of the child into the world of the adult (if that is indeed what occurred in mediaeval times) while capitalism and industrialisation remain. That is, in so far as Aries is correct in saying that the perception and treatment of children changed from the sixteenth and seventeenth centuries on (though varying with place and social class), and in so far as such change reflected broader social and economic change, it is not apparent that childhood should or could now fundamentally change again, and if so, in what direction. If 'childhood' was created for a reason (the need for a more prolonged period of education, most obviously) how can it now be decreated or deconstructed without a change also in that reason? It is not wished here to adopt the type of Panglossian complacency which accepts all to be for the best in the best of all possible worlds (so that if an institution exists it must have grown up to serve some useful social function and therefore is best left alone) – the condition of modern childhood, as the child liberationist authors show so well, leaves much to be desired. But a more searching analysis is perhaps needed of why children came to be seen as in need of special treatment, and the relationship of such special treatment to other aspects of social and economic organisation. How realistic or desirable is it to revert to an apparently mediaeval or pre-capitalist concept of childhood without reinstating mediaeval society? This may be an unfair comment, but it seems that Franklin, or certainly Plumb whom he quotes, is in danger of falling for another type of myth of a 'golden age' – of childhood long past. (Yet Aries' picture of children in the past is not altogether a favourable one – treating children 'as little adults' is not identified with treating them well.)

An additional and more minor point is that the evidence which Franklin cites on the political socialisation of children does not clearly support his argument about the similarity of children to adults. This research[25] shows, according to Franklin's own account, that the development of political knowledge and attitudes can be traced by a tripartite division into early childhood (five to nine), late childhood (nine to 13) and adolescence (13 to 18). In early childhood children view political authorities as benign – a more discriminating and critical attitude is developed in later childhood. There is a developmental process at work, in fact.

Finally, the evidence offered on the poor treatment of children by society and the state is convincing in its own terms, but does not unequivocally point to a 'children's rights' type solution. It may also point to the need for higher standards of *care*, and the greater regulation and resourcing of such care, in the paternalistic mode, rather than to more child autonomy. The paternalists might agree, for example, with many of the criticisms put forward of the state in its dealings with children, but differ in what they would see as the solutions. The argument of the children's rights supporters is essentially that the treatment of children would be better if children had more power. While such an argument can certainly be convincingly put on the basis of the evidence, it is not the only conclusion to which the evidence on child mistreatment leads.

## (b) *Problems with the implications for policy*

The implications of this perspective for state policy in the child care field are characteristically not worked through in the same detail as in the three other perspectives discussed, partly because the focus of the fourth perspective is much broader than the other three – it is on the role of children in society in its entirety, and all of the laws, rules, policies and practices which affect children, rather than the more specific role of the state in making decisions and providing substitute care or family support where child welfare is at risk. Nevertheless, it is clear that the children's rights perspective has far-reaching implications for systems of substitute child care and the maintenance of child welfare, as well as for the social rules governing childhood more generally. As indicated earlier, the very existence of a guardianship role for the state, involving decisions about where children should live and who should have rights over them, is called into question by the insistence on children's autonomy and their right to decide for themselves. And some children's rights authors have devoted considerable energy to criticisms of the way the state uses its power in relation to children, as shown. Both the implications for the general treatment of children, and for the specific child care role of the state, will be referred to here.

It is clear that the goals of the child liberationist writers would require sweeping legal changes. For example, Holt's proposals for the rights which he advocates would require changes in the law to abolish age restrictions on the various activities which he discusses, voting, driving, full-time employment etc. The implication of Holt's approach would seem to be that all existing statutes on child care and protection, custody, child education and labour and so on, would be swept away; nothing would be forced on children that could not be forced on adults; and children would make their own choices about their guardians. Franklin's book puts arguments for an extension of children's rights and autonomy in the various spheres discussed. For example, children should have the right to vote; should be freed from compulsory attendance at school; should have more say and better protection of their rights when in the state's care; and should have greater rights to sexual expression and sex education.

One obvious and pragmatic objection to the policy implications of the more radical children's rights position is that the changes intended are so drastic, and so out of line with child welfare as ordinarily understood, that they would inspire little support, and the proposals are therefore unrealistic. Unlike the pragmatic objections to the third value perspective, the argument here is not about cost (some of the proposed changes might well save money in the short-term – through closure of some schools and homes, fewer social workers and court cases, for example). The problem concerns the perceived legitimacy of the changes proposed – they, and the view of children on which they are based, conflict with the world of both common sense and psychological knowledge, and are likely, not just to lack widespread support, but to be actively resisted by those who believe that children do require special treatment, protection and control. It seems unlikely that any government would undertake such a programme of reform of childhood in the foreseeable future. There are doubts even as to whether children themselves would fully support the changes (as suggested by Farson, himself a liberationist writer).

Secondly, were such proposals in fact to be implemented wholesale, it may be argued that they would lead to a form of *laissez-faire* more extreme, and far more dangerous to children, than the *laissez-faire* embodied in the first perspective outlined in this book. It is submitted that such an absence of regulation of childhood would very probably lead to *more* exploitation of children, not less, and that the liberationists are naive in their understanding of the probable actual consequences of what they recommend, as opposed to the enjoyable freedom and excitement for children about which they fantasise. Take, for example, two of Holt's rights – the right to travel and the right to choose one's own guardian and where one should live. Holt's picture of what this would mean, drawn in the early 1970s, seemed naive by the end of the 1980s, when more was known about violence to, and the sexual abuse of, children. Increasingly, parents and teachers have found it necessary to warn children against the dangers of contact with strangers[26] (although it has to be acknowledged that most known abuse takes place within the family). Both Holt's right to travel without adult supervision and to leave home to live elsewhere would place children vastly more at risk from abusers of various kinds. Children could be enticed or coerced into various damaging or dangerous situations. Their problems could arise from other children, as well as from unscrupulous adults. In Holt's scenario it seems that neither parents nor the state would have any special right or power to intervene to protect them. Another obvious example would be the right to work. Holt envisages the right, but not the obligation, of children to work – children would still have the right to be maintained by their parents, and so need not work if they did not wish to. But the creation of an adult-type right to work for children would presumably mean the abolition of all legal restrictions on child employment and the ending of compulsory education. This would leave children formally unprotected from *de facto* coercion by parents and other caretakers who wished – or needed – them to work and bring in an income, rather than be economically dependent. It would, in fact, represent a reversion to the position of children in the early nineteenth century and before.

A third objection links the issue of parental coercion and manipulation, and that of how effectively children's rights could be implemented or enforced, given the physical and psychological vulnerability of children and their forced dependence on adults to at least some degree. Stating rights is one thing, but making them a reality, particularly where rights involve the imposition of duties on others for their realisation, is notoriously difficult, and could be particularly so in the case of children. A useful illustration is the proposed right to vote. How could such an independent right be exercised meaningfully, particularly with younger children? The child's right could simply become an additional right for parents. Admittedly both Holt and Franklin see the right to vote as only being exercised when interest is sufficiently developed to motivate the child to vote. Franklin states confidently 'Of course two-year-olds will not vote, since they are likely to be interested in things other than politics at this age'. The problem is that Holt and Franklin are talking about the absence of any lower age limit on a *legal* entitlement. Presumably if parents wished to place their child's name on the electoral register at birth, there would be no legal obstacle to prevent this. What, then, occurs when the parents arrive at the polling station with their baby or toddler? Are the returning officers to make a lightning judgement as to the genuineness of the child's interest? The right to one's own income provides another example. How could such a right be made effective in the light of the actual physical power of parents and other caretakers over children? Such an income could well be absorbed into general household income. It might be argued that this would be reasonable, given the parental duty to maintain, but such a situation does not correspond to the concept of an independent right to an income for children and young persons as a base for further independence, and highlights the difficulty of establishing the rights that the children's liberation authors seek, without, say, some protective system organised by the state.

This leads to the problems raised by the implications for state child care policy in particular. Holt sees children as choosing their own guardians, and being free to move away from parents and guardians whom they do not like. It seems clear that a developed machinery of state child care and child protection would not be compatible with the scenario of free and self-determining children whose status is near to that of adults or identical with it. This raises all sorts of difficulties. Babies and very small children are physically unable simply to get up and leave to live elsewhere. Older children may be physically able to run away but may lack the psychological strength or the know-how about where to run to.[27] Children can also be emotionally attached to those who ill-treat them. A useful parallel would be the case of women who find difficulty in leaving violent relationships. Legally adult, they may nevertheless remain in an abusive relationship because of an assortment of pressures, ties and needs. It may however be argued that separation from a violent partner is made structurally difficult for women, and that in the general scenario envisaged by the child liberationist authors it would be made structurally easier for children who wanted to leave an abusive, neglectful or unhappy home to do so. Nevertheless, without a protective machinery backed by the force of the law it seems highly likely that much abuse, neglect and poor child care could not be stopped. Again, children would be returned to the *laissez-faire* situation of the early nineteenth century.

However, the fundamental objection of the more extreme child liberationists to a child care and protection system, should be distinguished from the more specific criticisms of aspects of the current system put forward by more moderate proponents of the perspective. For example, to argue, as Lavery and Freeman do, that improvements should be made to the existing statutory child care system, is not the same as to seek to remove the whole protective system in the name of children's freedom to live where they like. One of the problems of the more extreme children's rights view is that well-founded criticisms of the way society treats children are met with what could be seen as an over-reaction – the demand to abolish virtually all compulsory structures even if designed partly for children's own benefit.

So far, objections to the policy implications of the fourth perspective have been put forward mainly from the point of view of children's interests. Children, it has been argued, would suffer some of the worst aspects of a *laissez-faire* system if paternalism and protection were to withdraw completely, leaving them to the exercise of 'rights' which could in practice spell greater exploitation. However, another practical difficulty facing the implications for policy of the children's rights perspective, is the resistance likely to be encountered from those adults who would see their *own* interests as threatened by the prospect of children having more power but not necessarily commensurate responsibility. Parents, in particular, might feel that they would face an impossible task, of accountability without adequate control, and even an impossible life, with children who come and go, and do more or less as they please without regard for adult interests. Notwithstanding the problems for *children* of more freedom, adulthood might *seem* to be a less preferable state in the society the child liberationists seek to build. Yet it is adults who are called upon to bring forward the necessary changes which would make children's rights a (legal) reality. Again, this seems unrealistic.

A final objection relates mainly to the abolition of compulsory education, but also to the general reduction of control over children, and concerns the need to prepare individuals for a place in the labour market and in society in general. This need concerns not just jobs essential to the economy, but those in various public sector services and the professions; at a broader level, it concerns citizenship, socialised behaviour, and participation in a range of institutions. Without compulsory education at key stages in development, it may be argued, adequate preparation for crucial occupational and social roles might be lacking. There is a limit to the extent to which missing childhood education and learning can be compensated for later. With less control in general over children, socialisation in a broader sense could also be inadequate. To this, however, the liberationists might reply that children would become socialised more rapidly if they were allowed to exercise adult rights earlier. For example, Franklin says: 'If adults acknowledged young people's capacities to discuss political issues, those capacities would be nurtured, enhanced and, perhaps, show signs of even earlier or accelerated development.'

## (c) *Problems of rationale and underlying values*

As indicated earlier, the rationale and underlying values of the fourth children's rights perspective centre round a perception of children's similarity to adults and their primary need to be free of adult control; the artificiality of the construction of childhood; a pessimistic view of adults and their treatment of children; the concept of rights; and a negative view of both the family and the state. Certain problems surrounding the concept of childhood have already been considered in the section on empirical support, and some of the problems of the withdrawal of the state from children's lives in the section on implications for policy. This section will focus on the problems of advocating rights in isolation from duties and of emphasising rights to the point of neglecting other values, and will also consider further some difficulties in the concepts of childhood and adulthood held by the proponents of this perspective.

Firstly, there are problems in the overemphasis on rights to the neglect of duties. Writings by political philosophers on rights in general may be drawn on briefly here to show the interconnected nature of rights and duties. For example, Arnold (1978)[28] argues that the concepts of right and duty can only be elucidated by reference to each other and to the rest of the system. Right and duty are connected to each other as correlatives; they are two different ways of describing a single relation tying individuals together. Flathman (1976)[29] makes a related point, suggesting the inextricable connection between rights and duties, in emphasising that the practice of rights is a social phenomenon which presupposes social arrangements. It seems that the individual only has rights in practice in so far as he exists as part of a set of arrangements and social rules. Ginsberg (1965)[30] argues that rights and duties rest on the same ethical foundation, and like Flathman he stresses that rights and duties define *social* relations. The point here seems to be that the existence of *rights* logically entails the notion of a *duty to respect* those rights; with both the rights and the duties being recognised as part of an ordered social system. Rights are held against others in society (so *others'* rights are held against *us*). As has been indicated, the children's rights authors are ambiguous over the question of children's duties. How, in the society they envisage, would children learn, or be made, to respect the rights of others in exercising their own rights? Holt suggests that children should have the right to choose formally to live as fully legally and financially responsible citizens. This would mean that the child was fully accountable to his fellow citizens and the law for what he did; he could sue and be sued, be made bankrupt, and so on. However, the child could also formally opt back again, to dependent status. Would this allow him to escape some of the consequences of his acts? Holt seems to be saying not. Holt does also speak of the *burden* of citizenship, which can have serious personal consequences, and suggests that young people might be required to meet certain conditions before becoming independent citizens.

In general, though, the emphasis in this perspective is on the institution of rights for children rather than the imposition of duties. This raises the spectre of a section of the community – the least experienced section, by definition – acquiring considerable unaccountable power. Such an end-product seems both difficult to justify and socially dangerous. For example, unsupervised young people with guaranteed incomes and freedom not to attend school, work, or live anywhere in particular, would presumably have more opportunity to commit crimes, but (except in Holt's specific solution) could apparently neither be sued nor be treated as criminally adult. This sort of implication is not spelt out in the child liberationist perspective, however.

Having made this criticism, it is worth bearing in mind that in the past traditional concepts of children and their role have emphasised *duties* rather than rights[31] – the reverse of the child liberationist emphasis. It is perhaps therefore useful, up to a point, to correct this balance by now emphasising rights.

A brief attempt has been made to show the difficulties of emphasising rights while overlooking duties. Another area of difficulty might be a strong focus on rights to the exclusion of other values in human relationships such as love and affection. Freeman (1983) stresses the importance of rights in enabling us, as Bandman (1973)[32] puts it: 'to demand what is our due without having to grovel, plead or beg or to express gratitude when we are given our due, and to express indignation when what is our due is not forthcoming', that is, a world without rights would be morally impoverished; but Freeman goes on to acknowledge (drawing on Kleinig (1976)[33]) that 'there are other morally significant values, like love, friendship and compassion . . . the absence of these from interpersonal transactions does diminsh the moral quality of relationships'. Freeman quotes Kleinig's comment that: 'A morality which has as its motivation merely the giving of what is due or what is conducive to the greatest all-round utility, is seriously defective.' Freeman suggests that it may be an indictment of contemporary civilisation that rights have assumed such importance; and that rights may reflect the inadequacy or absence of good moral relations (though adding that rights remain important, however benevolent society).

An emphasis on rights reflects a somewhat legalistic view of human interactions as transactions governed by claims which can be substantiated by reference to legal or moral principles. It suggests a rational and abstract approach in which, in a sense, how relationships should be conducted, can be 'worked out', and appears to owe more to a cognitive or cerebral approach to other persons than to the emotions and spontaneity. The relevance of such a legalistic, rational concept of interaction, within the intimate day-to-day relationships of the family in particular, is an issue that should be considered here. It may be argued that a precise calculus of rights and duties in such an intimate setting is not usually possible, and, if attempted, could result in destructive conflicts. It may be thought that relationships between parents and children are more appropriately construed in terms of love and care than rights and duties; the same might be said about relationships between children and adults in certain other roles such as teachers, residential care workers and child minders. However, a word of caution is needed – feminism has shown how, within the private world of the family, an ideology of love and care, and a denial of the appropriateness of the concept of rights, has resulted in great injustice and exploitation for women.[34]

Finally, some further problems with the perception of childhood and adulthood can be touched on. It was argued in the section on empirical support that evidence of childhood as a separate developmental stage is ignored or inadequately incorporated into the argument, and that historical evidence on children in earlier times is wrongly interpreted. It is suggested here that another problem with the liberationists' approach to childhood is that, while in a sense they argue for a continuity between childhood and adulthood (for example, no clear cut-off points are definable or acceptable), in another sense they overlook such continuity. One example is the contrast between the positive, optimistic concept of what human beings as children are like, and could be like given more freedom, and the rather negative, cynical view of the state of adulthood which these children will eventually reach. Perhaps, however, it is assumed that freer children would in time become nicer adults than the adults currently existing. Linked with this question of continuity is the tendency of the liberationists implicitly to perceive childhood's absence of rights and freedoms as *permanent*. This may be partly why the link with discrimination by race and gender is made. Franklin in fact states that 'a child, even if foolish enough to desire it, cannot grow old prematurely. In this way exclusion is a "permanent" exclusion, since *all* children are denied rights simply because they are children and can acquire them only when they cease to be children'. Yet from the point of view of the individual person, childhood with its special status is *not* permanent. Individuals only exceptionally find it possible to pass from one racial category or one gender category to another, and therefore racial or gender-based disadvantage must be considered permanent unless and until external change occurs. But – barring premature death – all individuals grow from childhood to adulthood and therefore move on from the deprivation of rights and special status to which the child liberationists object, gradually acquiring the freedoms of adults. In this sense the 'disadvantages' of childhood are different from, and, it may be argued, more justified than, the disadavantages of other groupings. The disadvantages are intentional and directed to a different purpose – socialisation, that is, learning to be adult.

## (v) *The perspective in practice*

As the child liberation/rights perspective is not as widely accepted within the field of child care law and policy as state paternalism, the defence of the family, or even *laissez-faire*, and is also a much more recent appearance on the child care scene than the other perspectives, it is less easy to point to particular times and places where this perspective may be said to have been in the ascendant. However particular aspects of policy which reflect a children's rights view, broadly defined, can be identified in certain countries. This 'in practice' section is thus briefer than those relating to the other perspectives; but it will discuss the system existing in Norway of a government Ombudsperson for children, and will look briefly at some other countries where *some* traces of a rights approach are in evidence.

## CHILDREN'S RIGHTS IN NORWAY IN THE 1980S[35]

Norway is one country where the children's rights viewpoint has been taken seriously to the extent that, since 1981, a *Barneombudet*, an Ombudsperson or Commissioner specifically for children, has been employed, as an independent official but part of the machinery of government. This was the first such government post in the world, and was seen as an independent public spokesperson to protect the interests of children and young people (up to the age of majority – 18).

The post is based in a single national office, with a secretariat, and an advisory panel which meets four times a year. The *Barneombudet*'s duties are defined by the Commissioner for Children Act 1981, which states that the Commissioner's responsibility is to promote children's interests in the private and public sectors and to follow up the development of the conditions under which children grow up. In particular, duties include ensuring that existing legislation protecting children's interests is observed; proposing legislation to strengthen children's security; protecting the interests of children in planning and policy formation; suggesting measures to resolve conflicts between children and society; and ensuring that sufficient information is given to the public and private sectors concerning children's rights and measures required for children. The Commissioner can act on her own initiative or on request. In carrying out these duties, the Commissioner is to ensure that the needs, rights and interests of children are given the necessary consideration in all areas of society. There is also a responsibility to ensure that the public is informed about the office's work.

The *Barneombudet* deals with individual cases but does not have the power to decide cases or change official decisions. Nor is the *Barneombudet* empowered to deal with conflicts between an individual child and her parents or with disputes between parents. She may, however, give information and advice on where the child or parents might obtain help. And where the problems raised by individual complaints give rise to issues of principle, these do belong within the *Barneombudet*'s field of action. But the office is not to interfere with the work of the courts, so any case being handled by a court has to be turned down. The instructions to the *Ombudet* in fact allow for individual cases to be rejected, or referred to other agencies including the Ombudsman for Public Administration, or shelved. Where a case *is* dealt with, a statement has to be made, in which the Commissioner personally adopts a standpoint; this would normally be a written statement giving the grounds for the opinion, the Commissioner to decide to whom the statement should be directed. This could include the media.

The *Barneombudet* can be contacted directly, in writing or by telephone, by children or parents, or by groups, with particular times set aside when only children may telephone. If an application concerns a specific child and is not from the child himself, she must obtain the child's permission to pursue the matter (and the guardian's, with younger children). There is some leeway to proceed without these consents, however.

The *Barneombudet* has free access to all public and private institutions for children, and is entitled to see their confidential records; information can also be demanded from others. She can make a formal statement on any matter raised and she herself decides to whom these statements shall be directed. An annual report is made to the Ministry and this is available to the public. As mentioned, the Commissioner also has to ensure that the public is informed about her work.

A report on the first five years of the scheme[36] found that annually the Office received approximately 2,000 complaints. A total of 4,066 cases were handled in the period 1981–6, approximately 500 of which were initially raised by children. The majority of complainants were parents, grandparents, professionals or local politicians, as well as organisations or local or national authorities. The report says: 'The telephone-calls and letters from children are of particular importance, because the children themselves tell what it is really like to grow up in their community and which conditions really create problems. Therefore children bring to the attention of the Commissioner problems of which adults are unaware.' While a decline in the number of complaints over time had been expected, the number had in fact increased steadily. Contact with the media had been important, with the number of interviews reaching approximately 350 per year. Local newspapers routinely received copies of statements given to municipal authorities, to keep the public informed of the Commissioner's views. It was found that two-thirds of cases originated in Oslo or the southern counties, where only a half of the population lived. To counteract this skewing to the south, the Commissioner lectured or participated in meetings more readily in the northern counties; and the Commissioner's telephone number (from 1985) was published in all telephone directories.

A seven-fold breakdown of case types is given in the report, with the largest categories being cases relating to family circumstances (279 cases in 1986); children in institutions, child welfare and child abuse (174 cases); and school problems (129). Smaller categories related to physical conditions and planning (112 cases); cultural and consumer questions (79); and child care and leisure facilities (55). In addition 10–30 cases a year were not covered by these categories. The total number of cases handled in 1986 was 855.

On the office's effectiveness, the five-year report comments that while the Commissioner's statements are taken seriously, actual results are difficult to point out. Nevertheless, the Commissioner had been instrumental in creating public awareness of children's needs, instigating debate, and lobbying for amendments of legislation such as the prohibition of physical punishment and a new law concerning the distribution of videotapes. At a local level, it was found that the Commissioner's statements were widely used as a source of information.

The weaknesses of the *Barneombudet* system include the lack of a *local* system – there is only one national office; the fact that the system can only handle a limited number of cases; and the lack of political power – the *Barneombudet* can make recommendations but is powerless to enforce them, and cannot change official administrative decisions. Nevertheless there would seem to be great value in an office publicly committed to children's well-being and able to campaign and make formal statements on children's issues. The fact that the office is part of government and has access to various organisations and their records is an asset, as is the right of direct access *to* the office. A children's rights emphasis is apparent in the provisions for children to initiate complaints, and for their consent to be sought when they have not initiated.

## OTHER SIGNS OF THE PERSPECTIVE IN PRACTICE

Other fragmented manifestations of the children's rights viewpoint can be found in other countries in recent years. In **Sweden**[37] there is also a children's Ombudsperson or *Barnombudsmannen*, in existence since 1973, but the system is different from Norway in that the Ombudsperson is employed by a voluntary organisation, Radda Barnen (Save the Children). While this makes the institution independent of government and freer to criticise, it provides no official, legal right of access to institutions and thus reduces the Office's effectiveness. Nevertheless, the institution is significant for its recognition of the need for an independent and separate spokesperson for children. It seeks to influence legislation and policy by working on its own initiative or with government bodies; publicises children's needs and rights; educates professionals on children's issues; and supports and publicises research. The Ombudsperson also takes on individual cases, including abuse cases, giving advice and assistance, and attempting to mediate an agreed resolution of conflicts – either with parents or with authorities (here apparently going beyond the Norwegian remit). As in Norway, telephone counselling is provided. Press campaigns might also be initiated. But the Ombudsperson lacks legal power (as indeed does the Norwegian office).

In **England and Wales**, while the children's rights perspective has not had significant influence in its more radical guise, it has been expressed in a greater concern for the child's own feelings and views. The 1975 Children Act contained two sections relating to the child's own 'wishes and feelings': Section 3, which stipulated that in adoption decisions, while first consideration should be given to the need to safeguard and promote the child's welfare, the court or agency should 'as far as practicable ascertain the wishes and feelings of the child regarding the decision and give due consideration to them, having regard to his age and understanding', and Section 59, which embodied a similar provision for decisions relating to children in local authority care. (However, the duty could be waived when there was a need to protect members of the public.) This provision was re-enacted in the 1980 Child Care Act as Section 18(1). The 1989 Children Act strengthened the provision regarding welfare, in that the child's welfare became the *paramount* consideration in court cases relating to a child's upbringing (Section 1); while the wishes and feelings of the child were to be ascertained in decisions about children in family or care proceedings or being 'looked after' (ie in care or accommodation), although in the latter case the wishes and feelings of parents or anyone else with parental responsibility also had to be ascertained (Sections 1 and 22). Such provisions are consonant with a moderate child liberationist position which emphasises that the child himself has a point of view which ought to be formally considered (although it is not necessarily the decisive factor).

The 1975 Act also made provisions for children in certain cases to be represented in court separately from their parents if there was thought to be a conflict of interests (Sections 64–6). This was achieved by the creation of independent *Guardians ad Litem*, court-appointed short-term social workers, to represent the child's interests and instruct the child's solicitor. The 1989 Children Act strengthened these provisions by extending *Guardians ad Litem* to more categories of children. Guardians were to be appointed routinely in care and emergency protection proceedings, unless the courts were satisfied that it was not necessary to do so to safeguard the child (Section 41); however there was some concern at one stage that children would lose the benefits of access to *both* a Guardian *and* a solicitor.[38] The concept of a separate advocate for the *child* – as distinct from the parents or the local authority – again rests on the notion of the child as an individual, a subject, with separate claims, wishes and feelings which ought to be heard. Another provision of the 1989 Children Act which may be mentioned in this context is Section 26, which placed a new duty on local authorities to 'establish a procedure for considering any representations made to them' by a child, her parents, a person with parental responsibility or a foster parent, about the discharge by the local authority of their functions relating to accommodation and the support of children and families – in other words, a form of complaints procedure. (The 1984 Short Committee Report, *Children in Care*,[39] had recommended more rights for children in care, and the 1987 White Paper on child care law[40] had recommended a complaints procedure for children in care.) Under the 1989 Act also, the child can take certain actions herself – for example, challenge an Emergency Protection Order (Section 45), seek an order on parental contact when in care (Section 34), and challenge the unmarried father's rights (Section 4).

Other changes in English child care practice which reflect a children's rights view include the admission of children in some cases (although it is not widely practised) to case conferences and reviews called to discuss their future, and discussion of access to the child's records.[41] The formation of organisations like the National Association of Young People in Care, and a Voice for the Child in Care, also reflect an emphasis on the child's participation and right to a say when in care. NAYPIC was set up in 1979 as an independent organisation to support local care groups and take up issues at a national level. It originated in a National Children's Bureau initiative, the 'Who Cares?' project, which ran in the late 1970s and helped young people in care to meet nationally as well as starting local 'Who Cares' or self-advocacy groups.[42] NAYPIC saw itself as a consumer group, the voice of young people in care. The organisation called Voice for the Child in Care described itself as a network of people concerned about children in care; it supported, for example, the idea of an independent spokesman for the child.[43] Other developments have included complaints procedures in some authorities prior to the 1989 Act, the appointment of a children's rights officer in at least one authority, and moves towards ending corporal punishment for children in care.[44] There have also been moves to outlaw corporal punishment by parents.[45] In this context, it is significant that corporal punishment ended in state schools in Britain in 1986.

Another development has been the giving of greater weight to **what children say**, firstly in facilitating, and listening more carefully to, children's disclosures of abuse; and secondly in allocating a larger role to children's evidence in court. In 1987 the Home Secretary announced his intention to change the law so that a conviction *could* be obtained on the unsworn and uncorroborated evidence of a child (under 14), something which had not been possible before.[46] Child witnesses were also to be enabled to give their evidence by live video link in some cases rather than actually in the courtroom.[47] These changes were enacted in the Criminal Justice Act 1988; while the Children Act 1989 allowed *civil* courts to accept unsworn evidence from young children, and hearsay evidence – including videotaped evidence – of abuse (Section 96). The importance of listening to what children say was also recognised in the setting up (within the voluntary sector) of telephone counselling services for children, of which 'Childline', established in 1986, was the most well known. Childline attracted an enormous response from children, and was in fact unable to deal with all the demand directed at it. Attempted calls reached the level of 8,000 to 10,000 a day (less than 10 per cent of which were answered).[48] Staff more than trebled in the first year. The significance of services such as Childline is that contact is child-initiated, and it is what *children* say that is listened to and respected.

The establishment of the Children's Legal Centre in 1979, in the International Year of the Child, and the publication of its journal *Childright*, have already been mentioned as an expression of the children's rights perspective. Another relevant pressure group was Justice for Children, founded in 1978 to bring about reforms in the juvenile justice system. This group has been mentioned in connection with the *laissez-faire* perspective, but in certain respects may be identified with a children's rights viewpoint. That is, it included among its aims the protection of the rights of children, as well as parents, in court, and access by children in care to an independent complaints procedure. The group also supported the principle of separate representation.[49] Another development of a rather different kind, a government advisory committee, the Children's Committee, may be mentioned. Originating in a report on child health published in 1976,[50] this had the function of advising the Secretary of State on health and social services in relation to children. It was, however, short-lived, lasting only from 1978 to 1981. Finally in the English context, the child's right to refuse a medical examination was upheld in the Children Act 1989 (Section 44); and the Labour Party Policy Review of 1989 proposed the establishment of a Children's Commissioner.[51]

Briefly, developments in a children's rights direction in **Canada** and **New Zealand** may be referred to. In Canada, a Charter of Rights and Freedoms in 1982 gave rise to debate as to whether or not children should be considered 'citizens' under the Charter and therefore be allowed rights such as the franchise. It should be noted that children's voting has been a subject of serious public debate in Canada.[52] Other Canadian developments include the office of Official Guardian for children established in Ontario since 1881. Since 1949 the Guardian has been responsible for investigating arrangements for children in divorce and separation. Where there are grounds for concern, an investigation is carried out and a report made for the judge. In British Columbia, Family Advocates are attached to Family Courts, and can intervene as the child's counsel where the court is of the opinion that the child requires representation. The Advocates ensure that children have representation where court decisions are made on matters affecting their interests or welfare; and one result of their presence is that many cases where they are involved are settled without the need for a court hearing. The Alberta Child Welfare Act 1984 provides for separate representation of the child in court. Several statutes in Canada allow courts discretion in determining the appropriateness of a child's testimony, and a statute in Quebec requires that children be given an opportunity to be heard.[53] Finally, in New Zealand a Royal Commission in 1986 explored the possibility of lowering the voting age to 16.[54]

While not altogether free of paternalism, developments of this kind do reflect a concern with the child as an individual with an individual set of interests, and with a right to have these interests represented. To a degree, then, they reflect a children's rights perspective.

## SOME REFERENCES RELEVANT TO THIS PERSPECTIVE

B. Bandman 1973 'Do Children Have Any Natural Rights?' *Proceedings of 29th Annual Meeting of Philosophy of Education Society* 234–6

R. Farson 1978 *Birthrights* New York, Penguin

B. Franklin (Ed) 1986 *The Rights of Children* Oxford, Blackwell

B. Franklin 1989 'Children's rights: developments and prospects' *Children and Society* 3(1) May 1989 76–92

M.D.A. Freeman 1980 'The Rights of Children in the International Year of the Child' *Current Legal Problems* 33 1–17

M.D.A. Freeman 1983 *The Rights and Wrongs of Children* London, Frances Pinter

M.D.A. Freeman 1987 'Taking Children's Rights Seriously' *Children and Society* 1(4) Winter 1987–88 299–319

M.D.A. Freeman 1988 'Time to stop hitting our children' *Childright* 51 October 1988

H. H. Foster and D. J. Freed 1972 'A Bill of Rights for Children' *Family Law Quarterly* VI(4) Winter 1972

R. Hodgkin 1986 'Parents and corporal punishment' *Adoption and Fostering* 10(3) 47–9

J. Holt 1975 *Escape from Childhood. The Needs and Rights of Children* Harmondsworth, Penguin

J. Kleinig 1976 'Mill, Children and Rights' *Educational Philosophy and Theory* 8 14

D.J. Macdougall 1985 'Children's Rights: An Evaluation of the Controversy'; in K. L. Levitt and B. Wharf (Eds) *The Challenge of Child Welfare* Vancouver, University of British Columbia Press

P. Newell 1989 *Children are People Too; the Case Against Corporal Punishment*

C. Rogers and Wrightsman 1978 'Attitudes towards Children's Rights – Nurturance or Self-Determination' *Journal of Social Issues* 34(2) 59

V. L. Worsfold 1974 'A Philosophical Justification for children's rights' *Harvard Educational Review* 44(1) 142

## NOTES AND REFERENCES

1. See Chapter 4, footnote 76.
2. J. Holt 1975 *Escape from Childhood. The Needs and Rights of Children* Harmondsworth, Penguin.
3. Ibid.

4. H. H. Foster and D. J. Freed 1972 'A Bill of Rights for Children' *Family Law Quarterly* VI(4) Winter 1972.

5. V. L. Worsfold 1974 'A Philosophical Justification for children's rights' *Harvard Educational Review* 44 (1) 142.

6. R. Farson 1978 *Birthrights* New York, Penguin.

7. J. Rawls 1972 *A Theory of Justice* Oxford, Clarendon Press.

8. B. Franklin (Ed) 1986 *The Rights of Children* Oxford, Blackwell.

9. P. Aries 1962 *Centuries of Childhood* Harmondsworth, Penguin.

10. M. D. A. Freeman 1980 'The Rights of Children in the International Year of the Child' *Current Legal Problems* 33 1–17; M. D. A. Freeman 1983 *The Rights and Wrongs of Children* Chapter 2, footnote 45; N.B. For Wald's framework on which Freeman's is based see: M. Wald 1979 'Children's Rights; a Framework for Analysis' *University of California Davis Law Review* 12 255–282; See also M. D. A. Freeman 1987 'Taking Children's Rights Seriously' *Children and Society* 1(4) Winter 1987–8 299–319.

11. R. Wilson 1988 'Protecting children's rights' *New Statesman and Society* 9 December 1988.

12. There were moves in 1989 (within the context of the passage of the Children Bill through Parliament) to eliminate *all* corporal punishment of children in Britain, although these moves were not successful. For a recent survey of the law on physical punishment of children see: M. D. A. Freeman 1988 'Time to stop hitting our children' *Childright* 51, October 1988; R. Hodgkin 1986 'Parents and corporal punishment' *Adoption and Fostering* 10(3) 47–9. Also see: P. Newell 1989 *Children are People Too; the Case Against Corporal Punishment.*

13. For a discussion of the social construction of dependency in old age see, for example, A. Walker 1980 'The Social Construction of Poverty and Dependency in Old Age' *Journal of Social Policy* 9 49–77.

14. C. Rogers and Wrightsman 1978 'Attitudes towards Children's Rights – Nurturance or Self-Determination' *Journal of Social Issues* 34(2) 59.

15. D. J. Macdougall 1985 'Children's Rights: An Evaluation of the Controversy' in K. L. Levitt and B. Wharf (Eds) *The Challenge of Child Welfare* Chapter 1, footnote 3.

16. G. Lavery 1986 'The Rights of Children in Care' in B. Franklin (Ed) *The Rights of Children* This chapter, footnote 8.

17. R. Adams 1986 'Juvenile Justice and Children's and Young People's Rights' in Ibid.

18. D. J. Macdougall 1985 'Children's Rights' This chapter, footnote 15.

19. L. E. Teitelbaum 1980 'Foreword: The Meaning of Rights of Children' *New Mexico L. R.* 10 236.

20. P. Aries 1962 *Centuries of Childhood* This chapter, footnote 9.

21. J. H. Plumb 1972 *In the Light of History* Harmondsworth, Penguin.

22. L. Pollock 1983 *Forgotten Children. Parent-child relations from 1500 – 1900* Cambridge, Cambridge University Press.

23. L. DeMause (Ed) 1976 *The History of Childhood* London, Souvenir Press.

24. L. Stone 1977 *The Family, Sex and Marriage in England 1500–1800* London, Weidenfeld and Nicolson.

25. The sources quoted by Franklin which are relevant here are: R. E.

Dawson, K. Prewitt and K. S. Dawson 1977 *Political Socialisation*; F. Greenstein 1974 *Children and Politics*.

26. For example, the Kidscape campaign of education psychologist Michelle Elliot, helps teachers and parents to alert children to certain dangers. (H. Franks 1989 'A world of secrets' *The Guardian* 5 July 1989.)

27. Seven year old Maria Colwell, it may be noted, was locked up to prevent her running away. See Chapter 3, footnote 62.

28. C. Arnold 1978 'Analyses of right' in E. Kamenka and A. Ehr-Soon Tay *Human Rights* London, Arnold.

29. R. Flathman 1976 *The Practice of Rights* Cambridge, Cambridge University Press.

30. A. Ginsberg 1965 *On Justice in Society* Harmondsworth, Penguin.

31. See for example: I. Pinchbeck and M. Hewitt 1969 *Children in English Society* Chapter 2, footnote 34; N. Middleton 1971 *When Family Failed* Chapter 3, footnote 54.

32. B. Bandman 1973 'Do Children Have Any Natural Rights?' *Proceedings of 29th Annual Meeting of Philosophy of Education Society* 234, 236; as quoted by M. D. A. Freeman 1983 *The Rights and Wrongs of Children* Chapter 2, footnote 45.

33. J. Kleinig 1976 'Mill, Children and Rights' *Educational Philosophy and Theory* 8 14, as quoted by Freeman, Ibid; and M. D. A. Freeman 1980 'The Rights of Children' This chapter, footnote 10.

34. See feminist writing on women's caring role, such as: J. Finch and D. Groves 1983 *A Labour of Love: Women, Work and Caring* London, Routledge and Kegan Paul; C. Ungerson 1987 *Policy is personal: sex, gender and informal care* London, Tavistock; G. Dalley 1988 *Ideologies of Caring: rethinking community and collectivism* Basingstoke, Macmillan.

35. Sources used for the Children's Commissioner in Norway here are as follows: Norway Information 1987 *Commissioner for Children in Norway* Oslo, Royal Norwegian Ministry of Foreign Affairs; Children's Legal Centre 1984 *Congress '84; Children and their Rights, Discussion Group Paper B: Representation of Children and Young People's Interests* London, Children's Legal Centre; B. Franklin 1989 'Children's rights: developments and prospects' *Children and Society* 3(1) May 1989 76–92.
   Additional sources on Norway include: M. Flekkoy 1988–9 'Child Advocacy in Norway' *Children and Society* 2(4) Winter 1988–9 307–318; M. G. Flekkoy 1985 'Speaking for Children' *Childright* 14 19.

36. Norway Information 1987 *Commissioner for Children* Footnote 35.

37. Sources used for the Children's Ombudsperson in Sweden here are as follows: 1987 *Facts about Radda Barnen. The Children's Ombudsman* Stockholm, Radda Barnen; Children's Legal Centre 1984 *Congress '84* This chapter, footnote 35; B. Franklin 1989 'Children's rights' This chapter, footnote 35.

38. See for example: M. Jervis 1989 'The "User-Friendly" Children Bill' *Social Work Today* 12 January 1989. This issue now appears to be resolved.

39. House of Commons 1984 *Children in Care* Chapter 4, footnote 20.

40. White Paper 1987 *The Law on Child Care* Chapter 4, footnote 23.

41. See for example: M. Stein and S. Ellis 1983 *Reviews and Young People in Care – Gizza Say* NAYPIC.

42. NAYPIC 1983 *Sharing Care.* See also: R. Page and G. Clark 1977 *Who Cares?* London, National Children's Bureau; M. Stein 1983 'Protest in care' *in* Ed. B. Jordan and N. Parton *The Political Dimensions of Social Work* Oxford, Blackwell 89–105.

43. A Voice for the Child in Care 1982 *Children's Spokesmen.*

44. See: Children's Legal Centre 1984 *Congress '84* This chapter, footnote 35; B. Franklin 1989 'Children's rights' This chapter, footnote 35; R. Hodgkin 1986 'Parents and corporal punishment' This chapter, footnote 12; P. Newell 1989 *Children are People Too* This chapter, footnote 12; M. Lindsay 1988 'Child's Rights Officer by appointment' *Childright* 49 July-Aug. 16–19; M. Jervis 1988 'Crossing the boundaries' *Social Work Today* 5 May 1988.

45. For example, an amendment to this effect was proposed to the 1989 Children Bill, as was an amendment to prevent foster parents using corporal punishment. See this chapter, footnote 12. Both amendments were lost, although with some prospect that foster parents *would* be prohibited.

46. Since the 1889 Prevention of Cruelty to Children Act; re-enacted in the Children and Young Persons Act 1933 Section 38(1).

47. In Sweden, children's evidence in abuse cases can already be given by video. (Source: letter from Swedish Embassy, April 1989.)

48. C. Doran and J. Young 1987 'Child abuse: the real crisis' *New Society* 27 November 1987; Editorial 1987 'Suffer the little children' *New Society* 18 December 1987.

49. Justice for Children leaflets on aims and objectives (no date given).

50. Court Committee 1976 *Report of the Committee on Child Health Services. Fit for the Future* Cmnd. 6684 London, HMSO.

51. Labour Party 1989 *Meet the challenge, make the change – final report of Labour's Policy Review for the 1990s.*

52. For example, two radio programmes: *Giving Children the Vote* by Ian Hunter. An Ideas documentary. May 30 1988. CBC-AM; *Phone-in on Children Voting* – An Almanac show broadcast May 27 1988. CBC-AM.

53. Sources used on Canada here are: K. Levitt and B. Wharf (Eds) 1985 *The Challenge of Child Welfare* Chapter 1, footnote 3. Especially chapters by M. Callahan 'Public Apathy and Government Parsimony: A Review of Child Welfare in Canada'; and D. J. Macdougall 'Children's Rights' This chapter, footnote 15; Children's Legal Centre 1984 *Congress '84* This chapter, footnote 35.

   See also: Berger Commission, British Columbia 1975 *Report of the Royal Commission on family and children's law* Vancouver.

54. B. Franklin 1989 'Children's rights' This chapter, footnote 35.

# CHAPTER SIX

# Convergences and divergences

The past four chapters (2–5) have each outlined one value perspective on child care law and policy, these being: *laissez-faire*; paternalism and protection; the defence of the birth family; and child liberation. For each perspective particular aspects have been considered: the **main elements** of the perspective; some of the most prominent **authors** associated with the perspective; its **rationale** and underlying values; and some **criticisms** that can be put. The criticisms have focused on the empirical support for the position, problems with its implications for policy, and problems with its rationale and underlying values. Each perspective has been considered in practice in particular times and places – mostly in England and Wales (from the nineteenth century to the 1970s), but also in the United States, Australia and Scandinavia. Developments in the 1980s in England and Wales have so far been neglected; it is submitted that they do not reflect any one value perspective in a clear way, but an attempt to analyse this decade will be made in Chapter 7.

As will be apparent from the discussion so far, the four perspectives contain both themes and ideas in common, and some important differences. This chapter will attempt to summarise both what the perspectives share and where they part company, under the title of 'Convergences and Divergences'. At this stage the differences between the positions are perhaps more obvious than the areas they hold in common. This higher profile for differences than similarities is a drawback arising from the attempt to define four *different* perspectives, show how they differ, and categorise child care authors according to one point of view or the other. The author acknowledges that the latter attempt has not been entirely successful. For example, it has been necessary to create a 'moderate' version of some perspectives in order to accommodate certain authors and assimilate them to the framework – Dingwall *et al.*[1] are seen as 'moderate paternalists' and Freeman[2] as a 'moderate children's rights author' – while there are doubts about classifying Morris *et al.*[3] and Taylor *et al.*[4] under *laissez-faire* with Goldstein *et al.*[5] Morris and Taylor perhaps occupy a position part way between *laissez-faire* and a liberationist perspective, although the author's conclusion is that they are in fact closer to *laissez-faire* than anything else in the framework developed in this book. Such intermediate positions, however, highlight the problems of attempting to classify views and authors in any definitive way. It may be noted at this point that the original article by the author under the name of Fox[6] on which the framework here is based, may be criticised for polarising and exaggerating the distinctions between the two 'value positions' which the article outlined. For example, Holman (1988)[7] commented: 'It should be noted that Fox's categories sharpen the differences between the two camps.' However, it should be recalled that Fox's article did devote some space to 'Areas of convergence between the two positions' before going on to enumerate the major differences. It should be helpful at this point, therefore, to consider the important common ground shared by the four perspectives discussed in this book, before outlining how the perspectives diverge.

## POINTS OF CONVERGENCE BETWEEN THE FOUR PERSPECTIVES

### (a) *The focus on children*

Firstly, all four value perspectives must be credited with some genuine concern for the well-being and interests of children. This fundamental orientation is indeed in large part the authors' motivation for writing in the field they do. Goldstein *et al.*, for example, start from a central interest in healthy child development. The paternalist authors are deeply concerned about child abuse and neglect and good standards of parental care, while the child liberationists are clearly shocked at the general societal treatment of children and desire passionately to improve it. Slightly less unambiguous is the focus of the third, pro-family perspective, but here too a central caring for children does manifest itself. For example, Holman's starting point in this field is an interest in *child care* – his sympathy for parents and families has developed from this. The following already-cited quotations from authors in the four camps illustrate their concern for the best for children:

> constantly ongoing interactions between parents and children become
> for each child the starting point for an all-important line of development
> that leads towards adult functioning. (Goldstein *et al.*)

Whatever beneficial qualities a psychological parent may be lacking, he offers the child a chance to become a wanted and needed member within a family structure. (Goldstein *et al.*)

children are not the property of their parents. Parents are trustees for their children's interests: as with any trust, if they fail in the duties involved, they should be discharged. (Dingwall *et al.*)

(to parents)
1. Give continuous, consistent, loving care . . .
2. Give generously of your time and understanding . . .
3. Provide new experiences and bathe your child in language . . . (Kellmer Pringle)

the conviction gained ground that a child's own family was, in most cases, the best place for him to be. (Holman)

(on families) the normal and rightful lot of most children. (Holman)

children have a right to make just claims, and adults must be responsive to those claims. (Worsfold)

(children) form a large, long-suffering and oppressed grouping in society. (Franklin)

The child-centredness of the thinking is apparent in the desire for children to be normal, healthy, happy, loved, wanted, respected persons whose suffering should be prevented. A value is placed on children and their experiences.

It might be thought that this point is so obvious as not to need stating. Why, after all, discuss and explore child care matters if one does not have a central concern for the welfare and happiness of children? However, in principle it would be possible to write on child care from the point of view of perceiving children as a management or social control problem, whose potential disruption of adult life should be minimised. A purely punitive or oppressive approach is also quite possible in focusing on the issue of children in society. Just as all policies relating to children and young persons are not necessarily benign, so all writing on this issue need not necessarily be motivated by benevolence.

Nevertheless, the authors discussed in this book may be credited with a high degree of concern for children's well-being, even if mixed with other motives at times. The problem, of course, in making sense of these authors' work, revolves around the question of how the child's welfare should be *interpreted*. Fox's article referred to some useful comments by Walton (1976)[8] on the interpretation of the 'best interests' of the child. Walton argued that the use of the phrase 'best interests of the child' had often confused rather than helped child care debates, creating the illusion that these interests constituted an objective fact.

He saw 'best interests' as contingent, rather than objective, the view of interests depending on the particular position and assumptions of the person expressing them, and often used as a deceptively simple slogan. The term was used to justify action taken with respect to children but was open to abuse, creating confusion and drawing a veil of ignorance over important issues. In Walton's view there was a need to consider factors to be taken into account if the phrase were to be infused with greater meaning; otherwise there was a danger that it would be used symbolically, to create an illusion of change, to deflect criticism, or to discredit opposition (because no one would want to be seen to oppose 'the child's best interests'). Walton stressed that there was no simple concept or criterion which could be applied in a crude rule of thumb way, and no group or individual which had sole authority to assume that generally it had the best conception of the child's interests.

It is clearly on this question of *interpreting* the child's interests or welfare that the four value perspectives diverge. Their central interest in the well-being of children, albeit differently defined, does however merit bearing in mind.

## (b) *The state and the blood tie*

A second area of convergence is that the four perspectives would all accept some role for the state in intervening between parent and child in order to defend or help the child; while none of them would argue for completely unfettered parental rights, or that the blood tie is always good for the child and ought to be unequivocally supported. The fourth, children's rights perspective is different from the others in that the role of the state it envisages is largely to do with taking steps to free children from any controls at all not imposed on adults. But none of the four perspectives would construe the child's welfare as lying in a return to the legal position of the early nineteenth century in the sense that parents (or fathers) should have virtually absolute control over their children, very much as though they were possessions or chattels, or that the principle of non-interference by the state or anyone else in the dynamics of the patriarchal family should be carried to extreme lengths. Indeed, it is probably the fourth perspective most of all which would find such a system repugnant and deeply antagonistic to children's true interests. Nevertheless the policy implications of the fourth perspective, as has been shown, do in fact seem to lead back to a form of *laissez-faire* in that compulsory education would be ended, there would be no restrictions on child labour, no specific juvenile justice system, and no system of state substitute care. But the difference from the early Victorian age is that parents, while retaining a degree of responsibility, would *not* have rights and powers of the same kind. And it is state action through changing the law which would bring this situation about.

The first and third perspectives, while showing a preference for parental control and family autonomy on the whole, do recognise some situations where the force of the law should be used to separate children from their parents and remove parents' rights. Goldstein *et al.*, as shown in Chapter 2, specify the precise circumstances in which this should be done, and the form of intervention envisaged by them when it *is* deemed justified, is draconian (permanent severance from the family of origin). The proponents of the third perspective are vaguer about compulsory intervention and play down the need for it, but would not go so far as to suggest that it should *never* come into play. For example, one defender of birth families interviewed by Fox and reported in her article, commented on the Maria Colwell case:

> I read the majority of that report the other day . . . given the obvious protests that she [Maria] made, I just cannot conceive of it [the decision to return her to her natural parent] . . . I don't think any of the reasons were valid . . . She did not want to be there . . . I just do not understand that social worker's decision.

The difference from the paternalist school is one of emphasis, of how and in what circumstances children should be removed and when parental contact should be maintained and restoration to the birth parent attempted. Differences arise, then, about the range and form of state intervention, but the principle of some action by the state to safeguard children's interests and rights held against adults, is accepted by all four perspectives.

(c) *Areas of convergence in the first* **three** *perspectives*
Finally, on convergences, certain common ground shared by the first *three* perspectives may be mentioned. One point is that all would give some role to support for natural families stopping short of compulsory intervention, although this is very muted in Goldstein *et al.*'s work. But Morris *et al.* and Taylor *et al.* argue for voluntary services to assist parents and children before the point of compulsory intervention. Tizard[9] mentions the need for support to the natural parents to enable them to care adequately; Kellmer Pringle[10] advocated payment for mothers who stay at home to care; and both Kellmer Pringle and the British Agencies for Adoption and Fostering in their later writings moved closer to a preventionist position in arguing for support for families to help them care for their own children.[11]

Again, the difference is one of emphasis: the pro–birth family position is more concerned to press for policy changes such as better day care and financial benefits as urgently necessary; the paternalists perhaps see such changes as more long-term and not immediately related to the needs of the children who are currently the subject of placement decisions, but they are nevertheless not entirely unsympathetic to birth parents. This is also the case with some moderate children's rights authors (notably Freeman).

As has already been made apparent, the first three perspectives converge on not stressing children's autonomy (with the exception of Morris *et al.* and Taylor *et al.*, who do put some emphasis on this) but on seeing children as different from adults, more vulnerable, of necessity dependent, and appropriately subject to adult decisions. The child's own viewpoint and separate set of interests are thus somewhat overlooked. This, as shown, is the radical difference between the first three positions and children's rights. *Laissez-faire*, paternalism and the pro-family position also converge on accepting *some* role for adoption and fostering. This is most apparent in the first two perspectives, where good adoptive and secure foster homes have a crucial role in caring for children who are not with their own parents; but the supporters of the third perspective would not *deny* a role for adoptive and foster parents. However, there are some crucial differences on the type of role envisaged for foster care and adoption, as will be highlighted in discussing 'divergences'. It can be mentioned here that the children's rights authors also see some role for 'substitute homes' – of a kind: those that children choose to go and live in. This is rather different from a home selected and supervised by a child care agency, however. Finally, all the first three perspectives generally favour the nuclear family structure (whether based on biological bonds or not) as in general a beneficial environment for child-rearing, and have reservations about alternatives such as residential care; although some role for the latter may be acknowledged.

## POINTS OF DIVERGENCE BETWEEN THE FOUR PERSPECTIVES

Having indicated these basic points of convergence between the four perspectives, the discussion will now focus on how the perspectives diverge.

## Perspectives in child care policy

### (a) *The understanding of child welfare*

Firstly, as will be apparent, the understanding of the child's welfare, of in what that welfare consists, is different. The first, *laissez-faire* perspective sees psychological parenthood, undisturbed by intrusions from outside except in extreme cases, as of most benefit to the child. This creates a sense of security and commitment and the opportunity for appropriate relationships to develop. The third, pro-birth parent perspective takes a similar approach but places more value on *biological* parent-child bonds, and envisages the parent-child unit as supported and helped from outside, not just when extremely vulnerable or on the verge of crisis, but at a much lower threshold of need; indeed, in this view, child welfare would be served if society through government extended more help to families with young children in general. While the first perspective stresses certainty, permanence, and a stable bond with a single set of parent figures, the third finds the child's interacting with a number of parent figures more acceptable, indeed often desirable – so the long-term foster child, for example, would usually benefit from contact with birth parents even if they are unlikely to resume full-time care. The second, child protectionist perspective, by contrast, sees child welfare as consisting of receiving the best possible care – as this is construed – which is not necessarily supplied by the original biological or psychological parents. Good care provided by devoted adoptive or foster parents is often preferable to the child's remaining with her early caretakers; the supporters of the protection position would be more prepared to cut early bonds in the interests of better quality care, and in so doing would give a higher profile to the decisions of professionals and experts as to whose care is preferable. Compulsory intervention to this end is seen as justified. But the first and second perspectives broadly concur on the need for any switch to a new caretaker to be final; 'permanence' must be established in the new home; and the child usually fares best if the original parent figures are excluded. The fourth, child liberation perspective takes the view that the child's welfare consists of maximising the child's freedom, including the freedom to choose her own guardians. Whether 'permanence' is more important than retaining contact with more than one home/switching between homes, whether the blood tie is more important than psychological bonds, whether a change of home should only take place in cases of extreme bad care – these issues tend not to be tackled directly by liberationist writing, but would presumably be for the child herself to decide.

The view of the child's welfare is dependent on various underlying ideas and assumptions mainly to do with child psychology. Differences open up as to the child's perceived degree of attachment to neglectful original parents; the child's capacity to relate to more than one set of parent figures; the strength of early bonds and memories; the importance of birth and genetic links; the effects of uncertainty and ambiguity; the effect on the child of intervention in the family by outside experts; the effect on the child of changing her home; and the extent to which children can be generalised about at all. Underlying these questions are perhaps three key issues. One concerns the nature of attachment; the second the importance of self-image; and the third the need to look at individual cases individually.

The first problem concerns to what extent attachment is formed in conditions of poor care, the dangers of disrupting attachment, and to what extent attachment needs to be *exclusive* to one parent or co-habiting pair of parents. Also, does intervention from outside and a change of home, or the threat of these things, seriously weaken attachment in a way which is damaging to the child? Secondly, the issue of self-image is important in considering knowledge of and contact with the birth family, and perception of why a breach with the birth family has taken place; are children damaged by loss of genetic links, or a negative view of their origins, even when they receive good care and become attached in other homes? The third point serves as a reminder that children are individuals and psychological theory cannot fully predict the effects of particular steps in every individual case; it is necessary, to some extent, to look at each child as unique and to absorb what *she* appears to be telling us.

## (b) *The view of the family*

A second area of divergence concerns how the family is perceived. The third perspective is the one most obviously concerned about the preservation of the family in a biological or kinship sense. This may include other relatives as well as the parent-child nuclear unit; for example, a respondent reported in Fox's article talked of children having a right to their own family 'and that doesn't just mean parents, it means grandparents, people who can talk to them about their past, the past of the family'. Kinship is seen as of great psychological benefit to individuals; and in this approach the parents' needs and rights are weighted and valued as well as those of the children. Although, as indicated earlier, the rationale for emphasising birth and biological bonds *per se*, does not seem fully worked out, it appears to be partly to do with a healthy sense of identity and with what is socially regarded as 'normal'. Children who have lost their original family suffer, in this view; and the parents' suffering in losing their children is also given some weight.

The first and second perspectives set greater store by relationships based on actual psychological interaction of a positive kind, rather than the blood tie. This position is most fully worked out in Goldstein *et al.*'s writings, the arguments being largely derived from psychoanalytic theory. In their view, as attachment grows out of relationship, interaction, and day-to-day care, it is the *psychological* parent figure who is important. When the biological parent is *not* also the psychological parent, she diminishes in importance, indeed may be of no consequence for the child. However, the proponents of the *third* perspective might also draw on psychoanalytic theory to support their view that the primary bond with the birth parents, when they *were* also the psychological parents, can only be severed at great cost to the child. The dispute arises over how worthy of preservation birth families as such are in the face of poor quality care, weak or non-existent actual relationships, or the disruption of relationships. The second perspective falls broadly into line with the first in advocating the superiority of good 'psychological families' to poor birth ones, but is readier than the first to attempt to create new families based on psychological bonds. These would be adoptive or secure foster homes probably without contact with the original family. All of these three perspectives, however, as mentioned earlier, see some form of nuclear family structure as appropriate for the care of children and are generally wary about alternatives such as residential care. The children's rights perspective, by contrast, has doubts about the nuclear family structure itself; but it must be said that their view of alternatives is not very fully worked through. However, Holt thinks that children need 'extended families' (networks of adults) and does propose some possibilities such as groups, communities and organisations where 'young people could live under the loose supervision of some older people who would be responsible for them'. These group settings would need to be small and informal. Children are also seen as having the right to go and live in other households if they wish and the adults there accept them – presumably in nuclear families other than their own. The children's rights perspective does not value any family structure for its own sake, however, but values what children choose for themselves.

In summary, then, differences exist between the perspectives as to whether families should be construed primarily in biological or psychological terms, as to how easy it is to create or recreate families, and, to some extent, on the primary importance of the nuclear parent-child unit.

(c) *The origins of child care problems*

Related to the differences in the perception of the family are differences of view over the origins of family malfunctioning, problems in families, and poor parenting and inadequate child care. For most writers supporting the first and second value perspectives, problems in families and unsatisfactory care of the children are seen as rooted largely in the parents' own psychological history. In particular, those who have not experienced the right kind of psychological parenting and good care themselves have a weak chance of becoming effective parents in their turn; there is thus a cyclical character to poor parenting. Treatment, therapy, social work and so on, might help, but, particularly for the second perspective, damaged parents are usually better replaced by psychologically healthier ones. The loss they might experience in having their children permanently removed must be offset against the prevention of further poor parenting by those children in the future. Young and immature parents may also be seen as a factor predisposing to poor child-rearing. In other words, it is factors relating to parents as individuals which are significant in child care matters.

For the third, pro-kinship school of thought, family and parenting problems are to a much greater extent due to external material circumstances such as poverty, environmental stress, and the inadequate provision of services. Parenting behaviour is altered by resources and the opportunities and life chances available and arising from external factors like social class and geographical area, rather than stemming from parents' own psychology. The lack of child care resources in the home and lack of stimulation, arising from low income, poor housing conditions and deprived neighbourhoods, constitute one type of pressure here, which might lead to child care being so poor that the family is separated. Psychological/behavioural and material factors are seen to interact. So Holman draws on research to show the psychological effects of poverty – lowered self-respect and self-image; and cites data showing two contrasting reactions to this: withdrawal and aggression.[12] Both of these may have an adverse effect on child care. And it is the poor whose children disproportionately come to the attention of child care agencies. Holman stresses that poor parents may well share the child care values and objectives of the wider society, but are prevented from achieving them by depriving environments. Parents are thus seen as less culpable in this perspective. Construing bad parenting in terms of personal indaequacy, as the first and second perspectives would do, may be seen from this viewpoint as 'blaming the victim'.

In the fourth perspective, the origins of unsatisfactory child-rearing are relatively unexplored, although it should be noted that Freeman shares many perceptions with Holman and the birth parent school.[13] The more radical children's rights proponents are aware of the way that the adult world *in general* treats children badly, but the reasons for this are not it seems enquired into in any depth.

As the causes of poor child care are construed differently, the remedies are seen differently too. In the first perspective, child removal is justified only when standards are extremely bad; certainly in the Goldstein view, little else is offered. For the child protectionists both help to the individual family experiencing problems and removal of the child to another home might be appropriate at different times and in different cases, but the emphasis would be more on the latter. For the birth parent defenders, the remedies involve help to vulnerable families, reducing social deprivation, and helping families with children more generally. Appropriate means would include child day care, financial support, and community action by groups of parents. Removal is not excluded but is given a lower profile. Loosely speaking, for the proponents of the third perspective, 'prevention is better than cure' (and is presumed possible). The children's rights authors seem to look again to removal of the child to a better home environment – but to self-removal rather than compulsory powers exercised by the state.

These different perspectives on the response to poor child care are linked with different perspectives on the role of the state, as will be shown in the next section.

### (d) *The role of the state*
A number of differences between the four perspectives are found here. In their general view of the state the first three perspectives differ markedly from each other. In the *laissez-faire* school of thought a minimal state is favoured; the state's role in child care is marginal in the sense that it is confined to severe cases, although the state should have very extensive powers *in those cases*. However, exercise of the power to remove the child to, and establish him in, an alternative home, although a strong power for the state, would mostly be followed by withdrawal – the new home having similar autonomy from external intrusion to the first. For the paternalists the state should have a much wider and more controlling role, intervening by compulsion in families on a much greater scale and at a much lower threshold of mistreatment; so in this perspective the state is anything but minimal and may indeed be seen as an over-authoritarian institution in relation

to families. Neveretheless its interventions are still individualised, focused on particular families and children rather than concerned with widespread family support. In the third perspective the state's role is seen as wider yet less authoritarian. The state should be concerned with providing for the welfare of children across a broad front through various supportive services offered on a voluntary basis; but it should use its coercive powers of child removal *less*. This is broadly consonant with notions of the 'Welfare State'.

The position of the fourth, children's rights perspective is of interest particularly because, starting from totally different arguments, it comes to resemble the first perspective. In this view the state should take drastic steps to alter the conditions of childhood so as to make it more like the status of adulthood; such legal changes must then be enforced and upheld; but otherwise the state's role reverts largely to *laissez-faire*, with children enjoying adult rights such as the franchise but apparently no compulsory education, no legal restrictions on child labour, no juvenile justice system, or child protection system backed by the law. The law would not discriminate between adults and children; it was shown in discussing this perspective how this seems to return us, in some respects, to an early nineteenth-century type of *laissez-faire*.

It is the second and third value perspectives which have the most optimistic view of what the state can achieve in the field of child welfare: the paternalists have considerable faith in the decision-making power of courts and social workers, and in the capacities of substitute parents, while the birth parent defenders have faith in the possibilities of broader child policy, preventive and rehabilitative work. The first and fourth perspectives are more sceptical about the state: for the minimalists the law is a clumsy instrument incapable of supervising complex parent-child relationships, while for the children's rights supporters, the state like individual adults may get in the way of the child's liberty. For both perspectives, in attempting to improve things for children the state may often in fact make things worse.

The perspectives also differ in how they see the details of state intervention in child care. Some of these differences, relating to removal versus help and prevention, were suggested in the last section when looking at the remedies for poor child care. Two further aspects will be mentioned briefly. The first relates to adoption. The first two perspectives look on adoption as a solution to the problems of inadequate child care much more favourably than the third; in particular, the legal security of adoption is seen as a positive point. To some extent the advocates of adoption can draw on research to

211

support their position. The pro-birth family school, however, tend to have two kinds of reservation about adoption, one relating to the effects of social class and the other to the *long*-term effects on the child. It may be that if social class is accounted for, and the long-term effects are looked at, adoption *per se* is not the superior form of child care that it appears to be. The second aspect relates to foster care, and has already been touched on in discussing differences over child welfare and child psychology. The divergence of view is basically over whether foster care should resemble adoption or birth family care, on the 'exclusive' model, or whether it should be seen more as a partial and temporary quasi-parent-child relationship which is open to contact with the birth parents and eventual return to them. Broadly, *laissez-faire* and paternalism support the first approach and the kinship school the second. While the children's rights perspective tends not to tackle this sort of issue directly, it would seem not to support exclusive parent-child bonds of any kind.

The differences between the perspectives on the child care role of the state connect with their wider views on society and social problems. These will be discussed separately, but firstly a short detour will be taken into the question of how the four perspectives view the concept of rights.

## (e) *The concept of rights*

The four perspectives have different implicit or explicit approaches to the issue of rights in the child care field. It is in the third and fourth perspectives that the term is most likely to be explicitly used. Some supporters of the birth parent school may raise *parents'* rights as a specific issue; for example, the National Council for One Parent Families did so in opposing the assumption of these rights by a mere resolution and calling into question whether this procedure was compatible with notions of 'natural justice'.[14] The fourth perspective, clearly, makes extensive use of the concept of children's rights, defining these as rights of self-determination and essentially the same as adult rights. However, it may be noted that the second, child protection position may also argue in terms of children's rights, although the rights referred to are to nurturance and care, not to autonomy. The moderate children's rights author Freeman occupies a mid-way position. Both the second and fourth perspectives give a very weak weighting to parents' rights. Finally, Goldstein *et al.* are advocating a model of intervention which in effect shows a strong respect for parents' rights, but their argument is advanced chiefly in terms of what is best for the *child*. This is also the case with much of the pro-parent writing – parental control is seen as better for the child; at the same time the distinction between what is in the interests of the *child* and what is in the interests of the *parent* can be somewhat blurred.

The notion of rights thus occupies an ambiguous role in this debate. Conflicting rights are recognised to a degree; arguments may be advanced in terms of rights but are often put in other terms which overlook rights; the concept of rights is given different meanings; and there is perhaps a (probably well-founded) reluctance to understand the child care debate primarily in these terms. At the same time the notion of rights – both parents' and children's – cannot be altogether ignored. Other rights may also complicate the issue – for example, those of substitute parents and of the state.

### (f) *The view of society and social problems*

A final important area of divergence concerns the broader social and political philosophy underlying the four perspectives. A crucial aspect of this is the awareness of social divisions, class and power as significant dimensions to the child care role of the state. It is the third perspective which is most aware of these. Parents who come into contact with child care agencies are seen to be of low social class and in a weak power position; and their child care problems are seen as originating in factors connected with social class. Social workers, judges, magistrates, and often substitute parents too, occupy a higher and more powerful class position, and apply middle-class or upper-class values and norms to child care problems. The result is a class-loaded system in which the poor are at much greater risk than others of losing their children – to higher class homes. Inadequate *middle*-class parents suffer less visibility, are less likely to become the object of the child care actions of the state, and have a wider range of private child care options open to them. Ethnicity is also a factor which operates in the system in a similar way. Preferred solutions to this bias in child care are basically an extension of the Welfare State and a reduction in inequality. This *is* perceived as possible within the framework of a capitalist society (despite the problems seen as generated by such a society). The position may thus usefully be classed as a moderately left-wing view of society and social problems.

By contrast to the child protectionist standpoint, birth parents appear to have too much rather than too little power, and often stand in the way of the best solution for the child. While not totally unaware of the impact of class and racial factors, the supporters of this position see the first priority as the child, in the sense that the best care must be achieved for her now, regardless of the structural antecedents of the problem. As has been suggested, the second perspective, in attempting to be non-political, perhaps only succeeds in being politically naive. Child care problems and solutions are construed largely in personal terms. The social structure is only weakly related to individuals' problems, and is not challenged. The preferred solution is not only individualised but essentially one of social control, and may be seen as treating symptoms while overlooking causes. The state is seen as politically neutral and benign, and its agents as 'a politically neutral expert elite and as legitimate decision-makers in the lives of citizens'.[15]

Interestingly, the first, *laissez-faire* perspective is aware of the class and ethnic element in child placement decisions, and uses this as one argument for minimising state intrusion in families. In many ways, however, a *laissez-faire* stance on child care connects with a right-wing view of a minimal state in general. The approach of Goldstein *et al.* would surely be congenial to a right-wing government which wished to roll back the state, curtail public expenditure, and uphold the traditional and self-contained family as a value. The Goldstein perspective legitimates all of these things. Yet Morris *et al.* and Taylor *et al.* challenge state intervention from a left-wing position. This confusion is compounded by considering the child liberation perspective. While Freeman concurs with the left-wing family defenders at many points, Holt, Farson and Franklin, it is suggested, are essentially advocating an anarchist solution which might also be attractive to a right-wing position favouring less state expenditure on welfare and a cheap and biddable labour force. The liberationists, it will be remembered, see oppression and powerlessness in terms of age rather than class. The solution is largely to emancipate children from dependency by giving them adult rights; and in their scenario much state machinery could be dismantled. The provision of a guaranteed income, it is true, *would* be expensive for government and would be quite incompatible with a right-wing market-oriented approach. But the children's rights proponents' emphasis on independence, on the adverse effects of paternalism, protection and help, uncomfortably echoes some extreme right-wing propaganda.

In conclusion, of the four perspectives outlined in this book, only one, the pro-parent position, can be clearly located within a political framework, and even this has its own inbuilt contradictions. Both the first and fourth perspectives might be convenient for right-wing governments but cannot be unequivocally aligned with the right. The paternalists, presumably, belong somewhere in the political centre, but are somewhat detached from a broader political debate.

## A FINAL COMMENT

This chapter has attempted to outline both the convergences and divergences between the four child care perspectives. Two additional general points may also be made. Firstly, there are differences in degree of empirical support for the four perspectives. The paternalist and pro-family positions appear to be better supported by reference to studies of child welfare and the child care role of the state than the other two. However, this is not necessarily to denigrate the *laissez-faire* and children's rights perspectives; and this leads to the second point, which concerns the quality of the argument. Goldstein *et al.* achieve some stature by their link with the respected body of theory associated with psychoanalysis, and have much to say on child psychology which is of great value (in particular, on the child's sense of time). But it is the arguments of the children's rights school, including Freeman, which the author personally finds most formidable (while not altogether agreeing with them). Holt, perhaps, is a lightweight, but the originality of his ideas still deserves close scrutiny. Franklin and Freeman present the greatest intellectual challenge. And if the rights perspective does nothing else, it compels us to re-examine our attitude to children in a fundamental way.

## NOTES AND REFERENCES

1.  R. Dingwall *et al.* 1983 *The Protection of Children* Chapter 2, footnote 3.
2.  M. D. A. Freeman 1983 *The Rights and Wrongs of Children* Chapter 2, footnote 45.
3.  A. Morris *et al.* 1980 *Justice for Children* Chapter 2, footnote 6.
4.  L. Taylor *et al.* 1980 *In Whose Best Interests?* Chapter 2, footnote 8.
5.  J. Goldstein, A. Freud and A. Solnit 1973, 1979 *Beyond the Best Interests of the Child* Chapter 2, footnote 4; 1980 *Before the Best Interests of the Child* Chapter 1, footnote 3.
6.  L. M. Fox 1982 'Two Value Positions' Foreword, footnote 1.
7.  B. Holman 1988 *Putting Families First* Chapter 4, footnote 11.
8.  R. Walton 1976 'The best interests of the child' *British Journal of Social Work* 6(3) 307–313.
9.  B. Tizard 1977 *Adoption* Chapter 3, footnote 11.
10. See Chapter 3, footnote 23.

11. See Chapter 3, footnote 15.
12. Holman refers to Haggerstrom: W. Haggerstrom 1964 'The power of the poor' in Ed. F. Riesman *Mental Health of the Poor* New York, Collier-Macmillan.
13. M. D. A. Freeman 1983 *The Rights and Wrongs of Children* Chapter 2, footnote 45. In Chapter 5 of Freeman's book particularly.
14. NCOPF 1982 *Against Natural Justice* Chapter 3, footnote 38.
15. See footnote 6.

# CHAPTER SEVEN
# *Law, policy and practice: an uneasy synthesis*

This book has outlined four different value perspectives on child care law and policy which, while sharing certain ideas in common, take different views of child welfare, the family, the origins of child care problems, the role of the state, the concept of rights, and society and social problems. While each perspective has a degree of internal coherence, and while each may be identified as influential in actual policy and practice at different times and in different places, the 'real world' of such policy and practice, it is argued, always represents an uneasy and incoherent synthesis of views. That is, the perspectives are not found in practice in anything like their pure forms, notwithstanding the broad prominence of particular perspectives at times. Many factors influence the movements in *actual* policies. Among these, nevertheless, are swings in professional and pressure group thinking which may correspond to the perspectives which have been outlined.

Such broad swings in thinking may be more apparent with hindsight than when considering contemporary and very recent change. For example, it is now fairly easy to identify the 1960s in England and Wales as the 'prevention' decade when policy and social work practice favoured supporting the natural family and minimising time in care, and the 1970s as the time of 'child protection' spurred on by concern about child abuse. There may be a tendency to oversimplify the past, however. It is perhaps because the 1980s – at the time of writing – were not yet over, that it seemed harder to generalise about this decade. At the same time, it is submitted that the 1980s in England and Wales were genuinely a time of polarisation, of contrasts, and of greater tensions and conflicts in child care policy.

This concluding chapter will attempt to accomplish two tasks.

Firstly, the chief factors which seem to be influential in determining the shifting nature of child care policy will be outlined. Secondly, a brief attempt will be made to analyse English child care policy in the 1980s in the light of the four value perspectives. The brevity and superficiality of this account of the 1980s is acknowledged; this complex decade merits a far fuller treatment as an exercise in its own right. This brief account may however illustrate the extent to which the world of *actual* policy always represents an 'uneasy synthesis' of views.

# FACTORS INFLUENCING LAW, POLICY AND PRACTICE

The following four broad areas are suggested as significant:

Scandals and enquiries and the response
Interest groups and their thinking
Reviews of legislation and policy
Wider policies and changes

## (a) *Scandals and enquiries and the response*

It is impossible to overlook the impact of individual cases which achieve 'scandal' status, on the development of child care policy, and difficult to overestimate their importance in English policy in the 1970s and 1980s. Even as far back as 1870, the case of Margaret Waters, a private foster mother or 'baby farmer' executed for the death of one of the neglected infants in her care, caused a wave of public consternation and prompted the infant life protection movement to press for legislative change to regulate private boarding out.[1] It was a scandal case, that of the foster child Dennis O'Neill, followed by a government enquiry,[2] which was one factor in the post-War realisation that the child care service was in urgent need of reform. Most famous of all scandal cases, perhaps, is that of Maria Colwell of 1973,[3] which was followed by a public enquiry and much media coverage hostile to social workers. In the fifteen years 1972–87 there were no fewer than 34 enquiries,[4] some public, some held in private, into deaths of children known to Social Services Departments. Most of these produced recommendations relating to the law, policy and practice. Among these cases the most well-known are probably a cluster in the mid-1980s – Jasmine Beckford, Tyra Henry, and Kimberley

Carlile; the latest scandal case at the time of writing was Doreen Mason (1987).[5]

Three points may be made about the significance of scandal cases, the enquiries into them, the reports, and the media and public response. The first is the degree to which blame for the child's death is popularly apportioned to the child care agencies of the state rather than the actual killer of the child. The second concerns the determinants of public response to such child deaths and to the responsibility for them. The third point concerns the perception of such child deaths as preventable through the manipulation of the state's response.

Firstly, cases in the 1970s and 1980s have been marked by criticisms of the social workers deemed responsible for the care of the child at the time of her death, and also seen as largely responsible for not preventing the death. These workers have been publicly pilloried in the popular press with headlines such as 'They Killed the Child I Adored'[6] and 'Kimberley: Social Workers Failed her and the System Doomed her to die'.[7] The Social Services Director in the Beckford case – herself exonerated by the inquiry report – had to remind herself that she did not kill Jasmine, Morris Beckford did. Criticisms were based on the view – blindingly obvious with hindsight, but often only with hindsight – that the child victim should not have been left with, or returned to, the birth parent. That is, social workers were castigated for not being firm and authoritative enough in relation to birth parents and children at risk. (A reversal of this type of criticism was found in the suspected sex abuse cases in the county of Cleveland in 1987 – not involving child deaths, but also the subject of an inquiry and report[8] – where social workers were portrayed by the press as over-zealous, as brutally removing children from their parents when there were no good grounds for doing so. These cases were an important influence on the emergency protection provisions in the Children Act 1989.) The issue raised here revolves round the location of blame in those state agents responsible for child protection – almost to the exclusion of the actual killer of the child. It is rather as though doctors were blamed for every death of a patient known to them.

A second and related point of significance is *why* the public response to children killed by their caretakers should have been as intense as it was, and should have taken the form it did. An often mentioned comment is that child cruelty and child murder are hardly historically new phenomenon, yet it is in the years since the 1960s, when the phenomenon of 'baby-battering' was identified, that the public and the media have been highly sensitised to the occurrence of child abuse, and much publicity has been given to discoveries of individual severe abuse cases where social workers were involved. It is not clear whether in fact the incidence of serious abuse has increased or merely that there is more awareness of it. In any event, the degree and nature of social concern, sometimes even seen as a 'moral panic',[9] requires explanation. Parton[10] is one writer who has set this trend in context – that of a more generalised anxiety about the family and the social order. Another aspect of the context is a general attack on the public sector in the 1980s.[11] Child abuse enquiries have apparently provided a useful weapon with which to attack one of the least popular groups of public servant. Of interest here also is the much lower profile given to children killed by foster and adoptive parents, than those killed by birth and step-parents.[12] The significance of this distinction must be left to speculation at this point however.

Thirdly, there is the assumption that severe child abuse and deaths from abuse *can* be prevented – by more vigilant social work, by changing the emphasis in social work, by changing the law, by improving training, and so on. Recommendations from inquiry reports assume that steps can be taken to reduce the danger of similar cases occurring again. There are problems with this assumption. Firstly, expectations of social workers are contradictory (as comparison of the child death cases and the Cleveland cases makes clear). Secondly, the crucial issue of resources in child care work is often not adequately tackled.[13] Thirdly, it may reasonably be argued that because of the complexity and unpredictability of human behaviour, no child care agency or child care law can ever completely eliminate severe abuse. Nevertheless, policy and practice have been subject to numerous changes because of scandal cases and their effects.

## (b) *Interest groups and their thinking*
A second factor in policy is the influence of relevant interest groups such as professional and pressure groups. These groups are themselves influenced by research, practice experience and ongoing discussion, and by the particular interests they represent, as well as by the scandal cases mentioned and the policy reviews and wider changes to be discussed below. From time to time new pressure groups appear, such as Justice for Children and the Family Rights Group in the late 1970s, and Parents Against Injustice (PAIN),[14] the Children's Legal Centre, and the Family Courts Campaign[15] in the 1980s. The thinking of certain groups may be broadly aligned with particular perspectives outlined in this book – for example, the British Agencies for Adoption and Fostering has been broadly identified with the

protectionist, 'permanency' position, and the National Council for One Parent Families with the pro-parent view. The social work profession as expressed in the British Association of Social Workers has been, certainly at one time, associated with a position sympathetic to natural parents and preventive work;[16] although the effect of child abuse enquiries on the social work profession should not be underestimated. These have resulted in great anxiety surrounding child abuse work, and some defensive practice. Finally, professional and pressure group thinking is subject to changing trends or, to put it more derogatorily, 'fashions'. As has been suggested, in the 1960s the 'fashion', broadly speaking, was in favour of natural families and preventive work, and in the 1970s, protection and permanency. It may be that each swing of thinking sets in train its own backlash, giving rise to a 'pendulum' effect.

Interest groups and their thinking may have both a direct and indirect influence on policy and practice – a direct influence on individual decisions and practice at the micro level; and an indirect influence in so far as they feed into the policy-making process at higher levels.

### (c) *Reviews of legislation and policy*

Apart from reports of individual case inquiries set up by government, other government documents which review child care policy in general are clearly influential. One category of review is the report of a government committee set up for a specific purpose. In the recent history of English child care policy three reports stand out – the Curtis Committee report, on children in public care (1946),[17] the Ingleby Committee report, focusing on delinquency and child neglect and their prevention (1960),[18] and the Houghton Committee report, initially on adoption, but coming to include fostering, and children in care (1972).[19] The three reports laid the foundations of the 1948, 1963 and 1975 Acts respectively. Their significance lay, broadly, in the construction of a new and better quality service for children in the care of the state (Curtis), the introduction of preventive powers to act on family breakdown, child neglect and delinquency (Ingleby), and the granting of greater powers of child protection (Houghton).

Another type of report is that of a standing body such as the All-Party Parliamentary Select Committee on Social Services (known for a time as the Short Committee), whose report on children in care in 1984[20] was influential in the setting up of the review of legislation which eventually led to the Children Act 1989. This review of legislation also demonstrates the influence of reviews and reports in the policy-making process. Consultation papers were issued in 1985 by an Inter-Departmental Working Party of civil servants set up immediately after the Short Report to look at options for the codification and amendment of the law. These papers formed the basis for further consultatiion, for costing, and for a White Paper on child care law and family services published in 1987.[21]

At a later stage of policy-making, White Papers prepare the way for legislation but are also part of the process of consultation. In the 1960s two White Papers on juvenile delinquency[22] – the first of which met with considerable opposition – fed into the process which eventually produced the Children and Young Persons Act 1969. The 1987 White Paper just mentioned formed, after more consultation, the basis for the Children Act 1989.

Another category of government document which may be mentioned here consists of regulations, circulars, notes of guidance, and codes of practice. These may lack the legal standing of Acts of Parliament, but have considerable force in policy nevertheless. Examples would be a code of practice issued in 1984 on access to children in care, and a circular in the same year on the passing of parental rights resolutions.[23] Also worthy of mention are reports by non-governmental respected bodies such as the Law Commission. The latter has reported on aspects of private child care law such as illegitimacy and custody after divorce.[24] Law Commission recommendations were incorporated into the Children Act 1989.

### (d) *Wider policies and changes*

Two aspects of wider change which impinge on child care policy can be referred to. Firstly, there are other aspects of government policy. One important aspect comprises government approaches to public expenditure in general and social expenditure in particular. Pressure on resources and the search for cheaper solutions have a long-standing history in the field of child care policy, and both foster care and prevention have at times been identified as means of reducing costs.[25] Where governments seek to reduce state welfare spending in general, social work as a relatively expensive form of labour might be expected to be under scrutiny;[26] but the pressure of public interest in child protection makes it difficult for even an avowedly expenditure-cutting government directly and obviously to reduce work in the child care field. *Indirect* curbs, however, may stem from reductions in local authority spending in general, adversely affecting child care services unless local authorities choose to divert resources from other areas of work. Other relevant aspects of government policy include policies in the field of health care, social security, education, and housing. Many policies here may be said to have implications, short and long term, direct and indirect, for child welfare and child care problems. A useful example of the intersection of policies in different areas is provided by homelessness. Affected by policies in both the income maintenance and housing fields, homelessness can have severe effects on the health and welfare of children – if families, for example, sleep rough, take refuge in grossly inadequate or overcrowded conditions, or are housed in squalid and dangerous 'bed and breakfast' hotels. Some children come into the care of the state solely because of homelessness.[27]

More generally, government policy on welfare sets the context and general climate of thinking surrounding child care policy. This is usefully illustrated by contrasting the situation in the late 1940s and in the 1980s in England and Wales. In the late 1940s newly popular collectivist ideas on welfare spread their influence to child care, where a much wider concept of state responsibility for children developed than had been accepted in the past. By the 1980s, although major Welfare State institutions were still in place, there was apparently an end to the post-War 'consensus' on a major state role, and prevalent 'new right' ideologies favoured free market economics, the reduction of the state's role in welfare, and the encouragement of independence from the state, of private and voluntary sector alternatives to state provision, and of family care. This was a totally different climate, and logically would not have supported a major state role in child care. However, the effect, as will be shown, was ambiguous, and actual policy did not take the *laissez-faire* form which might have been expected from the ideology.

The other aspect of wider change which is significant for child care concerns wider economic and social change, including levels of prosperity, poverty, unemployment, and demographic change. To take two examples from the 1970s and 1980s: increased unemployment and changing family patterns both have profound implications for child care within families and thus for demands on the state child care system. Unemployment has been shown to impose strains, both psychological and financial, on families, and there appears to be an association – though probably not a straightforward causal relation – between unemployment and referrals to child care agencies.[28] The poverty associated with unemployment itself causes child care problems, if the proponents of the third value perspective are correct. Secondly, changes in families connected with the increased incidence of marital breakdown and its consequences are significant – particularly more lone parent (usually mother-headed) families, and more 'reconstituted' or step-families often comprising a birth mother and 'step-father'. Lone parent families in general experience social, financial and work-related problems, and their children are disproportionately likely to enter care;[29] reconstituted families often have severe problems of internal relationships[30] while the prominence of 'step-father' figures in notorious child death cases has been notable.[31] Another family trend has been an increasing proportion of children born to lone mothers, and in cohabiting partnerships which may have less stability even than marriage.[32] Other factors in late post-War society which may be mentioned include smaller families, changes in sexual mores, changing gender roles and the influence of feminism, increasing demands on the 'middle' generations by the elderly, the demands from vulnerable and dependent groups discharged from hospitals into society at large, ethnic and cultural diversity, inner city decline, the increase of indebtedness as a pattern of life, and the very pace of social and economic change itself. Many change factors could be listed, and no doubt the reader has her own list of those to be considered the most significant. The relationship of all these variables to child care problems and the need for state intervention is complex, not clearcut; but the general point is that child care problems and the response to them do not arise in a social vacuum.

## ENGLISH CHILD CARE POLICY IN THE 1980S – THE UNEASY SYNTHESIS

To illustrate the extent to which actual policy is a pragmatic response reflecting a number of different, often conflicting positions, a brief account will be given of the 1980s in the light of *laissez-faire*, paternalism, the support of the family, and children's rights. The questions of conflict and balance will be briefly highlighted.

### (a) *Laissez-faire*
As already suggested, less has been seen of *laissez-faire* in English child care policy in the 1980s than might be expected from the government's declared ideology (or from the ideology of family 'traditionalists' like the Conservative Family Campaign). Rigid time limits after which a child must be returned to his family or adopted were not imposed, or at least not at a national level; the legal grounds for compulsory intervention were not clearly defined more narrowly as *laissez-faire* would require; the state did not withdraw from all but the most

extreme cases; children were not all cut off from their family of origin after a change of home. Certainly, 'permanency' continued to be generally favoured (although with greater grounds for doubt emerging towards the end of the decade[33]); but permanency, as said before, can also be associated with the second, protectionist perspective or, if return to the birth family is preferred, with the third, pro-parent view. Interestingly, while effecting swingeing reductions in local authorities' powers in almost every other field, central government in England in the 1980s did *not* attempt to remove from local authorities the primary responsibility for child care and protection work.

One way, however, in which *laissez-faire* did manifest itself was in certain provisions of the Children Act 1989 (Section 1), which set out the principle of 'non-intervention' in both public and private law. The principle stated that a court should not make an order regarding a child unless it considered it better for the child than making no order at all. This would mean, for example, that in matrimonial cases parents' arrangements would not automatically be judged by the court, and in care proceedings a Care Order would not automatically be made just because the statutory criteria were made out.

## (b) *Child protection and state paternalism*

While the 1970s in England and Wales have been shown to be the decade in which paternalism in its modern form made the greatest strides, in the 1980s the paternalist and protectionist approach was still influential, especially after the cluster of publicised child abuse cases and the enquiries into them in the middle of the decade – Beckford, Henry and Carlile.

The major legislative event of the decade was the Children Act 1989, which as, indicated, was the fruit of a lengthy period of preparation including the appearance of consultation documents and a White Paper. It was intended partly to clarify and codify a vast amount of fragmented legislation which had grown up in a confusing and incremental way. This Act contained *both* protectionist and pro-parent elements: it is the protectionist sections which will be considered here.

One change which may be seen as a step towards greater protection was a widening in the grounds for care proceedings: these now included *likely* significant harm to the child as well as such harm already inflicted (under Section 31). Where a Care Order was made, it would mean that mostly children would indeed be *in* care; the local authority would receive them into care (Sections 22 and 33). If a Supervision Order were made, it would give the social worker greater authority (Section 35). Another change was that the child's welfare should be the *paramount* consideration in court proceedings relating to a child's upbringing (Section 1); under the preceding legislation welfare was only the *first* consideration – not quite as strongly put.[34] An extension of local authority powers to care for and assist older 'children' – even up to the age of 21 – under Sections 20 and 24, might be seen as a further expression of paternalism, and Section 20 in some respects was wider than previous provisions for 'voluntary' care, and did not include a reference to returning children to their parents (this responsibility being placed only in a Schedule to the Act). Another change, which may suggest a fundamental shift in ideology and emphasis, was that parents were no longer defined as having 'rights' but 'responsibilities' (Sections 2 and 3). The Act thus underlined parenthood as a duty to care, although it also conferred the authority and power to do so (Section 3). This is in line with the general paternalist perspective. Another aspect of the Act of interest here is the provision that the Emergency Protection Order – the new shorter order which under Sections 44–8 replaced the old 28 day Place of Safety Order protecting children in an emergency – included a provision for ordering a child's medical examination (Section 44). The EPO was backed up by a Child Assessment Order for non-emergency situations, lasting seven days, and allowing social workers to seek an order for medical assessment (Section 43). Residence Orders (Sections 8–14) also perhaps reflected a protectionist emphasis, in that, for example, foster parents might ensure some security by this means.

As far as social work *practice* in the 1980s was concerned, planning for a permanent home for the child continued to be favoured in general, and it was the early 1980s which saw a considerable shift in this direction in many Departments' practices.[35] The social reaction to child abuse continued to exercise a considerable influence, as has been indicated. Awareness of child sexual abuse expanded, partly influenced by greater openness among women abused as children, partly by developments among paediatricians,[36] and there was more action on this form of abuse by Social Services Departments; however in Cleveland the circumstance of a large number of children being removed compulsorily from their parents in a short time on suspicion of sexual abuse led to something of a public 'backlash' against social workers for being *too* ready to protect, on insufficient evidence. Another practice trend was that foster care became increasingly popular as a form of substitute care, with the percentage of children in care fostered being as high in the mid-1980s as it had been in the early 1960s.[37] Some authorities closed children's homes. This was at least partly linked with a desire to reduce costs. At the same time, however, the total number of adoptions decreased.[38] The percentage of the child population in care also dropped.[39]

Meanwhile, notwithstanding 'traditionalist' defences of conventional family forms, and probably greater scepticism about the 'alternatives' to the nuclear family with which some had experimented in the 1970s, family diversity tended to increase: fewer children spent their entire childhood in the conventional model of a stable nuclear family with breadwinner father and mother at home full time. As indicated earlier, marriages increasingly ended in divorce;[40] more children were born outside marriage, and of these, more it seemed were born in the context of co-habiting relationships.[41] Some women chose to have children alone.[42] The stigma of illegitimacy was all but eliminated.[43] Hence – in part – the lack of babies available for adoption; as a result some infertile couples sought out surrogate mothers to bear children for them instead.[44] Thus, too, perhaps, a greater move to the adoption of children who came into care. Instability in family life might be used to justify a more strongly paternalist role for the state; but another implication of family diversity and change is the calling into question of how far a child can *ever* find permanence. Foster and adoptive families are not necessarily immune to these processes of change.

### (c) *The defence of the birth family*

In the 1980s the pro-birth family position also made its influence felt, although in a slightly different form from the 1960s, with more emphasis on parents' rights, and more action by aggrieved parents and pressure groups to defend these rights. In the early 1980s there was criticism of the administrative procedure used to take over parental rights by committee resolution, with the National Council for One Parent Families claiming that this was a contravention of 'natural justice'.[45] Two private member's bills sponsored by One Parent Families in 1982–3, which would have replaced the resolution procedure by a requirement to apply to the juvenile court for a Care Order, fell; but a circular in 1984[46] extended parents' rights in this procedure slightly by recommending that they be allowed to make representations to committee members. Meanwhile, a Section of the 1983 Health and Social Services and Social Security Adjudications Act (HASSASSA) extended the rights of parents of children in care a little by granting a right of appeal against termination of access to a child in compulsory care. A code of practice on access was also produced by central government.[47] However, the limited nature of the right of appeal, and the tendency for it to be pre-empted in practice by delays before hearings,[48] meant that it only marginally strengthened the power position of parents in relation to the local authority. The HASSASSA also facilitated parental objections in the parental rights resolution procedure by abolishing the provision for parental consent.

The 1980s saw other developments on the parents' rights front, including the formation of self-help groups such as PAIN, and appeals in child care cases to the local government Ombudsman and to the European Court of Human Rights.[49] The mobilisation of parents in the Cleveland sex abuse cases should also not be overlooked. Many fought the local authority's decisions on both the legal and a broader public front – there were wardship cases; some contacted the MP Stuart Bell who, as shown earlier, became very embroiled in the battle on the parents' side; and parents spoke to the media and involved other advocates such as a local clergyman. Some proceeded to sue for the damage they considered had been inflicted on their family life.[50]

The apparently 'pro-family' elements in the 1989 Children Act will now be considered. Firstly, it seemed that local authority 'preventive' powers, and powers of assistance outside the substitute care system, were being extended. Section 17 conferred a duty to safeguard and promote the welfare of children 'in need', and to promote their upbringing by their families, by providing services of various kinds, including, exceptionally, cash. Schedule 2 of the Act set out the details. This provision was broader than the old Section 1 of the 1980 Child Care Act (previously of the 1963 Act), in that the duty was not restricted to the diminishing of the need for children to enter care or go before a court. It therefore became easier to assist families, provided that these provisions were supported by adequate resources. However, the local authority had to consider the means of both parent and child, with an eye to repayment, which might be seen as a drawback from a pro-birth parent perspective. There were also some reservations about the possibly stigmatising connotations of the term 'in need'.[51] Another important development on the 'preventive' side was that health, housing and education authorities were placed under a duty to comply with requests for help from Social Services, if compatible with their own duties and functions (Section 27), and there was more provision for day care under Section 18.

Secondly, both parental rights resolutions and the need for a parent to give 28 days' notice of removal of a child in voluntary care disappeared with this Act. Care for the child – or 'accommodation' as it was now termed – was construed more in terms of partnership with the parents. However, the widened grounds for care proceedings, taking in the risk of harm, could be used to protect a child already in accommodation if the local authority thought a parental removal was inappropriate. Apart from this, the local authority was not usually to provide accommodation if the parent objected, and, in providing accommodation or care, the local authority had to consult the parents (Section 22).

Parental rights of access were further enhanced by the Act, and the shorter Emergency Protection Order might also be seen as a strengthening of parents' rights. Emergency protection (Sections 44–48) was now based on more explicit criteria, and the order lasted for a maximum of eight days rather than 28 (though with the possibility of extension for a further seven), with a right of appeal after three days in some cases (Section 45). The order carried a presumption of reasonable parental 'contact' (Section 44), this concept replacing 'access', and additional orders could be made regarding contact although it could also be refused. The time limit on police emergency protection was also reduced, from eight to three days (Section 46). The provisions helped to satisfy concern about the draconian nature of the former Place of Safety Orders.[52] There were also restrictions on interim Care Orders (Section 38). Where children were under Care Orders, the local authority was to be responsible for promoting reasonable contact with the parents, and the court could also order contact (Section 34). Contact could not be terminated without reference to the court. Under Section 26 a complaints procedure was to be set up by which parents, among others, could complain about the local authority in child care cases.

Local authority use of wardship proceedings was restricted (Section 100), and finally, the rights of unmarried birth fathers were enhanced, in that, for example, the father could obtain parental responsibility either through a court application or formal agreement with the mother (Section 4).

On balance, it appeared that the Children Act, while containing both state paternalist and pro-birth family provisions, leaned more heavily to the latter perspective. At the time of writing, however, it was too early to judge what effect the Act would have in practice. As mentioned, the adequate resourcing of the ostensibly wider powers is a crucial issue. The extra resources required to implement the powers could be considerable.[53]

A few additional points may be made about the pro-birth parent influence in the 1980s. Research evidence cast some doubt on policies of permanence;[54] and 'shared care' with parents was favoured to a greater degree in social work practice.[55] As noted, both adoptions and numbers in care dropped in the 1980s; it was also the case that fewer were in care under Care Orders than in the 1970s.[56]

### (d) *Children's rights and child liberation*

The manifestations of a children's rights perspective in English child care policy in the 1980s, including the relevant changes in the 1989 Act, have already been referred to in discussing the rights perspective in practice in Chapter 5, and the reader is referred back to this section. It will be recalled that signs of responsiveness to this perspective were found in the 1980s in the formation of pressure groups representing children in care, complaints procedures, moves to end corporal punishment, greater scope for children's evidence in court, and the setting up of telephone lines for distressed children; and in the Children Act specifically, in the provisions to pay heed to the child's wishes, extend separate representation for children in court proceedings, enable the child to take certain actions herself, and set up local authority complaints procedures. There were some signs of the liberationist perspective in practice, then, although it cannot be regarded as a dominant viewpoint.

## CONCLUSION: CONFLICT AND BALANCE

The 1980s, as the author has attempted to show, were a period in which both the paternalist and birth parent perspectives were in evidence, while *laissez-faire* and child liberation had a more minor influence. The 1980s appear, at the present moment of hindsight, to be somewhat polarised with no single perspective dominant. Concerns about *both* the child care agents of the state doing too much, too coercively, *and* about them doing too little, too ineffectually, resulted in a wish for legislation and policy to attempt to proceed in two directions at once – both towards better protection of the child and better protection of the parent.

This bi-directional policy may be be expressed in terms of **conflict**, or of **balance**. From one viewpoint, the two broad objectives are in conflict and cannot be realised simultaneously; more power for social workers in relation to children does mean that parents lose some of their rights, in this view. Therefore descriptions of the Children Act 1989 which refer to its providing both better protection for children and greater rights for parents[57] are simply a denial of conflict, an attempt to avoid the awkward dilemmas that the child care field inevitably throws up.

From another viewpoint, however, what legislation and policy is all about here is *balance*. While there are some conflicting objectives, it is argued, a better balance can be achieved. Thus it is reasonable, and not inconsistent, for the Children Act to attempt to proceed in two directions at once, adding to the power of parents here, strengthening the courts and local authorities there. What will be achieved, it may be argued, is not simply a redistribution of muddle but a genuinely more effective balance correcting tendencies both to over- and under-react, while helping parents and children as a unit where it is appropriate to do so.

## NOTES AND REFERENCES

1. See J. S. Heywood 1978 *Children in Care* 95–6. Chapter 3, footnote 49.
2. See Chapter 1, footnote 4.
3. See Chapter 1, footnote 2.
4. According to the Kimberley Carlile report 1987 *A Child in Mind* (Chapter 1, footnote 2) 34 child abuse inquiries had been carried out in the previous 15 years. See also: DHSS 1982 *Child Abuse* Chapter 1, footnote 2.
5. See Chapter 1, footnote 2. Doreen Mason was 16 months old when she was killed by her stepfather in 1987. An inquiry reported to Southwark Social Services Department in July 1989.
6. The headline in *The Sun* referred to Jasmine Beckford. It was placed next to the photograph of the social worker. See: B. Franklin 1989 'Wimps and bullies; press reporting of child abuse' in P. Carter, T. Jeffs and M. Smith (Eds) *The Social Work and Social Welfare Yearbook* 1 Milton Keynes, Open University 6. Similar headlines included 'Social worker lemmings let Jasmine die' *The Daily Telegraph* 3 December 1985; and 'Guilty ones who let Jasmine die' *The Sun* 5 December 1985.
7. *Daily Mail*, reported by M. Fogarty 1987 *Social Work Today* 21 December 1987. Franklin also quotes a headline from *The Star* 'Man who let Kimberley Die'. See B. Franklin 1989 'Wimps and bullies' Footnote 6.
8. See Chapter 1, footnote 6.
9. For the term 'moral panic' see: S. Cohen 1973 *Folk Devils and Moral Panics: The Creation of Mods and Rockers* St Albans, Paladin.
10. N. Parton 1981 'Child Abuse, Social Anxiety and Welfare' and 1985 *The Politics of Child Abuse* Chapter 2, footnote 53.
11. See references on the 'crisis' of the welfare state, chapter 3, footnote 78.
12. Chapter 3, footnote 37.
13. For example, the Kimberley Carlile report 1987 (Chapter 1, footnote 2) put the resource issue outside its remit.

14. PAIN was formed in the early 1980s.
15. The Family Courts Campaign was formed in 1985. See Chapter 2, footnote 7.
16. For example, during the passage of the 1975 Children Act BASW campaigned from a 'preventive' or pro-parent stance. See L. M. Fox 1982 'Two Value Positions' Foreword, footnote 1.
17. Curtis Committee 1946 *Report of the Care of Children Committee* Chapter 4, footnote 86.
18. Ingleby Committee 1960 *Report of the Committee on Children and Young Persons* Chapter 4, footnote 96.
19. Home Office/Scottish Education Department 1972 *Report of the Departmental Committee* Chapter 3, footnote 64.
20. House of Commons 1984 *Children in Care* Chapter 4, footnote 20.
21. White Paper 1987 *The Law on Child Care* Chapter 4, footnote 23.
22. Home Office 1965 *The Child, the Family and the Young Offender* Chapter 4, footnote 102; Home Office 1968 *Children in Trouble* Chapter 4, footnote 102.
23. DHSS 1983 *Code of Practice: Access to Children in Care* London, HMSO; DHSS 1983 LAC Circular on Access: (83)19; DHSS 1984 LAC (84)15.
24. See Chapter 2, footnote 12.
25. See J. Packman 1981 *The Child's Generation* Chapter 3, footnote 60; J. S. Heywood 1978 *Children in Care* Chapter 3, footnote 49.
26. As for example when the then Secretary of State for Health and Social Services, Patrick Jenkin, set up the Barclay Committee to look into the role and tasks of social workers in September 1980.
27. For example, the National Children's Home claimed 600 children in care because of family homelessness, in March 1989; NCH 1989 *Children in Danger – Factfile 1989* London, NCH, as reported in 'NCH report highlights dangers to children' *Social Work Today* 30 March 1989 4.
28. For the effect of unemployment on families and child care, see for example: R. Rapoport 1981 *Unemployment and the Family* London, Family Welfare Association; D. Piachaud 1986 'A Family Problem' *New Society* 13 June 1986; P. R. Jackson and S. Walsh 1987 'Unemployment and the family' in D. Fryer and P. Ullah (Eds) *Unemployed People. Social and Psychological Perspectives* Milton Keynes, Open University Press; J. Popay 1982 *Employment Trends and the Family* London, Study Commission on the Family.
29. See Chapter 4, footnote 34.
30. For reconstituted families, see for example: J. Burgoyne and D. Clark 1982 'Reconstituted Families' in R. Rapoport, M. Fogarty and R. N. Rapoport (Eds) *Families in Britain* London, Routledge Kegan Paul; 286–302.
31. For example, Maria Colwell, Jasmine Beckford, Kimberley Carlile.
32. See Chapter 2, footnote 51. There is some doubt about the long-term stability of these co-habitations. See: A. Spackman 1988 'Why the family is crumbling' Chapter 2, footnote 51.
33. See: J. Thoburn, A. Murdoch and A. O'Brien 1986 *Permanence in Child Care* Oxford, Blackwell. This study of a project run by the Children's Society found that, with some children, the new, permanent' family might need just as much help as the biological one if

placement breakdown was to be avoided. Successful placement required considerable staff input, and finding families and settling children took up to two years. The scheme was a more costly method than had been thought. So 'permanency' is not necessarily a cheap option.

    Meanwhile, an emphasis on 'shared care' was increasingly found in the mid-1980s.

34.   Under the Children Act 1975, Sections 3 and 59, and the Child Care Act 1980 Section 18, for children in care and adoption cases welfare was the *first* consideration. (Under the Guardianship of Minors Act 1971 Section 1, welfare was the *first and paramount* consideration.)

35.   See for example: M. Adcock, R. White and O. Rowlands 1983 *The Administrative Parent* Chapter 3, footnote 20; P. Beresford *et al.* 1987 *In Care in North Battersea* Chapter 4, footnote 27.

36.   The pioneering work of Wynne and Hobbs in Leeds had influenced Higgs and Wyatt, the paediatricians at the centre of the Cleveland controversy 1987. See: C. J. Hobbs and J. Wynne 1986 'Buggery in childhood – a common syndrome in child abuse' *The Lancet* 4 October 1986.

37.   While in 1980 only 37 per cent of children in care were fostered, by 1982 this had risen to 41.6 per cent, by 1984 to 48 per cent, by 1985 to just over 50 per cent, and by 1986 to 52 per cent. Sources: DHSS *Children in Care of Local Authorities Year ending 31st March, England*, various years. London, HMSO; DHSS *Health and Personal Social Services Statistics for England 1987* London, HMSO; See Chapter 3, footnote 60.

38.   The peak year for adoptions was 1968, when there were almost 25,000 adoption orders in England and Wales. By 1974 the number had dropped to 22,500, by 1976 to 17,600, by 1978 to just over 12,000, by 1980 to 10,600, and by 1983 (after a slight revival in 1982) to just over 9,000. The figure was just over 8,600 in 1984 – in other words about a third of its 1968 figure. (It appears that it dropped further after this.) Sources: Home Office/Scottish Education Department 1972 *Report of the Departmental Committee* Chapter 3, footnote 64; OPCS *Adoptions in England and Wales*, various years. London, HMSO; OPCS Monitors, quoted in *BAAF Annual Review 1985/6* London, BAAF.

39.   In 1976, for example, 0.75 per cent of the under 18 population were in care; the percentage was 0.77 per cent in 1980, but it had dropped back to 0.75 per cent in 1982, to 0.7 per cent in 1983, to 0.65 per cent in 1984, to 0.62 per cent in 1985, and to 0.6 per cent in 1986. Most children in care in the 1980s were aged over ten. Sources: DHSS *Children in Care of Local Authorites year ending 31st March, England*, various years. London, HMSO; DHSS *Health and Personal Social Services Statistics for England 1987* London, HMSO.

40.   In 1979 there were over 11 divorces per 1,000 married persons; by 1984 there were 13. The latest figure given by the OPCS in 1988 was 13.4. See: OPCS 1988 *Population Trends* 52.

41.   See Chapter 2, footnotes 50 and 51.

42.   See for example: J. Renvoize 1985 *Going Solo: Single Mothers by Choice* London, Routledge Kegan Paul.

43.   See Chapter 2, footnotes 12, 50 and 51.. Also see: R. Collins 1989 'Illegitimacy, Inequality and the Law in England and Wales' in P. Close

(Ed) *Family Divisions and Inequalities in Modern Society* Basingstoke, Macmillan.

44.  For surrogate motherhood, see for example: L. M. Harding 1987 'The Debate on Surrogate Motherhood' Chapter 2, footnote 20; DHSS 1984 *Report of the Committee of Inquiry into Human Fertilisation and Embryology* Cmnd. 9314 (Chairman: Dame Mary Warnock) London, HMSO; A. A. Rassaby 1982 'Surrogate Motherhood: the position and problems of substitutes' in M. Walters and P. Singer (Eds) *Test Tube Babies* Melbourne, Oxford, Oxford University Press 97–109; J. Montgomery 1986 'Surrogacy and the Best Interests of the Child' *Family Law* 16(37).

45.  NCOPF 1982 *Against Natural Justice* Chapter 3, footnote 38.

46.  DHSS 1984 LAC (84) 15 This chapter, footnote 23.

47.  DHSS 1983 LAC (83) 19 This chapter, footnote 23.

48.  M. Southwell, Leeds University; research as yet unpublished.

49.  See Chapter 4, footnote 56.

50.  Parton and Martin 1989 state: 'At the time of writing it is unclear whether the parents are pursuing claims for professional negligence, assault and battery, or defamation.' N. Parton and N. Martin 1989 'Public Inquiries, Legalism and Child Care in England and Wales' *International Journal of Law and the Family* 3 21–39, footnote 11 38.

51.  See M. Jervis 1989 'The Stigma of "Children in Need"' *Social Work Today* 16 February 1989.

52.  See for example: C. Ball 1989 '"Carlile factor" overlooked in proposed legislation' *Community Care* 23 March 1989.

53.  See for example: G. Stewart 1989 'Who will foot the bill?' *Community Care* 8 June 1989; J. Richards 1989 'The Bill: Resource Implications' *Family Rights Group Bulletin* Spring 1989.

54.  See this chapter, footnote 33.

55.  While the Short Report 1984 and the review of child care law 1985 favoured 'shared care', the White Paper of 1987 rejected the concept, feeling that the terms 'shared care' and 'respite care' were not advisable. (For these sources see Chapter 4, footnotes 20 and 23.)

56.  While in 1975 45 per cent of children in care had been under (1969 Act) Care Orders, by 1980 this percentage had risen to 47.5 per cent, and by 1981 to nearly 48 per cent. There was then a decline, however, and by 1985 the percentage was down to 43 per cent, and by 1986 to 41.6 per cent. Sources: DHSS *Children in Care of Local Authorities at 31st March 1986, England* London, HMSO; DHSS *Health and Personal Social Services Statistics for England 1987* London, HMSO.

57.  For example, the Prime Minister in introducing the Children Bill in the debate on the Queen's speech in November 1988 said: 'Children are entitled to protection from harm and abuse, and innocent families from unnecessary intervention by the state', as though the juxtaposition of these two aims was in no way problematic. See: J. Oliver 1988 'Introducing the Children Bill' *Social Work Today* 1 December 1988.

# Bibliography

Association of British Adoption and Fostering Agencies (ABAFA) (1976) *Practice Guide to the Children Act 1975*

ABAFA (1977) *Assumption of Parental Rights and Duties – Practice Guide*

ABAFA (1979) *Terminating Parental Contact*

Andrews C (1980) Is blood thicker than local authorities? *Social Work Today* 12(1) 2 Sept. 1980 19–21

Aries P (1962) *Centuries of Childhood* Penguin

Bandman B (1973) Do Children Have Any Natural Rights? *Proceedings of 29th Annual Meeting of Philosophy of Education Society* 234–36

Behlmer G K (1982) *Child Abuse and Moral Reform in England 1870–1908* Stanford University Press, Stanford, California

Beresford P, Kemmis J and Tunstill J (1987) *In Care in North Battersea* North Battersea Research Group

British Agencies for Adoption and Fostering (BAAF) (1985) *Good Enough Parenting*

Carter J (1983) *Protection to Prevention: Child Welfare Policies* Social Welfare Research Centre, University of New South Wales, Australia

Costin L B and Rapp C A (1984) *Child Welfare Policies and Practice* 3rd edition McGraw-Hill, New York

Department of Health (DH) (1988) *First National Survey of Child Protection Registers*

Department of Health and Social Security (DHSS) (1982) *Child Abuse: A Study of Inquiry Reports 1973–1981* HMSO

DHSS *Children in Care of Local Authorities at 31st March, England* HMSO

DHSS *Health and Personal Social Services Statistics for England* HMSO

DHSS (1985) *Review of Child Care Law: Report to Ministers of an Inter-Departmental Working Party* HMSO

DHSS (1987) *The law on Child Care and Family Services* HMSO

235

*Bibliography*

Dingwall R, Eekelaar J and Murray T (1983) *The Protection of Children: State Intervention and Family Life* Blackwell

Dingwall R, Eekelaar J and Murray T (1983) Times change and we change with them? *Community Care* 16 June 1983

Donzelot J (1980) *The Policing of Families: Welfare versus the State* Hutchinson

Family Rights Group (1982) *Fostering Parental Contact*

Family Rights Group (1984) *Permanent Substitute Families. Security or Severance*

Family Rights Group (1986) *Promoting Links – Keeping Children and Families in Touch*

Farson R (1978) *Birthrights* Penguin, New York

Foster H H and Freed D J (1972) A Bill of Rights for Children *Family Law Quarterly* VI(4) Winter 1972

Fox L M (1982) Two Value Positions in Recent Child Care Law and Practice *British Journal of Social Work* 12(2) April 1982: 265–90

Franklin A W (1982) Child abuse in the 1980s *Maternal and Child Health* 7: 12–16

Franklin B (Ed) (1986) *The Rights of Children* Blackwell

Franklin B (1989) Children's rights: developments and prospects *Children and Society* 3(1) May 1989: 76–92

Franklin B (1989) Wimps and bullies; press reporting of child abuse in Carter P, Jeffs T and Smith M (Eds) *The Social Work and Social Welfare Yearbook 1* Open University: 6

Freeman M D A (1980) The Rights of Children in the International Year of the Child *Current Legal Problems* 33: 1–17

Freeman M D A (1983) Freedom and the Welfare State: Child-rearing, Parental Autonomy and State Intervention *Journal of Social Welfare Law* March 1983: 70–91

Freeman M D A (1983) *The Rights and Wrongs of Children* Frances Pinter

Freeman M D A (1987) Taking Children's Rights Seriously *Children and Society* 1(4) Winter 1987–8: 299–319

Freeman M D A (1988) Time to stop hitting our children *Childright* 51 October 1988

Frost N and Stein M (1989) *The Politics of Child Welfare: Inequality, Power and Change* Harvester/Wheatsheaf

Goldstein J, Freud A and Solnit A (1973, 1979) *Beyond the Best Interests of the Child* Free Press, New York

Goldstein J, Freud A and Solnit A (1980) *Before the Best Interests of the Child* Burnett Books/ André Deutsch

Hardyment C (1983) *Dream Babies. Child Care from Locke to Spock* Cape

Heywood J S (1978) *Children in Care. The development of the service for the deprived child* Routledge Kegan Paul

Hodges P (1981) Children and Parents: Who Chooses? *Politics and Power* 3

Hodgkin R (1986) Parents and corporal punishment *Adoption and Fostering* 10(3): 47–49

Holman R (1975) The Place of Fostering in Social Work British *Journal of Social Work* 5(1): 3–29

Holman R (1975) Unmarried Mothers, Social Deprivation and Child Separation *Policy and Politics* 3 1974–5: 25–41

Holman R (1976 and 1980) *Inequality in Child Care* Child Poverty Action Group Poverty Pamphlet 26

Holman R (1978) A class analysis of adoption reveals a disturbing picture *Community Care* 26 April 1978: 30

Holman R (1980) A *real* child care policy for the future *Community Care* 18/25 Dec. 1980 340: 16–17

Holman B 1988 *Putting Families First. Prevention and Child Care* Macmillan Education

Holt J (1975) *Escape from Childhood. The Needs and Rights of Children* Penguin

Home Office/Scottish Education Department (1972) *Report of the Departmental Committee on the Adoption of Children* Cmnd. 5107 HMSO

House of Commons (1984) *Second Report from the Social Services Committee* (Session 1983–84) *Children in Care* (The Short Report) HMSO

Howells J ?(. . .) *Remember Maria* Butterworths

Ingleby Committee (1960) *Report of the Committee on Children and Young Persons* Cmd. 1190 HMSO

Isaac B C, Minty E B and Morrison R M (1986) Children in Care – the Association with Mental Disorder in the Parents *British Journal of Social Work* 16(4): 325–39

Katkin D, Bullington B and Levine M (1974) Above and Beyond the Best Interests of the Child: An Inquiry into the Relationship between Social Science and Social Action *Law and Society Review* 8(4): 669–687

Kelly G (1981) The lost cord *Social Work Today* 13(12) 24 Nov. 1981

Kleinig J (1976) Mill, Children and Rights *Educational Philosophy and Theory* 8: 14

Lait J (1979) Is less worse better than better? *Community Care* 14 June 1979: 24

## Bibliography

Lambert L and Rowe J (1974) Children in Care and the Assumption of Parental Rights by Local Authorities *Child Adoption* 78

Lasch C (1977) *Haven in a Heartless World. The Family Beseiged* Basic Books, New York

Levitt K L and Wharf B (Eds) (1985) *The Challenge of Child Welfare* University of British Columbia Press, Vancouver, Canada

Lewis J (1980) *The Politics of Motherhood, Child and Maternal Welfare in England 1900–1939* Croom Helm

London Borough of Brent (1985) *A Child in Trust: The Report of the Panel of Inquiry into the Circumstances surrounding the Death of Jasmine Beckford*

London Borough of Greenwich (1987) *A Child in Mind: Protection of Children in a Responsible Society. Report of the Commission of Inquiry into the circumstances surrounding the death of Kimberley Carlile*

London Borough of Lambeth (1987) *Whose Child? The Report of the Public Inquiry into the Death of Tyra Henry*

Loney M (1987) Pain in a Wider World *Social Services Insight* 13 November 1987: 20–2

Macleod V (1982) *Whose Child? The Family in Child Care Legislation and Social Work Practice* Study Commission on the Family, Occasional Paper 11

Martin J P (Ed) (1978) *Violence and the Family* Wiley

McGowan B G and Meezan W (1983) *Child Welfare Current Dilemmas. Future Directions* Peacock Publishers Inc., Illinois, USA

Middleton N (1971) *When Family Failed. The Treatment of Children in the Care of the Community during the First Half of the Twentieth Century* Victor Gollancz Ltd

Millham S, Bullock R, Hosie K and Little M (1985) Maintaining Family Links of Children in Care *Adoption and Fostering* 9(2): 12–16

Millham S, Bullock R, Hosie K and Haak M (1986) *Lost in Care: the problems of maintaining links between children in care and their families* Gower

Mnookin R H (1973) Foster Care: in Whose Best Interest? *Harvard Educational Review* 43(4): 599

Mnookin R H (1975) Child Custody Adjudication: Judicial Functions in the Face of Indeterminacy *Law and Contemporary Problems* 39

Monckton Sir W (1945) *Report on the circumstances which led to the boarding out of Dennis and Terence O'Neill at Bank Farm, Minsterley, and the steps taken to supervise their welfare* Cmd. 6636 HMSO

Morgan S and Righton P (Eds) (1989) *Child Care: Concerns and Conflicts* Open University/Hodder and Stoughton.

Morris A, Giller H, Szwed E and Geach H (1980) *Justice for Children* Macmillan

Moss P and Lau G (1985) Mothers without marriages *New Society* 9 Aug. 1985

National Children's Home (1989) *Children in Danger – Factfile 1989*

National Council for One Parent Families (NCOPF) (1982) *Against Natural Justice*

Newell P (1989) *Children are People Too; the Case Against Corporal Punishment*

National Society for the Prevention of Cruelty to Children (NSPCC) (1989) *Child Abuse Trends in England and Wales 1983–87*

Packman J (1981) *The Child's Generation. Child Care Policy in Britain* Blackwell and Robertson

Packman J (1986) *Who Needs Care? Social Work Decisions about Children* Blackwell

Page R and Clark G (1977) *Who Cares?* National Children's Bureau

Parton N (1979) The Natural History of Child Abuse: A Study in Social Problem Definition *British Journal of Social Work* 9(4): 431–46

Parton N (1981) Child Abuse, Social Anxiety and Welfare *British Journal of Social Work* 11(4): 394–414

Parton N (1985) *The Politics of Child Abuse* Macmillan

Parton N (1985) Politics and practice *Community Care* 26 Sept. 1985: 22–4

Parton N (1986) The Beckford Report: A Critical Appraisal *British Journal of Social Work* 16(5): 511–31

Pinchbeck I and Hewitt M (1969) *Children in English Society* II Routledge Kegan Paul

Pollock L (1983) *Forgotten Children. Parent-child relations from 1500–1900* Cambridge University Press

Pringle M Kellmer (1967) *Adoption. Facts and Fallacies* Longman

Pringle M Kellmer (1972) Better Adoption *New Society* 29 June 1972

Pringle M Kellmer (1974) *The Needs of Children* Hutchinson

Pringle M Kellmer (1980) *A Fairer Future for Children* National Children's Bureau

Rogers C and Wrightsman (1978) Attitudes towards Children's Rights – Nurturance or Self-Determination *Journal of Social Issues* 34(2): 59

Rowe J and Lambert L (1973) *Children Who Wait* ABAFA

Bibliography

Samuels A (1976) The Children Act 1975. A Critical Appraisal: The View of the Lawyer *Family Law* 6(1): 5

Secretary of State for Social Services (1974) *Report of the Committee of Inquiry into the Care and Supervision provided in Relation to Maria Colwell* HMSO

Secretary of State for Social Services (1988) *Report of the Inquiry into Child Abuse in Cleveland 1987* Cm. 412 HMSO

Seglow J, Pringle M L K and Wedge P J (1972) *Growing up Adopted* NFER

Smith Carole R (1984) *Adoption and Fostering. Why and How?* BASW/Macmillan

Spackman A (1988) Why the family is crumbling *Independent* 13 June 1988

Strathclyde Social Work Department (1980) *Strathclyde's Children. 111 Children Whose Parents are the Regional Council*

Taylor L Lacey R and Bracken D (1980) *In Whose Best Interests? The unjust treatment of children in courts and institutions* Cobden Trust and MIND

Thoburn J (1980) *Captive Clients: Social Work with Families of Children Home on Trial* Routledge Kegan Paul

Thoburn J, Murdoch A and O'Brien A (1986) *Permanence in Child Care* Blackwell

Thorpe R (1974) Mum and Mrs. So-and-So *Social Work Today* 4(22) 7 Feb. 1974: 691–5

Tizard B (1977) *Adoption. A Second Chance* Open Books

Tunstill J (1977) In defence of parents *New Society* 42(785) 20 Oct. 1977

Tunstill J (1980) *Fostering Policy and the 1975 Children Act* Brunel University Papers in Social Policy and Administration 2

Tunstill J (1985) Aiming to prevent misunderstanding *Social Work Today* 17 June 1985

Tunstill J (1985) Laying the Poor Law to rest? *Community Care* 20 June 1985: 16–18

Vallender I and Fogelman K (Eds) (1987) *Putting Children First. A Volume in Honour of Mia Kellmer Pringle* Falmer Press/National Children's Bureau

Verhellen E and Spiesschaert (Eds) (1989) *Ombudswork for Children* ACCO, Leuven, Belgium

Wald M (1975) State intervention on behalf of neglected children: A search for realistic standards *Stanford Law Review* 27: 985–1040

Wald M (1976) Neglected Children: Standards for Removal of Children from their homes, monitoring the status of children in foster care, and termination of parental rights *Stanford Law Review* 28: 622–70

Walton R and Heywood M (1975) Child care, culture and Social Services Departments *Yearbook of Social Policy 1974* Routledge Kegan Paul

Walvin J (1982) *A Child's World. A Social History of English Childhood 1800–1914* Penguin

Worsfold V L (1974) A Philosophical Justification for children's rights *Harvard Educational Review* 44(1): 142

# Index